CW01619224

MAKING PINK LEMONADE

Love your cycle

Sarah xox

MAKING PINK LEMONADE

SARAH O'MAHONEY

MAKING PINK LEMONADE

ISBN 978-0-9957636-4-7

First published in 2016 by Good Being A Girl,

London, England

http://goodbeingagirl.com

Cover design and typeset by Eva Megias

http://evamegias.com

To Mum who gave me my first pad
and reassured me that I was not
about to die on the bathroom floor!

INSTRUCTIONS

1. Please read this book - it's really not that yucky!

2. Please colour in any illustrations - you will definitely need a good red felt tip pen!

3. Use the chart at the back to follow your own Menstrual Cycle

4. Love your Cycle

THE BIG EVENT

The first time it happened I thought I was dying. It seemed the only reasonable explanation. Scarlet patches on my favorite Snoopy pants. That was Tuesday 8th June, the day of my first period. I was ten. The biggest event in a girl's life. Yeah, right. There was no special mention at Whole School Assembly, no Come to my Menarche* Party invites to give out. By the way Menarche is the proper scientific word for a first period, pronounced Men-ark.

No big family gathering. No me, clad in red velvet holding a single crimson rose. No fireworks, no party poppers. That's not to say it was totally ignored. No, to be fair, Mum did try to make a big deal of it in the following ways:

After assuring me, that of course, I was not about to a die a lingering death on the bathroom floor, she hugged me tight and said rather dramatically,

"Welcome to the World of Women"!

She meant well, I suppose, but I was horrified! How could that be, I had only that morning been combing my Barbie's hair and getting embarrassingly upset when I thought I had mislaid Mr. Pink (that's my teddy bear that I've had since I was one).

As my Gran says, I'm a big girl now - but a woman? I don't think so.

Gave me a special starter pack of sanitary towels... great! Nappies for grown ups.

We had a special tea with jammy dodgers and

strawberries. When Michael (that's my four year old brother) asked whose birthday it was.

Mum attempted to explain, accompanied by embarrassed coughs from Dad and giggles from my sister Tara.

Michael – *How come I didn't get a special tea when I cut my leg last week?*

Mum – *Michael, that's not the same thing*

Michael – *Why not? I got blood too!*

Mum – *It's something that only happens to girls.*

Michael – *But that's not fair. I want a period too.*

Mum – *Believe me, you really don't! Have another jammy dodger instead.*

The food distraction technique usually works without fail. Four biscuits later and Michael's minute attention span is already on to whether you could use jammy dodgers as wheels to make a truck.

That was it, an event as big as my birthday, but no real celebration to speak of. No renditions of Happy Menarche to Kali (that's me by the way), no cards in the post, except for Michael's gory handmade card with me looking like I was being tortured to death. Serious overuse of red felt tip!

How can something so important be swept under the carpet and not really talked about? It truly is the biggest cover-up of all time.

Over half the world's population has one, for goodness sake!

GRUFFALO DAYS

Two years on and Mum still delights in reliving how I screamed out to her on that fateful day,

Mum, come quick, I think I'm dying! As if she were recalling how I took my first step. As if it were a big joke, not potentially the end of my life on this

Earth, or so I thought.

Yes, thanks, Mum, for your ever-loving concern and sensitivity. Just because I'm your daughter, doesn't make my memories yours by right.

At this point I usually toss my head, take my leave, remembering, (VERY IMPORTANT THIS), to slam the door behind me. It's all in the exit. I find it almost as satisfying as having a whole Galaxy bar to myself. I seem to be doing a lot of that lately, slamming doors, tutting and generally being annoyed by the other hapless humans who live in the house (i.e. my family).

Michael calls them my Gruffalo days. Lots of stamping upstairs, growling under my breath and if you look closely enough, PURPLE PRICKLES spiking out of my back.In fact Michael is my unlikely saviour on those Gruffalo days, as the fearlessly brave and clever Mouse. As long as I stay in character,

Mouse is happy to transport essential supplies from the kitchen in his "special" Spider Man swag bag. Roast fox becomes chocolate biscuits and Scrambled Snake becomes strawberry yoghurt shake. It can get annoying when I forget and say chocolate instead of Roast Fox.

No the Gruffalo doesn't say that

Oh Michael go on I need it now.

Not till you do it properly.

At the point where he begins to walk away, I suppress my desire to break his Lego City to bits and dutifully follow the script. Mum can't work out why I seem to want to play with Michael, when generally I would be happy if he was permanently hung upside down on the washing line.

So now, at the truly mature age of 12, I suppose I should be pretty blasé about my monthly visit. Some of my friends haven't started yet. This half makes me feel grown up and wise beyond my years and half jealous that they don't have to worry about spots on their games shorts.

Someone has to be first, says Mum. Not first at landing on Pluto or going round the world in a washing up bowl but first to have boobs, hairy under arms and of course to get my period! No gold medals and cheering crowds for that!

Some of my favourite female firsts:

In 1932 Amy Johnson was the first woman to fly to Australia in a bi - plane with no radio or modern sat nav.

In 1975 Peggy Braithwaite became Britain's first female lighthouse keeper.

In 1953 Lita Rosa became the first woman in Britain to reach number one in the charts with

How Much Is That Doggy In The Window?

Strangely, each month, roughly every 28 days, it comes. But somehow it always takes me by surprise. It's as if when it goes I erase all memory of it, until the next time. Maybe it's because I wish it wouldn't come again or that as the world doesn't think its anything special, why should I?

Mum says it's because I am not thinking of it as really part of me but just this slightly annoying thing that happens that I have to just grin and bear.

Well it is a pain, having to think what to wear in case of a leak or dealing with cramps during Social Studies. Also it's how it makes you feel, all moody and cross all of a sudden. It makes me want to run and hide in a handy tree house, (definitely with a pull up ladder). It makes me feel like I am going slightly mad.

I usually love going to the Cafe after school to

mull over the day and to dissect exactly what Nathan flicking paper at my head might really mean, or at least pretend that I care. But when I have my period I just want to rush home and curl up in my duvet with Mog, my cat and reread Anne of Green Gables. She's funny and feisty and has red hair like me. I do like my hair colour but I do have to put up with some stick.

Believe me it doesn't matter that Lily Cole is a top model/genius and Dr.Who's sidekick was a red head too; I still get called Ginger and Carrot Top or worse Ketchup Head.

Basically it was only when I was about three, with Annie like curls, that people thought I was adorable and cute. I know its not the end of the world and I've never really been bullied because of it but it seems even PE teachers feel they can ruffle your hair affectionately and say *"Well done Ginger"*, when I intercept a pass in netball. Being small can be an advantage sometimes. Oh to have springs on my feet.

So, no, I have not reclaimed the nickname for myself. I am Kali, definitely. Apart from my Pre-Raphaelite burnished locks, which is now cut short with a floppy piece. I am over five feet tall, well five foot one. The one-inch is crucial. My Dad is always winding me up and insisting on measuring me to double check - the cheek. It's his fault I'm a redhead.

His hair is bright light ginger whereas mine is a darker tone. Mum has dark blonde hair. Tara is dark blonde and Michael is a redhead like me. Actually both parents have to have red head genes for children to inherit. It's 50:50. As if that wasn't enough I am short sighted and have to wear glasses.

Thankfully no longer the blue NHS plastic pair I first wore aged 9. I can still remember walking into class for the first time with my glasses on to a hush that even then I knew had to be the work of my teacher Mr.Price in collusion with Mum, to ensure no one laughed. It helped that two of my friends Ruthie and Siobhan (pronounced Shove awn) also wore them, in pink and tortoiseshell, respectively. That's a quick way of saying that Ruth had the pink, Siobhan the tortoise shell ones. Of course by explaining I have just made it ten times longer. I'm working on my tendency to use 100 words when 5 would do! We learnt that in essay writing skills.

Of course now I have these great black frames that are cooler NHS shape specs. Hurrah for geek chic! Glasses are so cool at the moment that people wear them even though they don't need to.

My eyes are a cat like green, which I like. I have loads of freckles even when it's not sunny.

My boobs have started growing and I have hair growing not just on my head, if you know what I mean! Thankfully clothes hide all that, except for the horror, which is communal showers after games, that is all girls not mixed! Friends try not to stare or gasp. Some our weirdly jealous and others just plain horrified that it will happen to them soon.

Why should I feel such a freak for just being the first to "mature"? That is definitely physically speaking only! I mean I can laugh hysterically for hours at my Dad's Churchill (the dog on the advert) impression. *Oh Yes!*

I freely admit that I still blub every time I watch The Lion King. To be fair Dad's the same when he watches ET. He says the opening bars of the theme tune are enough to set him off and as for the bit when the boys' bikes fly on their way to take ET back to the spaceship, he weeps.

Got something in your eye love? laughs Mum.

So I have probably made myself sound like a complete social misfit but really that's just drama queen embellishment. I mean who wants to be just normal.

GOING WITH THE FLOW

One Sunday morning I can be found slouching into the kitchen on the hunt for hot tea and toast to bring back upstairs to bed. I usually bring Mum a cup of tea up while she waits for Dad to come back with the papers. He puts his jeans on over his PJs so he can pretend he hasn't really got up.

Michael goes along too, with whatever wheeled contraption he has rigged up for the transportation back, of papers, milk, and pastry selection. It pays to be around when the booty is delivered, so to have first pickings. It's our breakfast treat of the week as Monday to Saturday it's usually healthy cereal with extra seeds and banana, which is quite scrummy but pain au chocolat dipped in hot tea is another league!! I think my French is coming along well. Croissant, chocolat chaud s'il vous plait... what more do you need?

On the kitchen table I found a package wrapped in polka dot tissue paper.It had my name on. I opened it, wracking my brains, for what I might have done to deserve this. Inside was the most beautiful crimson - coloured journal. It felt like it was covered in silk and the crinkle edged cream paper looked handmade. I felt like hugging it. Inside was a note saying:- **For my darling Kali, to chart her very own cycle. Love Mum xxx**

I ran upstairs straight away, barged into Mum's room and jumped right onto her bed.

Mum this is so lovely but what am I going to write? Glad you like it!

I love it!

Well it could be a bit like a diary that you can write down what you feel and do and then start to look out for patterns.

Patterns, how do you mean?

Well you may start to notice that on the same days each month you need to hog the bath, or would kill your own mother for a Kit Kat! And then maybe others you feel like hanging out with your friends downtown, that sort of thing.

Am I really that obvious?

Kali we all have our up and down days, but us girls have a special built in way of tracking them, so we can predict and plan things to make even those really, I-want-to-scream- and throw-plates-days, not quite so bad.

It might take a few months to see the patterns, but they are there.

Mum really knew what she was talking about. We all knew to give her a wide berth on those days when she began to mutter to herself or say extra loudly and sarcastically: *Oh look, another jumper for the laundry fairy to pick up and oh bliss no milk left for MY cup of tea. Is it just ME or is it not full milk bottles that go in the fridge, rather than empty ones?* It's usually my Dad who gets the glare at this point, before she rushes out the door to the surgery where she works part-time as Office Manager, banging the door so it rattles the whole house. We all look at each other and sigh. Then Dad says

I pity those poor patients who come to the surgery

today, unless there are literally about to expire! OK gang action stations. Kali clothes in washing machine, Tara plates in dishwasher, Michael, bulldoze Lego city now and relocate.

After dropping Michael and Tara at school, Dad will go to get milk, flowers and large Galaxy for Mum to find when she gets home. She will then run a bath, grab the chocolate and a Chamomile Tea and soak for hours, not to be disturbed at any costs. Even Michael has given up knocking on the door and asking can he come share the chocolate with her.

Go bond with your father Michael.

Mum calls this her Rose Garden time. I am going to smell the roses *or I need to do some pruning*. All euphemisms (funny ways to disguise embarrassing words) for it's my period and I need time away.

I have been trying to think of a special way to refer to mine, so this journal will hopefully sound poetic not like a biology textbook. My Gran Adelaide still calls it the Curse, although hers is long gone.

GRAN *In my day it was rolled up newspaper not these new fangled tenpins.*

KALI *They're called tampons Gran*

GRAN *Whatever, it's just not natural is it?*

KALI *What having a period or tampons?*

GRAN *Well sticking stuff up your nether regions o course.*

My auntie Eireen, calls hers Gerald, which before I knew what periods were I thought was some very unreliable boyfriend who turned up each month!

I thought of calling mine Justin, after Justin Bieber, just so I could say Oh yes Justin's come to stay, or must go, Justin's coming. To be honest I don't really see what all the fuss is about but you can't be seen to be lame or "such a child".

Here are some more euphemisms for I'm Having My Period: From Rolling out the Red carpet, Riding the Cotton Pony to the Japanese Little Miss Strawberry and the slightly scary CRIMSON TIDE. All brilliant. Eventually I decide on my favorite, which I think is quite subtle and would not easily be decoded by others – Making Pink Lemonade or MPL for short.

DAY 1 ALERT ALERT

THOUGHT FOR THE DAY

In Ancient Rome, it was commonly believed that menstrual blood could cure certain illnesses.

How come when I know it's due does it still come as a total surprise?

I suppose I should have realized how desperate

I was for my Sunday pastry treat yesterday and come to think of it, how tired and a bit heavy I felt. I went up to bed even without having to be asked.

It's Monday and of course I didn't have any pads with me. Of course not. Hopefully keeping this Menstrual Cycle Diary will help me to know when the next one is due. Mum has agreed to let me take responsibility now and not to remind me. As she says I will know best about my own body and how it works. I think I am beginning to.

When I noticed a slight pinkness on the toilet paper, during morning break, I knew IT had come. There is always a feeling of slight relief,that my body is doing what it should. Then for the rest of the day it is hardly visible and I think maybe I dreamt that it had started. But during RE I could feel the flow start and was glad that Ava had some tampons on her.

Tampons are the small sausage shape towels that

can go inside and soak up the blood...too much detail...well that's what they do.

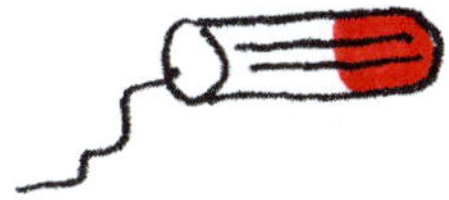

Ava is my best friend, since we were 5 and started Primary together. She is almost 6ft tall, well 5 ft 10, that's almost a foot taller and has long dark hair that does literally shine, like in the ads. I love it when the rain makes it go all curly but she just hates that and would rather wear a bobble hat.

Nonetheless she is on the school swim team, which she adores so much that she puts up with weekly practices, which of course result in wiggly jiggly curly locks.

Now, Ava is the same age as me but hasn't started her periods yet.

I know so why the tampons? Well Ava is also a Girl Guide so prepared for every eventuality, even those yet to happen. If anyone needs a spare pen, Ava's your girl. Desperate for just one chunk of Galaxy, then Ava has a constant supply. About to sneeze all over Mickey D, a tissue appears as if by magic under my nose. She is the perfect best friend, loyal, funny, silly, practically my own PA and most people seem to think she is totally sure of herself and not someone to mess with. This is great because those scary girls in Y10/11 leave me alone.

Only I know that she gets scared watching Doctor Who, talks to her pet guinea pig Freda and thinks she's gawky. She worries that all the swimming might stop her period coming. I usually give her, the- don't-be-such-a-twit look and pull her hair for good measure.

KALI *More likely that the chlorine has pickled your brain!*

AVA *Do you think so? That may explain why I am*

hanging around with a Leprechaun!

KALI *Ooh now that's mean.*

Ava has a big brother Marcus, in Y11, who everyone thinks looks a bit like Joe from Life of Dillon. I've known Marcus since forever. When you've seen someone dressed up as a kangaroo its hard to think of them as fanciable.

You must see him all the time people like Francesca ask, what's he really like...Well he has a bedroom that stinks of month old underpants and pet newts called Dipsy and Laa- Laa. (They are almost 10 years old now!) -

What Francesca seems to hear is, he is manly and loves animals...

Yeah? Your so lucky, he's so fit.... And you've been in his room?

As for Ava, she is just plain bewildered when Francesca or Leanne asks to be her study partners:

just to catch a glimpse of Marcus. She calls them her frenemies.

Marcus is my explainer of all things Planet Boy and vice versa, I let him know the complexities of being female. He seems to be oblivious that most of the girls in Y8 and 9 thing he's a God.

Thanks to Ava I am safe from free flowing all the way down my grey pleated school skirt and cream woolen tights. Tip for worst case scenario: period starts in class and you are wearing a white cotton skirt (why because you believe all that princess rubbish).You wouldn't catch me wearing pink either. Pink Stinks. Would make a great T-shirt! However I have to confess I loved it when I was three and four. There is photographic evidence of me with a pink tutu and fluffy pink jumper. I cannot deny it! Also pink and red hair not great combo! Although my cute factor was higher back then. I was a real girly girl. Ugh! Even Katie Price's daughter has gone off pink and she's actually called Princess. Apparently she has asked her parents not to call her by that name anymore.

Good for her. I tend to wear jeans and trousers and sneakers (I love that term better than plimsolls or trainers). In fact my ideal look is currently Jodie Foster's, jeans baseball top and sneakers combo from the original Freaky Friday film. Anyway back to the Period alert scenario. Ask teacher to leave the room,saying you think you are going to be sick. Wink at Ava - code for need you to come too. *Ava you'd best go with her*. Then tie jumper around waist and walk casually down the hallway, with Ava on stain alert behind. So far this has not happened, but we have the plan, in case. Actually, as you can probably guess it was Ava's idea and by the way I would not wear a white peasant skirt under any circumstances. It was as Miss Dias, my English teacher would say, dramatic license.

It's almost the end of school and I text Mum in advance to say: **PINK LEMONADE IS SPILT!** This means please treat me gently from the moment you hear my key in the door, no ordering me to get on with homework or to help with making dinner. The rest of family may also be informed in order to be understanding (unlikely) or to give me a wide berth (more likely).

Mum replies" **Preps underway! Auntie Eireen is here is that OK?**

I love my Auntie Eireen, that's my Dad's younger sister. She is hilarious and talks to me like I'm grown up, which is mostly good. She is usually just splitting up with or just starting to go out with some guy.

When I get home I suddenly feel a heaviness in

my whole body and feel I could just lie down on the doormat and sleep right there. I slouch wearily into the kitchen and collapse with a big sigh onto a chair. Mum hands me a glass of bonafide Pink Lemonade (see below for the recipe)

HOW TO MAKE PINK LEMONADE – TO DRINK

Take 1 and half cups of sugar

4 cups of water

1 cup of cranberry juice

1 cup of lemon juice...

Or you can just buy white lemonade and add food colouring

My ten-year old sister Tara also has one and shouts cheers big ears to me and gulps it down.

Mum can I have rose Viv Clicko when I start,

says Tara.

Well get her ladyship over there, laughs Auntie Eireen

I think you'll find that's Veuve Cliquot, which if you make it to any secondary school, you will soon learn, is the correct way to pronounce it!

I blame the eyes myself. Transformation is now complete. I have become a cross between the Queen of Sheba and Cleopatra, which as Mum says is just the right balance of regal bearing and viper tongue.

She who must be obeyed and not crossed under any circs. Poor Tara took it well, considering she is in the midst of trying to get into my secondary school. Gone are the days when having a sister at the school meant automatic entry.

Mum and Eireen are having grownup pink lemonade, aka Rose Cava.

Gosh I wish I had such a fuss made when I started my periods or even now. Imagine going into work and Steve and the rest toasting me with pink gin!

Eireen works at a Mini cab firm answering the phone, in between acting jobs.

Mum and Eireen have hysterics at the thought and the bubbles from the Cava go right up their noses and they end up spluttering. I mean who are the kids here.

I give them a contemptuous look and pour another glass of Pink Lemonade.

Then I decamp to the best TV seat in the house with a couple of chocolate biscuits to keep me going until dinner is ready. I start watching Pretty in Pink, my favourite film. I first watched it with Mum. It's her favourite too. It's all about a girl who makes her own clothes.Oh yeah and she has red hair, has a boy best friend and doesn't quite fit with the wealthy kids at school. I won't say too much more because it'll spoil it but believe me it is sooo good. Makes me feel better about being me. Tara comes to watch too but keeps asking stupid questions so I give her the Paddington Bear super stare and she pipes down. I don't mind having her there as long as she understands the rules. I even give her one of the biscuits and she cuddles up beside me. I find it hard to be cross with her for long. She is two years younger than me and totally bonkers. Dad says she's the artistic one of the family, which seems to excuse any weird kind of behaviour - like painting the kitchen wall yellow with pink spots.

When I weep at the end Tara is sweet and pretends she doesn't see, hands me the bit of biscuit that she didn't eat and cartwheels out of the room. Being left alone to softly sniffle into a cushion feels strangely good, like all the pent up irritations of the day have been sobbed away.

In some places in the world women and girls are confined to their rooms or huts when they bleed. Is that so bad? I suppose it is, if someone else says you have to, because you are unclean or unfit to be around. Voluntarily confining myself to my room would be OK, with chocolate supplies, books, cat and own en suite. However I can hear all the laughter still going on without me in the kitchen. It half makes me want to join them but the other tearful- cushion -hugging half of me says go lie down upstairs with Mog the cat.

I remember there was this one time, about a year ago when Dan had his 10th Birthday and in my gut I really didn't feel like going. I think I had only started my period for the first time a few months before and didn't feel confident prancing around on the bouncy castle with sanitary towels stuck on my pants. I was terrified that they might fly out! I had no choice about going, as Dan would not have forgiven me and I wasn't about to tell him why I couldn't go! I've known Dan since Nursery but he goes to Edmund Burke, the all boys' grammar now.

Our parents are best buddies so we all hang out a lot together.

Anyway I survived the party by spending most of the afternoon entertaining Dan's little sister Alicia, who is 5. We played with her vast collection of Sylvanian families and tree house. I never had the treehouse! It did make me feel grown up and a bit like I had a secret that no one knew, whilst everyone else was jumping up and down on the castle and getting hiccups from too much juice and laughing.

Of course us girls do mature earlier. But now scientists have discovered for the first time that their brains can develop up to ten years earlier than boys. It's true really. At Newcastle University they found that the brain does a lot of re-organising during puberty, when changes happen in the body. Honestly. Mum was reading this article in the paper.

Could it have something to do with girls starting periods around then I wonder?

You really notice it in Y7/8 how the girls tower over some of the boys.

Auntie Eireen says that she's not sure boys ever really do! Mature that is.

Michael: *What's women's trouble, Auntie Eireen?*

Eireen: *Men my love, all except you of course my sweet little NEW man*

Michael: *But I'm a boy*

Eireen: *New boy then*

Michael: *No way Liam's the new boy and no ones likes him.*

Eireen: *Ok Auntie's little helper then*

Michael: *Do you have men trouble too?*

Eireen: *Oh yes all the time!*

THINGS NOT TO DO ON DAY 1:

Don't wear white trousers

Don't decide to run the marathon

Don't leave your history essay to do

DAY 2 CLEOPATRA TAKES TO HER BATH

Women of Ancient Greece used their blood to fertilize the fields

Woke up with slight cramps. I don't usually get major pain but today I felt bloated and heavy. I rubbed some of my Sassy girl oil mix – geranium, rose and lavender on my tummy, which smells good and feels calming.

I didn't feel like school – AT ALL

Me: Do *I have to? Can't I have a duvet day like*

they do in Holland?

Mum*: Imagine if you weren't allowed to go to school...*

Me: *Oh I do all the time believe me*

Mum: *No I mean because you're a girl. Even since the Taliban, girls in Afghanistan struggle against cultural stigma to stay at home.*

Me: *Mum I know it's my duty and before you mention the suffragettes and Malala I will remind you that is was me who insisted 3R girls take turns with the boys carrying chairs and equipment back to the storeroom.*

You can imagine how popular I was after that suggestion, especially with hair flicking Sonya and her crew who can barely seem to lift a comb without having to take a rest. Ava did query whether we could keep chivalry and still be feminists? The humiliation of not being able to lift the projector and Stephen

Miller having to do it instead, kind of defeated the whole purpose.I carried the power leads. To be fair he was one of the few boys who didn't jeer.

Mum: *Yes and very proud I am that you take a stand.*

Me: *It's just when I'm ON and pink lemonade is a pumping away (bit gross sorry) - I really need to be somewhere quiet.*

Mum: *In an ideal woman-run world you would be able to relax in your red tent and honour the need to be quiet BUT the best I can offer is a Lush bath bomb ready to explode the minute you get home. How's that?*

So I trudge to school grunting as off-puttingly as I can if anyone says Hi or wants to talk, putting my bag in that annoying way people do on the inside seat next to me on the bus. It is a day for an invisibility cloak, which I wrap around myself in my own mind and hope that by sheer force of will I be transported to a parallel universe; at least for the duration of the journey. I bury myself in To Kill A Mockingbird, which is homework but doesn't feel like that to me. I so love Scout. Love the way I can completely lose myself in a book even on days when I feel snarky. They really do transport me to another place. I look up surprised to find myself on the bus and not sat swinging my legs on a stoop with Scout someplace in the Deep South with the sound of crickets chirruping over the swamp. I wonder if it happens more when I am ON. Must check it next month. Note to self.

I almost miss my stop, only the general pandemonium of my fellow students careering down the stairs like they are actually in a rush to get there, makes me realize I have to get off too! Walking at a brisk pace makes me feel a bit lighter and brighter. I even manage a smile when one of the sweet year 7 girls called Maddie; calls out *Hey Kali...love your bag!* My beloved bright green satchel, which I got for my birthday.

It's what all children back in the 1950s used to have. Yet another thing that's come back into fashion. My Mum has a smaller handbag version in yellow that she uses when she's going "out on the Town". Which is really cute. Just big enough for a mobile, purse and a paperback book.Perfect.I am building up to asking if I can borrow it someday.

As I approach the main school gate I almost bolt and turn around and run home.

I need to be alone. If only I had that Marlene Dietrich cold sophistication that freezes the very words on peoples lips as I sweep past them in the corridor, dressed in one of those satin 1930s

Hollywood gowns, that look like nighties really I think. Bit tricky in a school of 1000 plus lunatics. I do have a tendency to sweeping statements but on this day pretty much everyone annoys me.

Mr.Hailpin's laughter for example. How can hypotenuse and right angles be funny?

Then I miss getting any smiley face chips by just 2 people in the lunch queue. There really should be a fast lane for those most in need.

Even lovely Mrs. Brennan one of the school lunchtime supervisors, (we can't call them dinner ladies anymore) fails to cheer me up with a "will you look at her with her cool floppy fringe. Oh she's like that one in what is it the ZZ...I can just about tolerate Ava, as long as she knows the dos and don'ts:

1. Immediate availability of chocolate
2. No stupid questions, apart from, Would you

like another bit of chocolate?

3. Give me in hours and minutes how long until I'm home

Strangely the only other person I can bare to speak with is the school librarian Miss Cranley, who seems to know when I need to be left reading quietly in the Myths and Legends section. I creep in at lunchtime and hunker down with The Red Fairy Book...Ssh don't tell! She always gives me a bit extra online time to research my new pet subject –which at the moment is periods of course!

Here's what I found out:

In South India, among the Brahmin community to wish a girl a fertile life they give her a raw egg prepared with ginger oil, then a milk bath!

Give me a foamy bath and a bowl of Malteasers any day! However the tradition in some societies where women and girls are confined to their rooms while bleeding so they can commune with the moon seems ok as long as I could commune with One Direction.

Imagine says Mum if you weren't allowed to go to school...IMAGINE

I daydream of being home in the bath with a LUSHous bath bomb whizzing around and my book. In fact having my period would be fine as long as I knew I could just lie in a bath for a few days and read and not be expected to do the usual.

Definite downsides:

Wearing sanitary towels. At first I felt like an overgrown baby. They felt weird and the sticky bit would sometimes end up giving me a mini wax in a certain area. When I complained to Mum, she suggested: *You could always do what the Rungus tribe of Borneo do and let your blood flow freely, whilst sat on dried moss or bamboo slats*

Yuck, sorry I spoke!

Actually it's not yuck as they regularly wash themselves and freshen the mats.

Gran Adelaide says that when she was a "gel" she used newspapers and that's if you were lucky. One day she was forced to use one of her Dad's old socks!

OK so perhaps we do have it slightly better THESE DAYS

Reasons to be cheerful about Periods in the 21st Century:

Slave girls in America were sold off when they had their first periods, for breeding and suckling purposes. How horrendous!

We have proper sanitary towels or tampons

In India girls get given clothes and jewellery when

they start. Definitely a custom we should adopt here

Without them who would populate the world. No periods. No Bables. No world.

Or as my Auntie Eireen says al least you know you're not pregnant!

Got through the day OK, almost forgot I had my period during Art when I got completely engrossed in my Matisse cutouts, which Miss Moxley then collected up and displayed along one wall in the Art room. They looked brilliant. Just like when Matisse decorated his own house. He was quite old then, about 80, even older than Granny Adelaide (that's Mum's mum) and as Dad jokes, she's practically from the Paleolithic era. Miss Moxley is great. She took us to see the Matisse exhibition at the Tate Modern. She even let us run down the slope and didn't get cross when we got excited but she did expect us to be quiet in the exhibition. We all went quiet anyway with wonder...we all went WOW miss!

Finally. As promised my luscious bath did await, foaming invitingly, ready for her serene highness, her most venerable crabbiness. Bliss! Only my nose is above water and my mind floats random thoughts like: There is a Native American ritual where menstruating girls are rubbed all over with stinging nettles, given no food and water for 3 days and left alone in a hut!

How is that a celebration? It's like a really bad I'm a Celebrity

Get me out of here!

I mean being confined to your room to commune with the moon or maybe Zayn- might be ok! I begin howling at this point and then splutter bubbles as I choke with laughter.

You OK in there Kali?

Yes dearest mother I am merely communing

with La Luna.

Mum: *Oh you have finally gone completely bonkers then.*

Kali: *Aoooooo*

DAY 3 MY PRETEND LIFE

Slightly yucky fact but your period flushes out all the dead cells with the blood, which is your uterus lining. So it cleanses you and keeps you healthy.

NO PERIODS NO BABIES NO WORLD! Thinking of having a t-shirt printed! This is the thing that really gets to me, not being able to say to the world; look I am having my period. It's totally natural, normal and a way bigger deal than getting 80/100 in my Maths test. I haven't managed that yet!

Nowhere close.

I mean, if you've just got a cold, you can go about sneezing and coughing and everyone is *Oh are you*

OK, maybe you should go home and rest up.

People go on about details such as being bunged up or snotty...and that's *not* disgusting?

It's hardly life or death but periods we don't speak about them apart from to our mums or maybe, sisters and friends. Anne Frank called it her "sweet secret". How sad it is to read her amazing diary and the way she talks about ordinary things going on in her life, like periods and fancying boys and what she wants to do when she is grown up; but yet she is hidden away with her family and never to go on to live that life. Take a look in any French or Spanish phrase book and you won't find sanitary towels or any mention of periods. Excuse moi, avez-vous des tampons?

Time for an update I think. Imagine a world where a girl's first period would be celebrated with gifts, proper gifts, not an at out-of-date Kit Kat Michael found at the bottom of his swim bag with his wet swim shorts...let's not go there.

There would be a full card rack of Happy Menarche cards in Smiths, parties and recognition at school assemblies. Girls would wear a special red rosette and expect congratulations from people in the street. It would be customary for all menstruating girls/women to celebrate their monthly cycle by wearing something red. Rita Ora, Rhianna, Katy Perry, Jessie J and her majesty Lady GaGa would wear slogan t-shirts like Hurrah it's My Period!

I have often thought boys have it way easier. Is it easier to be a boy,no periods, run the world? When I talked to Marcus about it, he said it's not all its cracked up to is. Depending who're your with you

DESIGN A T-SHIRT

have to keep up this macho thing.

Admitting you have a sensitive side is like asking for a kicking. It's a bit like your Period cover up theory it's the same for boys we keep up this old style macho rubbish but really we all would rather just be ourselves. Marcus can be pretty profound at times.

I told him about these girls in Afghanistan who disguise themselves as boys, called badia posh. It means they are freer to study and move about without so many restrictions. *That makes sense. It would be cool finding out how the other half live! Not that I'm saying I want to dress up in your clothes...don't get me wrong.*

Me: *No I think you want to go the whole hog and dress up like that Grayson Perry in a Bo Beep costume!*

At this point he gives a serious pinch on my arm.

Ouch that hurt. It was meant to.

Oh did I hurt your male pride.

Explain to me again why I come around here when all I get is insults!!

No I think weighing everything up I'm glad I'm a girl.

Checking to see what my school timetable is like today, my heart both lifts and falls. The morning will involve large-scale role -playing. I will have to be bright and breezy, as I am helping with the Open Day for new victims (I mean, new pupils), who seem desperate to come to Fawcett High.

Uniform will have to look crisp and smart and hair combed flat. At least I get to miss double Maths, which my floaty Day 3 brain could not have coped with. On a good day I can even make sense of logarithms, Mr.Hailpin even explained what we use them for in the real world; which does help to understand why on earth we have to learn them. The Richter scale, which measures earthquakes, is logarithmic, as are decibels (sound levels). Engineers use them. Anthropologists use them even people on the Moon use them. Let's do it let's learn our logs.

Anyway, I am left in charge of four Y6 girls from my old primary school St Brigit's, one of whom is at least 5 inches taller than me.Rising to the challenge I show them around. Wish I had had le grand tour before I came. It would have made it less scary and maze like. I remember the crisp cardboardness of my new green blazer and scissor sharp-ironed pleats in my grey skirt and my dorky briefcase. All from the school outfitters'. We were like so obviously green in every sense and easy targets for merciless older students who got pleasure in sending us the wrong way. So I deliberately introduce them to non-scary Y11s such as Gabby who edits the school zine and Joel who is a good friend of Marcus and plays keyboard in a band, which rehearses in the school music room.

They are called No Direction, at the moment! Joel is so funny and even though he is kind of skinny and gawky and wears silk scarves he seems to tread the line between the he-men and the sensitives. When he had some trouble with some boys from another school, all of Y11 boys and girls went out to show support, every single one of them wearing silk scarves!

One of the newees needed the loo and I made a point of pointing out the tampon machine and that the school medical room always has towels available. If not my friend Ava supplies me, as I always forget to keep some in my bag...they laugh.

We go to lunch and I encourage them to try the healthy options even though I am desperate for chips! Actually having the chicken salad made me feel less bloated. Must remember that when next those tasty chips whisper EAT ME EAT ME...

I then take them to the library and show them my cozy corner; a must on Days 1-3.I introduce them to Miss Cranley, the Librarian and Jacob her library assistant. He looks a bit like Ron Weasley, a fellow ginger nut. We have this thing where we tug our hair at each other in greeting.

After being a record breaking pilot like Amy Johnson or a writer like Jacqueline Wilson and Charlotte Bronte I think working with books all day must be the best thing. They are my escape, my quiet time, funny, sometimes sad and the best ones are those that seem to put into words exactly how I feel about certain things like what I look like, being friends, feeling sad. The idea that someone else understands how I feel can be better even than caramel filled chocolate biscuits... there I go again about eating chocolate...well it is Day 3! When I deposit them back at the Deputy Head's office, they all thank me and say that it has made it seem less scary. See you all in September gels, I say in my best St.Trinian's voice.

The idea is that when they start at the school properly I will be their mentor and tear-mopper-upper for the first few weeks!

Just as well I was named after a Hindu goddess with many arms!

DAY 4 HER BLOOD IS GOLD!

It's the only kind of blood that's not linked to death or dying.

Funny true story. One poor girl saw a brownish stain on her pants and didn't know her period had started for the first time. The night before she had eaten a caramel and thought it might have come out the wrong way...hilarious!

Worse even than having to keep it all secret is the remembering to have towels or tampons with you and to change them. There are only so many times you can put your hand up for the loo! Can't say please Sir I need to change my pad? Can you imagine? I do make a point of changing whenever I can, breaks and lunchtime, especially on the first 2 days when the flow tends to be heavier.

Of course it seems like we lose pints of blood but the reality is it's only about two tablespoons or a very small cup full. I was thinking that I suppose it's just like a snake shedding its skin, ok maybe that's not the best example! OK how about like dogs and cats shedding their winter coats or better still like us humans taking off a jacket when we are too warm. I know it's like blossom that falls from the tree when it's time or the autumn leaves that just know when to fall...must try to think of some more. I feel a Period Poem coming on. Get it!

The whole Tampons v pads thing... well I started on pads. At first I felt like an overgrown baby. It just felt weird and that surely everyone could tell I was wearing them. Not so much VPL as VNB (visible nappy bulge). Of course no one can tell. Tampons are great as an emergency measure and easier to carry about... and you can swim in them.

But try putting a tampon in, in the school toilets! I know you should be able to do it standing up but I need to practically lie down to get it up there! You need to be a contortionist and get just the right angle, which always seems to involve me bashing against the sanitary bin.

What are you doing in there Kali...sounds like you are falling down the loo...

The shame....

Might try using a Moon Cup - a silicone cup that you insert instead of a tampon or wearing a towel...I know sounds a bit scary but really is supposed to be gentle and easy to wear... when I am older, maybe?

When Mum was at school you didn't do games when you had your period, or anything mildly strenuous like gymnastics or swimming. A discreet word to the teacher and she was able to help tidy up the school library instead. Not fair.But now with the invention of those tampons and leak free towels we can carry on as normal...whatever that is! I blame those adverts with girls galloping around on horses in; you guessed it pristine white jodhpurs!

But there it is again that attempt to hide the fact that us girls do have our periods. Let's pretend nothing is happening. What we really need to do is lie down and curl up with a hot water bottle. I'm sure even Olympic decathletes take it easier around that time. I feel like writing to Jessica Ennis and asking her what she does.

Downsides:

• Pain, that can be stomach cramps

• PMT or PMS (pre menstrual tension) emotional irritability and sensitivity.Ava says it should stand for **P**roduce **M**ilky **W**ay **S**oon or **P**erfectly **M**ad **T**oday

• Oh yes it happens EVERY month

• The big wide world acts as if they don't exist

• We have to pay for sanitary towels but at least we no longer pay as much tax on them but why should we pay any? In Canada they don't and Republic of Ireland.

• No longer a viable excuse to get off games!

DAY 5 Hint of Pink...

Just a hint of pink on my pad, it's virtually gone. So no need to bother changing

DAY 6

Energy surge but still a bit reluctant to get into full High School dance routine mode. Somehow that energy doesn't make me want to dive into my homework. Having to do something never seems right, best if it at least seems like my idea, my choice. I will do almost anything but settle to my homework. I have exhausted all possible ghastly domestic tasks; I even offered to clean the oven.That bad.

I decide to dust my Mum's beloved ceramics collection.

Mum's a step ahead as always and prizes the cloth from my hands talking in that soft, slightly patronizing way I expect psychiatrists speak to their patients. *Come on Kali, enough is enough go upstairs and engross yourself in the Treaty of Versailles. Then to coin a famous phrase, you may later eat cake. See if you can find out who said that.*

Avoidance tactics exhausted. All possible excuses used up and of course can't use period one. I sit down at my desk, lean on my hand and stare out the window at the street hoping for inspiration from the pigeons and the horse chestnut tree with its spiky conker cases about to drop...hey there's another metaphor!

When Mum calls up to see how I am doing, I have managed to write the title and underline it twice. *I've started*, I shout and *it was Marie Antoinette who was supposed to have said, Let them eat cake,* which in French translates as Let them eat brioche, which is a sweet bread, quite nice but not as good as pain au chocolat, in my opinion and by all accounts Marie Antoinette as well! But anyway she didn't say it. Poor thing was only 14 when she was married to the 15 year old, future King of France, Louis XVI...scary or what. She was practically a teen idol, thousands came out to see her on her first appearance in Paris, and some were even crushed to death in the excitement! Now all this is very well but not sure Mr. Morgan would consider this relevant to the actual essay title: Did the terms of the Treaty of Versailles lead to the Second World War? Discuss. The fact that Marie Antoinette had her own fairyland built at Versailles is not connected in the slightest. Shame...however if the essay had been about The French Revolution then perhaps...might be a way to put that in as a comparison. Suddenly I am thinking like an historian and am finally in essay writing mode. Phew! I manage to do the Introduction, which is always the hardest bit. At least once you've done it; you have said how the essay's going to go. I then put down all the main points of the treaty to be discussed and expanded once I have some refreshment! Kali you may eat cake.

Mum? Let me eat cake or brioche or even a half a digestive biscuit I have important world affairs to think about! I write this now lying on my bed sunbathing in the late afternoon light with my sunglasses on. Kali sur-la-plage...I am really on the Cote D'Azure with a 20's style swimsuit like in those amazing Vogue magazines, waiting to be invited to cocktails at Gatsby's. I blame Miss Dias for giving us such brilliant books to read in English. I heart Miss Dias. She is small but strict.

DAY 7

Feel invincible, if slightly dreamy. Calm, full of yippee, joy, like dogs when they run into the sea and splash like crazy, or Michael when he crunches a poor snail...its true that old rhyme... What are little boys made of?

What are little boys made of?

Leftover sprouts

And smelly socks,

That's what little boys are made of.

What are little girls made of?

Chocolate and roses

And they definitely rock!

Anyway you get the gist right? I feel sociable and ring people I have been avoiding. I call my Gran Adelaide and ask after her bunions.

Something chronic they are but a nice warm footbath will sort them out and I'll be right as rain for me Bowls match. We'll beat that bunch of no hopers from Neasden easy. Anyway can't stand here gassing all night I've got bingo tonight.

Bye love...Click

What has the world come to when your 82-year-old Gran has a better social life?

DAY 8

Motivated. Finally that essay gets done; easily...I even enjoy checking all the references.

Mum jokes: Can *I have actual photographic evidence of this? Kali at her desk working and oh my goodness apparently enjoying writing her history essay.*

OK OK...ha ha ha

DAY 9

Not much happened which means I must have felt OK and just did the usual. It's the sort of day that when I was 8 and first writing a diary I would have written something like this:

Got up had breakfast. Went to school. Had maths and games. Came home had fish fingers and went to bed. It was rainy!

I mean why bother! All that 8-year-old angst left out, like when our old cat Sid died, not a mention or even when Tara broke her arm.

DAY 10 I can do anything!

Felt really confident today, perhaps bit too assertive, finding it hard to NOT say how I really feel. I am the ruthless truth teller...not a good day for Ava to ask me how she looks in her beret style hat.

Also felt twinge in my right side, which Mum says is where my ovaries are...its proper name is perhaps the best word in the world...mittelschmerz–good one for Scrabble. These twinges usually mean its ovulation time, when gloopy bits appear on your knickers...bit yuck but again perfectly normal.

DAY 11 I feel fabulous

I even think I look half way decent, Mirror Mirror... you are the most beautiful girl in the whole of Y8... maybe even the school...believe me I make the most of feeling this way because usually I compare myself to ridiculously gorgeous females, like Jourdan Dunn or Cara D.I know hardly my look- a-likes!

I have a strong desire to eat apples. This is slightly too Snow White and making a healthy choice over a finger of fudge is quite an achievement for me.

Decide to walk home from school. Don't suppose I'll get a sticker like we used to in Primary school. I go through the park and check on the swan family. Oh my there are four signets that have beautiful soft

grey fluffy feathers. They are bigger than babies, like teenagers, more..

When I get home I even agree to a cuddly toy puppet show for Michael.

Yes I know it's a bit Freaky Friday and I wonder if I have been transplanted into the body of not my Mum but maybe Mother Theresa?

DAY 12 All OK

That's the thing I find with diaries I tend to write reams and reams when I'm feeling sad, cross or just moany. Today I don't have anything to complain about apart from the ever heartbreaking fact that Zayn will probably never be mine.

DAY 13 Ditto!

DAY 14:The Switch Day!!!

It's always hard to pinpoint just when I 'switch', as I am usually feeling completely fine. Then someone will say something in all innocence like – "*I really like those specs on you?* Instead of hearing the compliment, I hear- you looked an idiot in your old glasses. It's like my brain calculates 2+2 to make 6,789 instead of 4. Malfunction Malfunction...

Or it might be someone brushing past me on the stairs up to Geography and I feel instantly outraged... Excuse me, am I invisible or what to some poor innocent Y7. On another day it would hardly register on my annoying-o-meter, but on this day I react way out of all proportion.

It's like I have travelled with Bilbo to Mordor

and am staring up at those dark towers. A definite move to the Dark side...I feel a shift...an outer layer coming off, leaving me raw. All the grumpiness sort of protects me although not everyone else!

Good friends can normally tell when you switch and be understanding and not take any catty comments too personally! Although poor Ava did look crestfallen when I said she looked like she had a pancake on her head...remember the beret? On a good day I would have said oh you look just like Amelie in that film and meant it. Of course I can now spot this switch in others too,friends, teachers,my Mum,my Aunt,even the lolly pop lady...you really don't want to dawdle on the crossing on one of her off days!!

DAY 15 Who's that girl?

First time I saw her was on my way to PHSE. A buzz

of loud whispers who does she think she is and oi what's it like up there...then the wave of sneerers parted to reveal the tallest girl I have ever seen, and she was wearing flats too! She should have looked gawky and awkward but she moved with the grace of a giraffe. All the buffalo and antelope made way for her and she merely stepped elegantly through and proceeded on her way.

KALI: *What's all the fuss*

AVA: *Oh her names' Freya, she's new and she's American and you should see her breaststroke! She's the star of the swim team, been used to swimming in Olympic size pools. Personally I think she's really a mermaid.*

She was gorgeous too, but in a way only model scouts can see, not teenage boys. Golden brown skin, spirally corkscrew afro curls, pointy nose and clear brown eyes. She was wearing a beautiful red rose on the lapel of her blazer and it caught the light and seriously shone.

Before I had a chance to think, fairly typical me, I called out, just as she was passing us:

I really love the rose.

Wasn't sure she'd heard amidst all the mayhem, which is changing classes, but then slowly like a gazelle turning back in the forest, she rotated to face me.

I gulped and thought oh no she's going to cut me dead. Instead she said: *Thanks; it's for my Lady Day,* in her soft American accent. She smiled and walked away down the corridor towards the art rooms.

Oh right? Not quite understanding, I thought she must have meant Our Lady, Mary. That it must be a Catholic Feast day.

It would make sense.

It was only when I got home and mentioned it to Mum that I realised:

It was another euphemism, one I hadn't heard before.

She meant it's her period and she is celebrating it. Well good for her. Brave girl.

I suppose nobody else knew either, is that still brave if it's her secret?

Mum: *Well you know as well now.You should try to talk to her again*

Oh I don't know...she is well if you saw her...a bit goddess like and probably would swat me away if I bothered her.

Mum: *I expect she was chuffed you noticed that the rose was significant. You could tell her about your diary.*

Sometimes Mum shows her ignorance, not often. Parents don't understand all the school rules not written down in the School Handbook when you first start!

For a start she's in Y11 and really does look like Jourdan Dunn and probably has a big gang of scary friends that hate red headed people.

Mum: *Oh come on Kali, did you really get the impression that she was that kind of girl? I thought Ava said she was new, she might be glad of a friend.*

Well no but she will think I am just some silly Y8, which I am...

DAY 16 OK

DAY 17 Monster in the mirror...aargh!!

Two- headed monster. I was perfectly fine and then completely without warning, what I see is not Beauty but The Beast!! It's kind of freakish how this happens, like those funny mirrors at the fairground that make you look like Hagrid!

It's a bit like the first time I really "saw" myself in a full length mirror, a couple of years ago when I was 10, in hand me down faux purple denim trousers, that I used to love and would have worn every day if I could...but suddenly it was like oh no I look like an overgrown little kid with no dress sense...not so much the fashion police but sergeant major of the fashion army giving me a short sharp reprimand... what do you look like...why had no one said anything. How could I have let my Mum dress me for so long?

Just realized I have written perhaps the longest, most gabbly sentence of all time. Miss Dias is trying to encourage me to be more succint.Write less words.

The horror of suddenly being self-conscious. A sudden realization that I was no longer a little girl but still walking around in clothes only fit for a six year old! It's not that I want to dress all womanly or sexy. No way but I did need a decent pair of jeans

DAY 18 It'll end in tears!

And it did. Elated slightly hysterical/manic seriously emotional. Then me and Tara watched that programme where people send in videos of their pets doing silly things like falling down the toilet. We laughed so much Tara started snorting and I called her a pig, as a joke and then she started crying. If it had been me oinking she would have said the same thing.Mum came and told us both to calm down and maybe watch Life on Earth instead. Only later did I wonder maybe Tara's first period,is not long away. She seems more sensitive some days...?

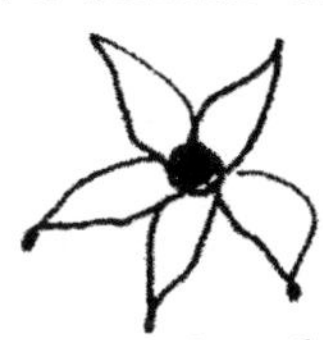

DAY 19 Super Brain

I love this kind of day and also very surprised when

my brain seems to be working at 100% capacity! Instead of daisy brain I have high voltage light bulbs going off. My problem solving is excellent. Without effort I can attempt to connect electricity circuits up and even understand how. Mrs. Kaplinsky was astounded: *You'll be an Ida Noddack yet.*

Ur thanks Miss, I think?

Had to look her up.

Ida Noddack, a German chemist, who co-discovered the chemical element rhenium and first proposed the idea of nuclear fission.

Might rather be British-born American astronomer Cecilia Payne-Gaposchkin who discovered that stars are made mainly of hydrogen and helium and established that stars could be classified according to their temperature?

Actually even cooler still, Delia Derbyshire who created the electronic version of the Doctor Who theme tune with her synthesizer machine. Dun der dun der dun...theme tune.

As well as being Mastermind and Marie Curie all rolled into one, I was even able to help Ava out when she couldn't work out how to change her ringtone from Waves, which is lovely but too soft to hear, to something like elephants trumpeting! if I could only trap this day in a bottle and open it when I have the opposite kind – lame brain, what is my name again?

DAY 20 CACTUS GIRL – WATCH OUT!

Mum says on days like these she is on red alert for the inevitable tipping over, the boiling point moment! She can tell the signs. I might suddenly decide to clean my room or tidy the living room. I have even been known to offer to clean out Michael's hamster cage! Out of love and generosity? Oh no, purely

because I cannot settle to anything like homework or practicing netball footwork.

It's that restless feeling, that I am trying to keep a lid on by doing boring, mind numbing cleaning. My seething brain is strangely comforted by the dull hum of the hoover as it picks up cat hair, hamster droppings and chocolate biscuit crumbs. Even the identification of these different bits of rubbish somehow calms me. As Mrs.Kaplinsky would say, it's a small sample of life. We can deduce a lot from even what may appear to be nothing. I suppose that's how detectives work out who murdered who by lipstick found on a discarded cigarette butt or a single stray hair teeming with DNA. Of course you may find treasure if you look hard enough, like the metal detectors that we see when we walk by the river. *Time to lock me away if you ever see me down there with one of those, says Dad*

Michael: *But you might find some real treasure that pirates have dropped.*

Dad: *A few rusty old cans and lost door keys if you're lucky* I found a pound coin under the sofa cushions and was well pleased with that for a half hour's work!

So was cleaning away quite happily until Dad makes a deliberately provocative remark, something really original like I think you missed a bit and BANG!! It's like a match striking touch paper; I explode, becoming a ball of fury. I throw down the hoover, slam out of the room seething and muttering and rush upstairs to fume in peace. Gruffalo spikes are out big time!

Dad: *Where's your sense of humour gone Kali? Did you suck that up along with the crumbs!*

Me: *AAAH !!*

Transformation complete I am the demented daughter from hell! I wish I didn't lose my rag quite so easily over a silly jokey comment. (Euphemism alert: On the rag is another code phrase for being on your period)! I want to feel strong and in control like my namesake the goddess Kali, fierce with many arms.

I could do with joining something like the Asgarda, a Ukrainian girl power movement, where you learn life skills and martial arts. Like a warrior version of the Girl Guides, with pick axes chains and scythes instead of string to make knots in, or is that the Scouts? When I told Ava about the Asgarda she said but don't they have badges or a special salute. Oh please Ava these are warriors not members of basically the junior wing of the WI!

Ava: *Actually Kali you know they did loads during the wars to help. Guides were earning badges as* *electricians, mechanics, first-aiders, and signalers. The telegraphist badge required them to construct their own wireless receiver and send messages in Morse code*

Me: *Oh right. I didn't know that.*

Ava insists on reciting The Guide's Promise right there in the dinner queue

"I promise that I will do my best:

To be true to myself and develop my beliefs,

To serve the Queen and my community,

To help other people

And To keep the Guide law."

I promise that I will do my best to eat this entire Galaxy bar.

There is a Guide badge for eating chocolate - it's true!

I lay on my bed trying to thing of things to calm me down:

1. My cat Mog, who had managed to get upstairs again. She wouldn't win any prizes in hide and seek, as she is currently a give away mound under my duvet. Mum gets cross if she comes upstairs. It is a battle of wills that usually Mog wins paws down by either streaking up the stairs through the slither of an open door or just stops, looks up at Mum with that I know I am adorable and you cannot possibly be cross with me, really, look. Works every time! I mean what animal gets away with cruelly playing with a baby bird dropped as a gift for Mum with a Well it is in her nature!

2. Imagining a day spent messing about on the river with Moley and Ratty from Wind in the Willows.

3. Reading the first 2 chapters of Wind in the Willows

4. Sitting quietly and breathing in and out slowly, like Miranda who came to do yoga with our class,

back in primary, showed us.

5. Watching Chocolat...the film...yes I do seem to be fixated!

DAY 21: DRAMA QUEEN

Well-behaved women rarely make history.

I feel it welling up inside me, this strong almost overwhelming feeling...quite scary, which seems to have overtaken me. The hormones are rising!

Usually the one who steps out of the way; today I collide. Usually so focused and sharp; today I float off and have to be called back to the here and now, which today is History with Mr. Morgan. I am daydreaming that I am charging along on my stead, sword in hand, but not much help if the lesson is actually about the Reunification of Germany...just a few centuries out.

Usually multi-tasker extraordinaire; today I have

to give the simplest thing like choosing a sandwich extra attention, its like I am being asked to explain the coding behind a complex computer system when in fact it's do you want the cheese and pickle or the ham?

I get pushed aside by those assertive others and don't even notice. It all seems too much.

For goodness sake Kali it's not a life or death decision. She'll have the ham. Ava to the rescue. She guides me to a seat and hands me the unwrapped sandwich and some water.

Eat. Drink. Think you can manage that? OK OK stop hassling me.

If I didn't you would still be agonizing over which poxy sandwich to get

Sorry Ava, I just feel a bit out of it.

I'd say on another planet!

Usually I don't have to think but just do; today

I need concrete boots to stop me floating up and away to lie on soft clouds with small birds taking a rest from a long flight from Africa.

Once I make it home, having got on the wrong bus and only realizing when I ended up at Ridgeway, I can just about make it to my room where I swoon dramatically onto my bed calling *Michael my liege can you get your poor Queen some sweet delicacy, a small trifle...you will be justly rewarded*. Thanks best brother (as Michael hands me a slightly squidgy half packet of chocolate buttons) you may indeed play with my beloved Pink Ted. *But don't try giving him a bath again please otherwise you will be hanging on the line with him, okay?*

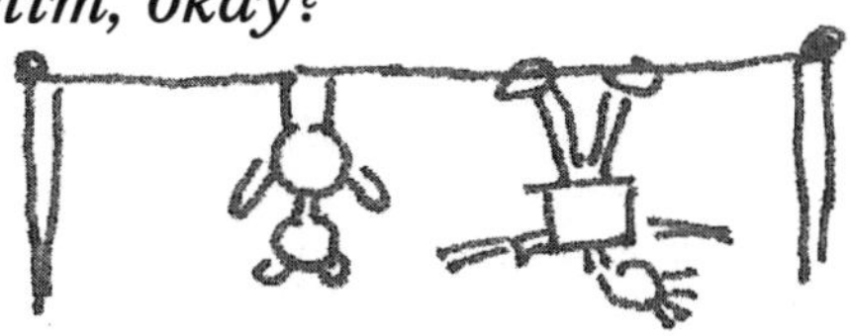

I could sit for hours watching rain fall.

I lie and listen deliberately to songs that make

me cry like:

Playlist TO BE MELANCHOLY TO:

1D - Summer Love

Taylor Swift – Last Kiss

Paloma Faith – Picking up the pieces

Amy Winehouse – Love's s Losing game

As long as he needs me (sang by Nancy in Oliver)

Anything from the Lion King

Later when I do go down for dinner I sniffle and watch wateryeyed when the ads for Dog Rescue come on. The odd tear trickling at some small tender thing like the baby meerkat in the advert.

Best thing about today, I almost forgot was seeing Freya from Y11, striding through the throng, giving the mean eye to all who got in her way and giving me a fleeting smile and a wink.

DAY 22 Bang on

Quick witted, alert focused, assertive.

All of the above adjectives describe moi today! Telling Y9 boys to move on the stairs and they did! Just said without a second thought, when most days I would be mumbling under my breath about the lack of gallantry and manners in today's world but outwardly saying "Excuse me please just trample on me it's fine!"

Ooh get her and what, is it your period?, followed by guffaws.

No she's too young mate

If only I had the nerve to say, yes actually it is and if it wasn't for us women none of you would be here in the first place...another fantasy when I am Kali the warrior rather than Kali the Coward...more worried about what others will think...which is fair enough in this school, you really don't want to draw attention to yourself for the wrong reasons.

Take poor Edmund who when he first came to Fawcett was a sitting duck target for the toughies - or they think they are anyway. Two years down the line and he has finally sprouted a few inches and grown into his biceps and no one gives him any more grief! Hurrah.

He is always getting down on one knee and pleading with me to accept his hand, usually in as public a place a possible, like the dining hall! He writhes around on the ground in mock pain.

Oh if she would but deign to look my way I would be happy! Seriously embarrassing but kind of flattering, even though I don't LIKE him in that way.

So the complete opposite from yesterday. Today I feel powerful and invincible striding down the steps to next class, parting the sea of people with the sheer force of my will. It's almost as if I am wielding a large shield and waving a sword.

Then from what seems like the mists of time I hear a lone female voice shout:

You go girl!

It was her; at least I think it was. Freya. As graceful as a giraffe nibbling leaves off the tops of trees, gone in a swish. I feel invincible like I have a whole legion of Amazonian warrior women following in my wake, backing me up. The Queen doth deign to notice me.

When I get to Citizenship, I who usually get told to speak up; am the Queen Bee ordering around my group. We discuss and put together a presentation on whether giving to charity really helps. We include a quite funny drama piece with Sonya being one of those annoying chuggers who stop you on the high street to try to get you to sign up. I know it drives Mum mad and she deliberately crosses the road to avoid them. Myself and Ava on the other hand will check to see if there are any cute looking ones and then smile sweetly and coo as they tell us about stranded whales or climate change, until they realize that we are after all only 12 and have no money to give!

Great organization and presentation, well-done Kali's group, Miss Samuels beams.

Other times I would be mortified to be singled out for praise but today I bask and preen.

Might get Hersha to print me a Q for Queen Bee t-shirt in her screen-printing class. She's in Y11 and really cool. I know her because she babysits for us sometimes.

DAY 23 don't mess with me

Women who inspire me and who have guts to stand up and be counted: Emma Watson at UN...you know Hermione from Harry Potter.

It's getting cool to say you're a feminist now Mum.

Mum: *It's about time*

As the power grows instead of involuntary outbursts of grrrrl power I become more premeditated. Too honest, opinionated assertive but potentially in a cutting hurtful way.

Feel it my duty to be the truth teller...watch out if you ask me what I think today.

There is a welling up of joy and I feel so brave and fearless. Wish I felt this way more often.

On the way home I saw a girl about seven, in a glittery dress over jeans with trainers, leapfrogging over her friend. She was having fun, being herself and not caring what anyone thought. I sometimes wish I could go back to before my period started, when I was about 8 and was happy in my cords, doing handstands, playing hopscotch and drinking milk.

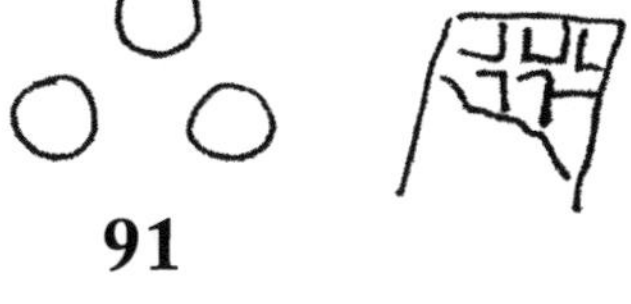

DAY 24 GIVE ME CHOCOLATE NOW!

Anything even a button or chocolate covered raisin will do, even the teeniest Lindt bear but preferably a very large bar of Galaxy Cookie Crumble. Just a smidgeon on the hour every hour prescribed by Dr Ava, a renowned expect on the healing powers of the sugar rush! Without chocolate I feel like screaming louder than a police siren. Even louder than Michael cries when Mum makes him have a bath. She says she used to have to lock herself in the loo when she was younger at home and curse for ten minutes, now she goes to karate and even teaches some of the classes now. Dad has learnt to be very careful about upsetting her at certain times, otherwise in a couple of smart moves she has him on his back on the floor.

I am liable to lash out verbally, prone to Torette's like swearing under my breath or have a tantrum equivalent to a two year old. I usually manage NOT to stamp my feet! Am trying to bite my tongue or to just step away, as Ava instructs. Reaching home the smoking dragon Smaug retreats to her lair calling for Mouse...

DAY 25 Almost there..

Sometimes when I drift off I start imagining all sorts of stuff like the world of swans and how come they return to the same pond each year and have their cute signets and why those crazy daddy long legs spider things parachute down at you. They are so delicate and graceful, the ballerinas of the arachnid world. Then in a blink I am back to reality with a bump, usually at school. In the void you are Kali, says Mum. The days just before your period starts are like you are in the wardrobe wrapped in the fur coats, just before coming out into Narnia. Dreamy days when nothing sticks but I might get a really out there thought come in. PING! It can be like the answer to a question I have asked the universe and having circumnavigated the galaxies for wisdom has brought an answer back. It feels like there is a big space in my brain...yes yes I know but seriously this space lets important thoughts in because its not crowded out with the usual mindless stuff like what I might fancy to eat, or should I try a pink streak in my fringe.

I had been asking why is it that we girls feel the need to be quiet and hide away when we bleed. This is what came back like a gentle tinkle in my mind's dropbox.

Well its because then these thoughts have a chance of coming in and being heard. I am waiting now for major wise and profound thoughts to start coming in. Nothing yet. *So Kali would you like to share your thoughts on the Weimar Republic?*

Snorts and giggles from the rest of my class and Nathan saying "Hey Space Girl!"

As Nisha said in the café after school, at least he noticed you, which in our book is practically a marriage proposal!

Intellectual pursuits are no good for me today I need to hide away in a mediaeval style tent with a red flag atop it, guarded by unicorns and waited on by squirrels in aprons bearing Minstrels and Hula Hoops. See what I mean. I really am in a different dimension, more likely to meet The Doctor than be sat in History next to Clint, who gives my elbow a friendly nudge when my dream state has been discovered. I wander into my house sighing and miss the hook that my blazer goes on and step out of my shoes and then drape myself on the nearest chair. My energy is spent I have become a human puddle, a floppy rag doll.

I do try to be helpful and offer to do the washing up. Oops CRASH!

Oh Kali not another one...

Oh yes the dropping of plates, mum's favourite mug, anything breakable seems to happen on this day. They just slip out of my hands. Or I tip something over, my arm or hand seems to have a will of its own, or there is a naughty poltergeist that probably looks like the imp in Harry Potter.

It is a scientific fact that during this part of our cycle we are prone to dropping crockery and a general aversion towards any kind of housework. Mum thinks Dad may suffer from this condition most of the time...ha ha

Low levels of testosterone and estrogen can cause poor coordination, due to lack of fluidity in the joints which leads us to feel clumsy and can also

cause fuzzy thinking, which could be another reason for perceived clumsiness during your period and the lead up.

FACT. The Yurok tribe forbids women to do any domestic tasks when they bleed. Very sensible. I have tried to pretend I am on Day 25 when I'm not, to get out of washing up duties. Basically I do need to retreat to my own Moon Lodge or Red Tent. I just need to be horizontal, without a tea towel. Now this minute, preferably on my lovely Orla Kiely duvet or failing that on a soft rug made from the down of baby signets- oh no that's so wrong...I mean fake fur equivalent! Maybe surrounded by protective wolves and a sentry that looks just a bit like Harry from ID.

I need to commune with the moon. In France they call periods Le Moment de la Lune. How more romantic does that sound. The Maoris call it Mala

Maraina – moon sickness.

I am definitely going to try that excuse one day. Can't do games as I have moon sickness...oh yes very contagious...

DAY 26 Demented?

Dad raises eyebrows and sinks deeper into The Guardian. Mum gives me the I'm disappointed -in-you- look because they think I swore in front of Michael. I really didn't.

M Oh you said a bad word Mum Dad Kali said a bad word

K ...*Michael I didn't what I said was oh bother*

M Well it sounded bad to me

K *Oh Michael go rattle the pea that is your brain*

Mum *OK Kali he doesn't understand there's no need to be mean what's got into you?*

Me: Is *it impossible to have any space around*

here without being subjected to The Family Interrogation. Can't you just all leave me ALONE!

Dad braving it, puts his head over the parapet -

Oh grow up Kali, you're acting like a 2 year old having a tantrum!

Me: *Grow up that's just the point. I can't drink, smoke, watch x-rated films or vote but I could have a baby.Is that grown up enough for you?* Maximum impact point to storm out of the kitchen, slamming the door-I felt!

For a split second Dad's face has a look of horror and he looks anxiously over at Mum who gives him the of course she isn't look.

Dad: *Well I must say that door hinge holds well. That's because we went for the Maxi Hold chrome with flexibility and strength.*

Mum: *Connor (that's my Dad's name) is this really the time for another of your DIY lectures?*

It really is amazing how your mind works...no your 12-year-old daughter is not with child!!

I couldn't help chuckling to myself as I stomped upstairs feeling much less angry but felt I owed it to the Wicked Witch of the South West to follow up my dramatic exit with another wall shuddering slam of my own bedroom door.

Oh no the handle.. Sugar x 3 It's come off! The force of the slam knocked it off! Now I'm locked in my room. I have locked myself in my own room!!

Sugar Sugar Sugar

I have two options. Either stay put or just hope someone comes to check on me later but because I now need to go to the loo I will be forced to be nice and beg to be let out...you can see how this will pan out after my performance downstairs.

My only hope is Tara who didn't witness the kitchen drama, who should be back from her football practice soon. I could text Mum with lots of sad face icons.

I decide I need the loo quite desperately so I text Mum: *Mum I'm sorry and if it makes you feel any better I slammed my bedroom door so hard the handle fell off and I am locked in, please help pretty please???* xx

I heard her let out a huge laugh and then tell my Dad who seemed to have become the laughing policeman he thought it was so funny. I could hear him saying Classic classic between belly laughs. Michael wanted to know what's so funny. When he realized what had happened he immediately ran up the stairs and called out to me its *Ok Gruffalo Mouse is here, I'll get you out!* Yes I did feel super guilty about how I had got at him earlier. He never seems to bear a grudge. He is really a sweetheart but don't tell him I said so! I am such as cow. But at least I know why. Next month I am really going to look out for those days when I do turn into a monster me. On days like today, I wonder what happened to that sweet girl child, laughing happily in her Matey bubble bath. I bet my family do too! Come back little me with scraped knees and pixie hair. Happy just to play Please Mr Crocodile or sit with old Mr Cornell over the road on the step while he told me stories of pirates and gold.

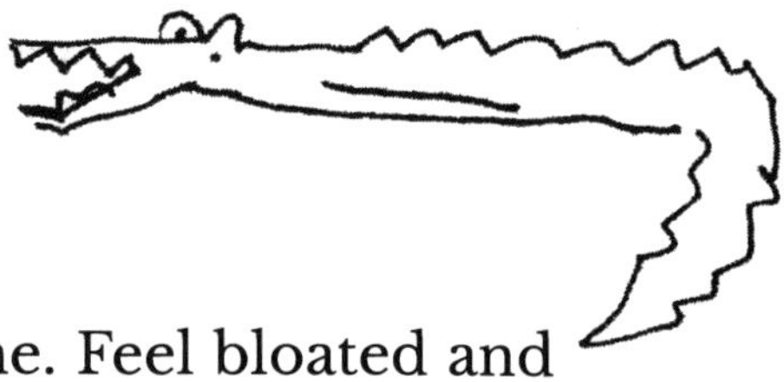

DAY 27 The Day before

Really want my period to come. Feel bloated and fit to burst. Got through the day somehow. Went home. I screened calls, all 2 of them. Made Tara answer. She is great at giving outlandish reasons for my being indisposed.

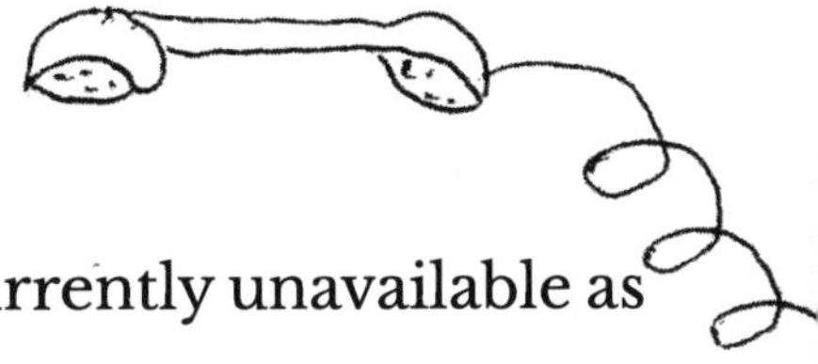

Tell Nisha I am in the bath

What Tara tells her: she is currently unavailable as she is floating off the coast of dreamland and won't return for some time.

I did talk to Ava. Well we do every night. *What can you still have to talk about you've just seen her all day at school?* Dad

Well only the whole journey back from school and the possible sightings of boys that look a bit like any of ID. We have separate journeys so that's a whole conversation in its self.

DAY 28 / DAY 1 It's here at last!

30 Million women have them. I come to visit every month. I am red all over. What am I?

The average cycle is 29.5 days in length, which is the exact time the moon takes to orbit the Earth. Good fact for geeky friends and the science teacher!

Mine seems to be pretty much 28 days long every month. Every girl is different.

The last day of the cycle becomes the first day of the next. The first day of your period...confused you will be! It all starts again. My bleeding lasts about 4-5 days but that will vary from girl to girl and woman to woman. The first 2 days will be heavier flow and then it seems to tail off and then practically be gone by day 5.

Thank goodness Day 1 falls on a Sunday, this month, so I do have pads to hand and no need to ask Ava or find reasons to keep going to the loo. Of course it won't always come at the weekend but it is so much better when it does. I can keep out of people's way if I feel grumpy and rest up in my room. I can take a bath or read. We haven't any family visiting to do either. phew!

FACT: It's usual for Native American groups to

hold a big party for young women who have started their periods – they are taken out to sea and left to make their own way back by swimming! Cor I just about managed my 50 metres and that was sheer fear of Mr Edwards the swimming instructor and his stick (which was of course to hook us out should we need help not for wacking us over the head!) Then on their return the whole village greets them. Symbolically she is bringing new life to her people.

As it's Sunday I spend most of the day in my room reading and musing about things and stroking Mog, She is overjoyed that a human is enjoying one of her favourite past-times, i.e lying around. Because I'm not rushing around I feel exactly when it starts. It does feel like the return of a long lost friend. I feel the relief and all the tension that built up the last couple of days disappear.

If I get those why me thoughts I remember the

reality. All women whoever lived, bled.All those living in caves 20,000 years ago, priestesses in the pyramids in Ancient Egypt, Queen Elizabeth I, (another impressive redhead),all bled with the Moon.

In Japan family and friends are invited to a party but aren't told why. Red rice, beans and an apple are given to the girl on her first period. What no marshmallows or chocolate...some party! Mmm talking of food think I can smell roast chicken. Mog wakes up at that point and sniffs the air. We both bound downstairs.

DAY 2 Monday

Period Poem

Bright redness of raspberry and scarlet like berries – I bleed.

I'm working on it OK?

Dreamt I was running fluid like a cheetah, graceful

as a deer, able to jump over tree tops and land lightly on marble steps, knowing that a mere twitch of a thought would allow me to rise again and fly. I told mum about this. I don't usually remember my dreams. She said it is a common dream for girls who have recently started there periods symbolising the transition from child to teenager. Felt a bit bloated but no cramps this time. Had a light lunch soup with bread. Can you believe no chips and there were smiley ones!

I decided to wear something red today that only I would know about, bit pathetic I know after all my ranting...so red pants it is.

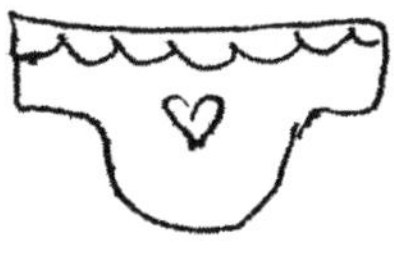

DAY 3 Tuesday

Was in the loo at lunchtime and I heard an Oh no its started!

I knew exactly what was happening.

Hello can I help. It's Kali. There's no one else in here. Kali, my period's come and I haven't got any towels.

It's OK I'm on Day 3, I can give you some. Just a minute. I'll slip it under the door.

Thanks.

Who should walk out of the cubicle but Sonya?

Our secret right? Course.

DAY 4 Going with the flow

Went swimming after school with Ava. She was having her practice and I just messed about in the shallow end and did a few pathetic widths. I thought I would brave it and try tampons in and have a swim. Felt a bit nervous that the little string thing would show or worse still that the pool would suddenly turn red and everyone would know and the lifeguard would shout: *Evacuate! Evacuate!*

Girl with period in pool.

Of course it was fine and being in the water made me feel lighter. I even joined Ava's swim group for an end of practice volley ball game. It was fun and I soon forgot I had IT in!

DAY 5 Where'd it go?

Not even a trace or a drop. But I thought I would put a pad on just in case!

DAY 6

Whether it was the swimming or just my energy returning but I felt full of beans.

DAY 7

Went into town with Ava and Tara and bought a new pen with red ink, rubbers shaped like squirrels and number stickers to decorate my you-know-what-diary! Just the essentials really.

Day 8

Decided it was time to sort through my old toys and donate to the school fair, offer to Tara and or Michael or just get rid.

Another photo opportunity Mum couldn't resist! Kali is tidying her bedroom voluntarily!
It was quite an emotional clear out. I kept Mr. Pink, obvs but Barbie was relocated to join Daisy and Action Girl in Tara's room. Humphrey the one eyed dog made of felt, went on the jumble sale pile, as did my out of date world globe and my faux purple trouser suit. Michael came in to rummage through the to go pile and rescued Humphrey. I was secretly glad.

I made a special space to keep my Menstrual Diary with a red candle beside it which next month I am going to light when it's the first day.

Day 9 Period Party...yes that's what I thought when Mum suggested it. Could be fun? They are very big in some parts of the United States. Has to be girls only, you can have your Mum and aunts there, even your Gran if you can bribe her with cocoa and cake.

I might think about it. See if Ava can come over on that day, which should be a weekend day, if all goes to plan. Would I want to invite anyone else? Tara obvs.

I was amazed to see an article all about Period Parties in Sugar magazine, perhaps it is coming out into the open a bit more? It gave me some ideas.

Definitely not the dunking tampons in water and pin the ovaries on the uterus games. Don't want to freak Tara and Ava out, or me come to that!

It does encourage you to explain menstruation to your brother...you can imagine how that would go!

Usually you would have this kind of thing for your Menarche, first period. Remember my non - event? But there's no reason not to have a belated party and celebrate this month's flow.

I like the buy yourself something special idea, like mum does. I would go for a new book or some red roses,

The thing is I like the idea of a party, now on Day 9, but what if when it gets near to the next period I don't feel like it? Have to keep it small and relaxed. Will talk to Mum.

I suppose I can always just have a sleepover and not say why. Only I would know the true reason but then what's the point and I would still be keeping it a big fat secret. Perhaps I could invite Sonya...not!

No I will keep it simple and see what Ava says.

DAY 10 Ask Ava

Ava thinks it's a great idea. No surprise that she had loads of ideas of things we could do.

We could all wear something red and bring red eats. Then we could light candles and watch a Jodie Foster film or swap stories of feisty girls. We could all tell the others about a girl or woman who inspires us.

Little brothers and dads would be banned. I know Marcus would love to be a fly on the wall, but no it has to be girls only.

Yeah definitely!

We could read passages from our favourite books and play songs.

We worked out that the first day of my next period should be a Saturday, which would be perfect. I would have lots of time to prepare and then the next day would be Sunday, so if it all got too much

I could hide under my duvet all day! I do feel like telling the world, shouting it over the school tannoy system like in Grease! But only for a second, until I looked around and came to my senses.

I did float the idea of asking Sonya to Ava. She stopped in her tracks and gave me her are you stark staring mad look, why? *Well its up to you its your party.*

DAY 11 Well Hello!

Found myself winking at cute boy in Y7. Kali really, you cradle snatcher. The temperature is rising...feel like its raining boys. Every turn on the stairs to Maths another cutie makes himself known.Uh oh must be ovulation time, when the little eggs go go go...most of the time I am happy in girl world but suddenly mid way my eyes go all twinkly and I wouldn't be surprised if Robbie Williams appeared, sliding down the banisters to sweep me up Hollywood style onto a flower swathed swing. I blame my Gran for making me watch all those Gene Kelly films. I start to see the world in technicolour and tweeting Disney birds blowing out hearts from their beaks.

DAYS 12 AND 13

Pretty fine

DAY 14

As the last couple of days had been so fine I completely forgot it was day 14 until I saw the same boy, the one who I thought was cute on Day 11 and scrowled as he got in my way on the stairs. He looked surprised and I thought uh oh. I'm switching. Took some deep breaths and told myself not to react should some other poor innocent knock into me by accident or say something unfortunate that I might take the wrong way.

I was quite proud of the way I didn't get upset when a Y9 girl stepped on my foot, by mistake. I smiled and said no worries even though my teeth were clenched tight and it took a lot of control to not scream, Look where you're going clod foot.

More deep breaths.

Cool as a cucumber I replied to Sonya's Go sista go sista how goes it for you?

Kali: *Well its half time and I'm gonna swing for somebody.*

Sonja: *I'm close behind you and could scream at the slightest.*

K: *Thanks for the warning shall I evacuate the building for you?*

S: *If you could.*

Since the-pad-under-the-loo-door bonding, Sonya and I have perfected our own private language to let each other know what day we are on. Not when she's with her gang then it all defaults to how it used to be and she makes some comment on my clothes, which will raise a laugh from her lot. She usually manages a wink that only I can see. It's like two worlds colliding, the pretend, fake one and the real true.

I am building up to asking Sonya to the Period Party but not sure that might be a step too far and Ava doesn't know why I should even want to. Tricky.

DAY 17

Nothing looks right. My skirt looks skew whiff, my blazer shabby, my hair just won't lie straight and of course it's a day when Nathan says *"Alright Kali"* as we get off the bus. Usually I would be thinking oh my he speaks to me and I need to tell Ava immediately but because I think I look crappy I just presume he means nothing more than that and I say Alright back and mooch onwards to school. I can almost see a black cloud hovering just over my head as my Eeyore mood takes root.

Ava: *What's up Kali, you look dangerous!*

No just feel a bit sad and that I look like a jammy dodger on legs.

Ava: *I'd say more of a fondant fancy! Ah hah almost saw a smile trying to happen then!*

Oh Ava why must I beee a teenager in love...Boop shewaddy waddy boop shewaddy waddy boop...

We both sashay down the corridor licking our fingers and laughing until I stop in my tracks and say *-Ava you witch you did it again. You made me stop being moody and now I am actually feeling good! You knew I wanted to be in a foul mood all day but no you had to make me feel better didn't you!!*

Ava: *Shucks I promise I won't do it again!*

And then the rest of the day that could have been miserable became OK.

Did I tell you Nathan spoke to me this morning?

NOOO...tell tell tell

Much embellishment and exaggeration ensued as I made Nathan's "Alright Kali" into a sonnet recitation akin to the balcony scene in Romeo and Juliet.

DAY 18 Salt Pepper Vinegar Mustard

All the mixed emotions of yesterday should have been a warning of my delicate state. Ava had jollied me out of my fug, my gloomy mood. I was feeling OK until I wacked my leg on a cupboard on one of the school corridors' its always been there and usually I would automatically avoid it, like you do when you are daydreaming and find you have walked home without realising it. Like your legs and brain decide you need to be on autopilot. There she goes again in daydreamer mode, suppose we'll have to get her home.

Well Ava thought it was hilarious as did half of my class:

Thought having four eyes instead of two you might have spotted large obstacle in your path!!

Oh you traitor!

I stormed off into registration and sat avoiding Ava, who sits beside me.

Oh come on Kali, I was only joking.

I decide to ignore her, despite all her efforts to apologize. We hardly ever argue, so it's really horrible when we're not talking.

I am trying to think when the last time was, unbelievably it was probably back in Primary school when we got cross with each other over a game called Salt Mustard Vinegar Pepper, where you jump on the right step. We didn't speak for the rest of playtime but really couldn't keep up the silent treatment for longer than lunch - time play.

We have different first lessons so I sit in my French class feeling annoyed with myself for being so touchy, especially with Ava. She was in Spanish class.

We almost collide coming out of our lessons and both laugh nervously and then say sorry at the same time.

Me: *Je suis desole*

Ava: *Lo siento*

We hugged and I said sorry again, in English.

You're such a good friend and put up with a lot from me and still I am horrible to you.

Ava: *Oh Kali, I think I probably knew what I said might annoy you as I could tell you were a bit tense, so I was being equally mean.*

All I can say is Salt Pepper Ava: Vinegar Mustard!

DAY 19 Cooking on gas!

An electric current is a movement or flow of electrically charged particles, typically measured in amperes.

Exactly right Kali, well done, said Mrs.Kaplinsky in a slightly amazed tone.

She was amazed – so was I. I didn't know I knew that. My brain is spitting facts today, without me having to try at all. Usually I would be dredging my memory for something vaguely related that might sound right but today it's on the tip of my tongue.

I was so chuffed I repeated my answer to anyone in my house that would listen. Dad was impressed and said next time a bulb goes its over to you Einstein!

DAY 20 Just a bit touchy....

I knew the minute I woke up that I felt a bit sensitive and second that it was Friday. Ok I can do this I can get through the day without weeping or screeching at anyone. No really I can! If I can just avoid any human contact and conversation, then I'll be fine! The universe must have aligned to Kali central because when I got into registration our form teacher Mrs. K said those with double drama will have to do study time, as Mr. Bell was away. I usually love this lesson but today it would have been hard to be bouncy and smiley.

While everyone else groaned. I was secretly going YES thank you universe.

Sitting quietly reading and writing an essay on our favourite film was just up my sensitive street today. I pretended to moan like everyone else but I was cheering inside. I wrote my essay on Chocolat the one with Johnny Depp. I love the main character Vianne and how she sweeps into the small French village and whips everyone up and of course those scenes when she makes the chocolate, well, pause, rerun, pause, rerun

I managed to keep my head down for the rest of the school day and avoid any situations that might involve noisiness and lots of people. I even went the long way round to history, up the quieter staircase.

Ah so you've found the secret staircase too Kali, I see! Jokes Mr. Morgan.

Keep it to yourself won't you.

Yes sir!

We had a great lesson all about the sad fate of the Tsar Nicolas and his family in Russia. I even went up afterwards and asked what he would recommend to read to find out more. Mr. Morgan was so pleased he wrote me a list. *Avoid the ones written by various women who claim to be Anastasia.*

Do you think they definitely all perished?

I would say it's a certainty but there's always a possibility

DAY 21 It's S.A.T.U.R.D.A.Y hurrah!

Anyone would think I hated school. I really don't most of the time. It's just I am glad to be home and if I start to feel tetchy can flee to my room to avoid my mighty wrath coming down on poor Tara or Michael. It seems too easy to take it out on my family. I make the effort for people at school so I should do the same for my beloved familia! But you know how it is, even when I am as calm as calm can be one of them will usually annoy me. It's a fact that families are annoying, right?

Hasn't it been scientifically proved that there are more rows on Christmas Day than any other day? Families forced to be together and under pressure to have fun. A recipe for disaster. But I am determined to try. I say of course Michael do tell me all about the dead pigeon you saw on the pavement, the more detail the better please!

When Tara starts singing along to Kylie loudly in the kitchen I smile sweetly and make tea. It does take a huge amount of self-control not to shout oh shut up can't you. I retreat to my room with a sigh of relief and start reading one of Mr. Morgan's non recommended books on is she or isn't she Anastasia, daughter of the Tsar. If you read it as a story then it doesn't matter if it's not true. The historical facts might be useful for the essay we have to write, but I might not mention this book in the references at the end!

Gran came round for dinner.

You're a bit quiet love, everything alright?

Yes thanks Gran just thinking about the Russian revolution and what happened to the Tsar and his family.

Course you know he was the cousin of our king and the Kaiser and should have been easy enough to get them all out safely but that's family for you...

No I didn't. Do you think it was wrong what happened to them?

No one should be put to death for any reason I don't think but they were living in a rich old wonderland while the rest of the country had hardly a crust to eat. I wouldn't mind reading that book after you?

Sometimes they surprise you. Family. Who would have thought Gran and me would bond over the Russian revolution and that she would think it was a perfectly normal thing to be thinking about on a Saturday evening.

Gran can also tell that I am feeling tetchy and she pats my knee lovingly and winks. Its like she knows. I suppose having lived as long as she has she must be able to tell a premenstrual girl a mile off!

DAY 22 Let's do stuff!

I woke really early and felt full of energy. I even beat Dad and Michael downstairs.

Think I'll come with you for the papers. Shall we get baguettes for a change?

Yes lets. Come on you two lets get going!

Dad: *OK hold on Kali, its still only 7am, even the corner shop won't be open yet!*

Kali: *Oh yeah well we could take the long way round via the park and Michael can take his bike.*

Yea said Michael can I bring the dinosaurs too.

K: *No we need the basket for pastries and papers.*

M: *How about one?*

We set off at a fast pace, led by me.

Dad: *Hold up Kali, aren't we having a leisurely Sunday stroll not a power walk.*

We reach the corner shop and the papers have just arrived and haven't been sorted out yet.

Next stop the new deli on the high street. It smelt divine. Such a choice. I forget about baguettes and go for an oat cookie.

Michael took forever and decided on what was a very large jammy dodger! Dad chose croissants for himself Mum and Tara. Mog the Cat is also partial to a few croissant crumbs. Weirdly she also likes Parmesan cheese. I think she must have been born of at least one continental cat parent. We should have named her Cherie or Pampelmoose instead of Mog.

We march back home to get at those goodies. Well I do anyway! It's still early. After breakfast, which I finish in about 5 minutes flat, I feel I can't sit still. Shall I do some hoovering? *Kali, while the offer is generous the hour is not conducive to such noise and your mother and Tara are still in slumber land, lucky things.*

But I need to do something.

OK Kali how about you sort out the recycling, quietly!

Here is a list of what I achieved today:

Sorted the recycling in the correct bags (quietly)!

Put the washing on

Cleaned Mog's bowls and fed her

Washed up breakfast things.

Bought tea and croissants up to Mum and Tara (at reasonable hour)

Hoovered and cleaned my room.

Made notes for my essay on the Russian Revolution

Planted some bulbs in the garden with Dad and Michael. 9. Helped Michael build a Lego spaceship whilst Dad got lunch on the go.

10. Asked Tara to help me make invites for the you-know- what-party!

I love days like this when I get loads of things done.

It feels like I am clearing the decks, making sure all work is done before My Period comes around again. Everyone else seemed to like it too!

You're a human dynamo today Kali, says Dad. It's like having a live in au pair!

Mum: *I'll have to make sure there's a list of jobs to do next time you feel like this!*

Michael: *I'm going to bring my Spaceship into school for Show and Tell.*

Tara: *Breakfast in bed. I could get used to that. How about being my personal Lady's maid?*

Think I will draw the line at picking up dirty knickers but thanks for the thanks!

I beamed with goodwill and love for my family. Make the most of it I thought because tomorrow might be a bumpy ride!

DAY 23 Shall I tell you what I think?

The warm fuzzy feeling was still with me, as I got ready for school. Michael's slurping of his cereal provoked only a sweet sisterly smile and an Ah Bless!

Dad's usual has anyone seen my keys scenario prompted me and Mum to roll our eyes in unison and laugh.

Mum: *Try your pockets? Me: Try your bag*

Tara: *Aren't they on the hall shelf?*

Michael: *Bet you wish you had one of them metal finder things now!!*

I wasn't even forcing it so I got a shock when some Y9 pushed in front of me getting on the bus and I yelled for the whole queue and everyone already on the bus to hear: *Hey oh my goodness I must have put on my invisibility cloak today, as everyone seems to think they can jump the queue.*

Hello I am here and with my hair hard to miss!

I was pleasantly surprised when what seemed like the whole bus erupted with laughter and clapping. Even the bus driver grinned and said:

You've made my Monday! Then he whispered have you got a ruler on you?

Yes why? You'll see.

When the last person got on the bus, the driver turned, waved my purple plastic ruler in the air and shouted ***Colloportus*** and the bus door closed.

Those Harry Potter fans are everywhere. Hurrah for that. Now that's the way to start the week. Sometimes speaking out can be a good thing.

DAY 24 Ha Ha it's Harriet Potter!

Well of course there was inevitably going to be a downside to my public performance.

Ava: *Why are they calling you Harriet Potter?*

Oh I've had Hey Ron and where's your broomstick but I think Dobby was a touch hurtful...

Ava: *Can't believe you didn't tell me about the bus, everyone is talking about it.*

Well it was spontaneous and great at the time; I thought the driver was going to burst into song. But now, today it's just embarrassing, what could have possessed me?

Ava: *Well clearly my Sonorus spell must have worked on you then!*

What's that, I've forgotten?

*IT AMPLIFIES YOUR VOICE...*Ava shouts and gets a reproving look from Mrs. Dillon, the Office Manager.

Ava: *So that's one more point on the who really knows their Harry P scoreboard to Ava, aka Hermione and Ginny rolled into one!*

Me: *Hhm more like Moaning Myrtle. I've heard you in the girls' loo*

*Now give me a finger of fudge...*immediately or I shall make you explode!

We have a pretend wrestle and Ava wiggles the chocolate just out of reach.

Me: *Give give give, you know what will happen if I don't have my regular dose...*

Ava: *OK OK spare us the Wicked Witch of the West impression. Silence as I swallow my medicine!* All is well as the chemical magic flows through my veins averting the transformation from sweet Y8 girl to witch.

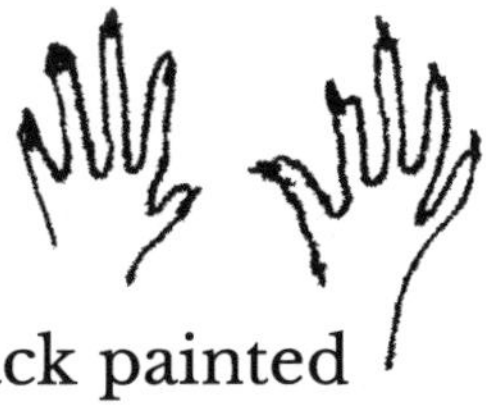

Ava: *Close call! Phew.*

Me: *Are you sure...*I show her my black painted fingernails...I start running after Ava making cackling sounds.

Must remember to keep my hands out of sight

as nail varnish not permitted on the premises of this educational establishment. Why? Who knows, maybe there is a scientific report that shows beyond any reasonable doubt that it impedes the intake of mathematical formula. Basically not allowed.

Could be DAY 24 is a rule breaker day. But black nail varnish hidden under cardigan sleeves pulled down hardly counts as revolutionary activity. It's about my limit. No putting my hand up today!

Have managed not to have a go at anyone today and as I am now sat in my bed with some kindly made by Mum hot chocolate and Mog the cat, there is unlikely to be any opportunities for conflict. Might need to breathe deeply if when I clean my teeth a family member who might hog the basin or make annoying gargling noises joins me. All went OK; I just shut the bathroom door on Tara and said I need privacy when I floss!

I think what made the difference this month was anticipating what might come up and then trying to control my reaction. There has definitely been less ranting...of course there is still 3 days to go...

DAY 25 Oops butter fingers!

The day started with me lost in thought, thinking about why it is that do-gooders felt the need to insist that all children should be able to go to school and at the same time whether Scout in To Kill a Mockingbird is in danger. My brain drifts from thing to thing not always with an obvious connection.

Then my brain and my right arm seem to disconnect and before I know it my breakfast cereal is all over my lap!

Oh no look at my skirt, its all milkified! Mum help!

Oh Kali you are all fingers and thumbs today. It'll be fine if you sponge it down.

But it will be wet and people will think I've had an accident!

Well you have.

Not that kind, you know what I mean.

It'll be dry by the time you get to the bus stop.

Sit self-consciously with my satchel on my lap. Not that anyone is looking at me. Decided against doing a tap dance down the aisle today!

Sonya got on and sat down beside me.

Sonya: *How's you?*

Kali: *Wet patch...*

Sonya: *Would have had your back if...*

Kali: *Good to know. Sonya?*

Sonya: *Yes?*

Kali: *Wanna come to a party, Saturday?*

Sonya: *What's the occasion?*

I raise my eyebrows and look down at my lap

Sonya: *A party for that? I dunno seems a bit*

weird, who's goin?

Kali: *Probably just Ava, my sister, my aunt and Gran, girls only.*

Sonya: *What will we have to do?*

Kali: *Oh no it will really just be like an afternoon tea, with cake and silly games and we can all choose music...*(I slip her an invite)

Sonya: *Sounds all right I'll see.*

Kali: *Don't tell anyone else will you?*

Sonya: *As if!*

So looks like I am having the party then. I don't suppose Sonya will come but well Auntie Eireen has already said she has penciled it in and quote: *I'll be there with my tampon tassels a shaking...*

She's joking of course, right Mum? Mum raises her eyebrows and says very unconvincingly, *I'm sure she is!*

Tara slid her handmade RSVP under my bedroom door with a large red glitter pen YES.

Mum says she has got the food sorted but says it'll be a surprise. She has sworn not to do anything like tampon shaped sausage rolls...she says she still has nightmares about her Hen do even now! Apparently it involved an unexpected waiter man wearing only an apron. No surprise that Auntie Eireen organized that little surprise!

I think I can trust Mum to know what not to do. Can't I? Gran's coming too although she did say what will THEY think of next and all seems a bit strange making a song and dance about yer monthly. Mum says Gran wouldn't miss it for the world, she loves a party! I feel sure there will be a few Back in my day anecdotes up her sleeve. Oh God why did I invite Sonya? Real friends you don't mind making a fool of yourself in front of.

Big mistake. What if she comes and thinks it all stupid or embarrassing. Or maybe she won't come and just decide to break our pact and shout loudly in the school corridor, *how'd your little Period Party go Kali?*

Oh now the whole idea seems ridiculous or just plain gross. I want to cancel but everyone is getting excited.

Ava says she decided on her outfit, which will be subtly red with some sort of flower corsage. I haven't even thought of that...I don't have red or pink clothes. Well the hair for one thing...just not my colours...will have to be clever accessories, shoes, hair slide maybe, necklace, and bangles. *Ava, will you come to Claire's Accessories with me after school?*

Sure, we could do Top Shop too; remember I've got that voucher.

Yeah but that's for you. I gave it to you.

So this is a special occasion and I've only got a fiver left on it anyway, I mean I wasn't going to let you have it all...please...

We both stuck our tongues out at each other and grinned.

So after school we went Period Party shopping, as you do! As we should do!

First off, Claire's where I got some red sparkly nail varnish, a hair slide with a red flower and a red belt. In Top Shop we giggled and dared each other to ask for the Menstruation range.

Of course all the loud giggling prompted one of the cool girl assistants to ask if we needed any help, were we looking for anything special? Which of course made us laugh all the more.

Actually, said Ava, where are your mainly red clothes. Well we don't keep them all together but I can show you what we have.

There was a gorgeous red top with lace that would have looked great on Ava, but not for Le Ginger Nut.

In the end we spent the rest of Ava's voucher on cute red heart sweets and some lovely red ribbon with pink spots that we both spotted at the same time for Tara.

DAY 26 Return of the Gruffalo

Haven't spoken to Sonya since but she has winked at me a couple of times. Not sure whether to interpret that as, I am coming or maybe she'd just got a nervous twitch. Can feel the purple spikes trying to poke through and hibernation mode setting in. Bears do it, hedgehogs do it, even menstruating girls do it, let's do it let's hide away.

When I got home I signal to Mouse that the Gruffalo is at large and may be in need of sustenance. Obliging as ever with his bottomless Spiderman bag he braves the Great Downstairs seeking eatables for a grumbling monster.

DAY 27

It's definitely on its way, heavy tummy and a desire to lie down anywhere. Doormat will do. Just step over me its fine. **Michael:** *Mum think Kali's turned into a dog*

DAY 28/ DAY 1 It's my party and I'll cry if I want to...

Getting just a little worried that my period hasn't started, what if there's no blood before the party, wouldn't that be a bit fake to pretend. I know, who's going to know? It's not like they'll want proof... will they?

Calm down Kali, you're getting all worked up and stress can stop it coming.

OK I have decided just to get on with the preps and make a final decision on my outfit!

Mum and Auntie Eireen are cooking up a storm

in the kitchen, all smells really good, but I am under strict instructions not to go anywhere near.

Michael and Dad have gone off on a Male Bonding day to the zoo.

Mum talked for ages about what to include at the party. She thought it best to have a vague plan so everyone knows what's likely to happen. I did emphasize that I didn't want any embarrassing surprises. No naked waiters

Course not, as If I would, winks Mum, worryingly! All I know is that there is going to be a group nail varnish activity. I know it's starting to sound terrifying. Mum and I thought we could all sit in a circle and paint the nails of the person next to us.

Well that should last five minutes max. So then what?

I have decided to wear my black pinafore and white shirt underneath with red belt, hair slide and red tights. Best of all I will be showing off my little red satchel, bought by Mum and Dad as a belated Menarche gift. I shed my first tears of the day. I love it!

Oh yes by the way IT started, just as I was deciding whether to wear my fancy red pants or some snoopy pants, as a nod to my first time. No, not the same Snoopy pants, a new updated pair.I decided to wear both just in case! Phew won't have to fake it. I am starting to get seriously nervous now about the whole thing.

Ding Dong, my heart skipped a beat and had a few moments of oh no what have I done...suppose it is a bit late to cancel now.

Gran arrived first with a beautiful mohair red scarf she had knitted.

Congratulations Kali, you're a woman now, gawd help you!

Ur thanks gran, I think?

Ava came straight from swimming and changed up in my room. When she came down the stairs she had let her gorgeous hair go all curly and she had on a maroon coloured dress with a white Peter Pan collar. Really lovely. *Just today, never to be repeated outside of this house understood.*

You look wonderful Ava

So do you, I love the touches of red. Here this is from me...

Me: *Really the hair was enough but this is so beautiful, a bloodstone on a chain.*

We hug and both pretend we haven't got a bit tearful and cough.

Every little thing was becoming very emotional, super charged with feelings All these lovely girls and women all here for me but quite different from a birthday. I started to cry and Ava said *oh don't blub or I'll start too.*

Well it is Day 1 so on top of the Party is the usual sensitive feelings.

If we're all here, shall we go in?

Just then the doorbell rang and who should be standing on the doorstep but Sonya with a huge bunch of red roses. I really didn't think she was going to come.

Hey blood sister! You been crying?

Hey yourself! Yeah getting a bit emotional already. Sonya the flowers are gorgeous!

You can thank Ava for the idea.

I looked at Ava with amazement and she nodded and winked at Sonya...

Mum begins to get everyone to go in to the living room and sit on cushions or chairs arranged in a circle.Gran surprised me and went for a cushion.

I mightn't be able to get up again mind you!1

Kali, you sit here so we can all see you!

Mum leads me to one of the dining chairs, which has been covered in rich red velvet.

A throne at last! Perhaps being a princess for a day is not so bad!

Did I really just say that? It's Day 1 I don't know what I'm saying...

Everyone followed me in and Tara did a curtsey.

We started with the nail varnishing, I did Gran's and then Sonya did mine.

Then to give it time to dry, Auntie Eireen did a brilliant rendition of Aretha Franklin's Respect.

We all got up to wiggle our fingers and shake our stuff. Thankfully no tampon tassels in sight! R.E.S.P.E.C.T. Ava read this poem by Mary O'Neill:

"What is Red?"
Red is a sunset
Blazing and bright.
Red is feeling brave
With all your might. A spot on your nose.
Sometimes red, is a red red rose.
Red squiggles out when you cut your hand.
Red is a brick
And the sounds of a band.
Red is hotness You get inside
When you're embarrassed
And want to hide.
Fire-cracker, fire-engine
Fire-flicker red –
And when you're angry

Red runs through your head.
Red is
A Valentine heart,
The trimmings on
A circus cart.
Red is a lipstick Red is a shout
Red is a signal
That says, "Watch out!"
Red is a great big
Rubber ball.
Red is the giant-est
Colour of all.
Red is a show-off,
No doubt about it –

Mum: *Well how do I follow that! Darling Kali, I thought we could give you a ritual bath and scrub you, I thought about giving you a raw egg and then* *rubbing you all over with stinging nettles and then maybe leaving you alone in a hut for 3 days with no food and water. But I was overruled*

Lots of laughter and oh nos

Instead I thought we could take it in turns to think of reasons why we love you....

Me: A*m I going to wish I WAS locked on my own in a hut?*

Mum: *I will try to make this as embarrassing and excruciating as possible. That's what Mum's are for. I'll start then shall I?*

Well Kali. Certainly has her moments, usually on Days 25 and 26 but I have to admire how she has coped with having periods at such a young age. My girl is growing up!

Gran: *She always rings her old Gran and makes me laugh!*

Tara: *Thanks for being the best sister and always*

lending me your stuff even when you don't know I've borrowed it! I can't wait for my period to start now, if it's going to be this fun.

Sonya: *Kali's cool because I can trust her I don't have to pretend with her.*

I was really touched by that. Of course that will probably be all forgotten at school on Monday!

Ava: *Kali is the best friend anyone could have. She's funny and silly and never boring. Sometimes cranky but at least she let's me know and I can always let her know if I feel moody.*

By this time I had given up trying to keep the tears back and just started blubbing big time.

Oh Kali, don't think you're going to get out of making a speech.

I laugh and cry at the same time.

I breathe deeply and blow my nose, not

very princess like I know and say a few words, which I really hadn't prepared: *Thank you all for coming and for all the lovely presents and for all the lovely things you said. Can we do it again next month! Ha ha*

This is the best Day 1 I've had. It really makes if feel like a celebration and not a curse, as Gran calls it! It makes me feel good to be a girl!

They all clapped and cheered until Auntie Eireen said, OK *that's enough being all serious and weepy, le party!* We all danced to *Girls Just Wanna have fu* and tucked in to the food and drink.

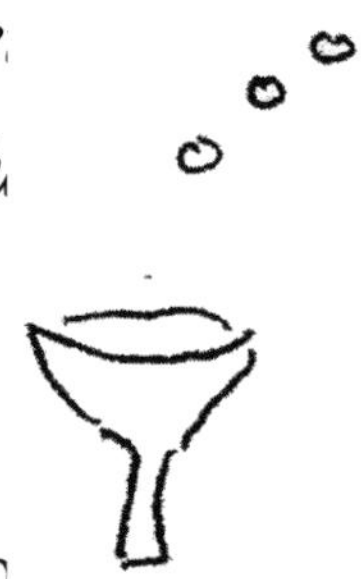

There was:

Pink Lemonade and Cava for the grown up Apparently I am not grown up enough for that!

We had: pizza topped with extra tomatoes, red peppers and pepperoni,

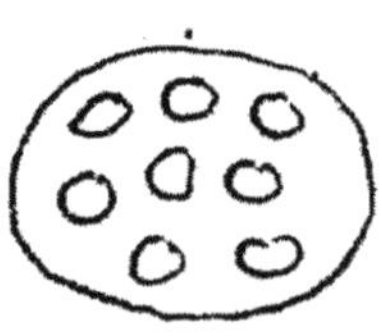

Fairy cakes with red and pink icing. Those healthy beetroot and parsnip crisps for the colour, red and pink only Smarties.

I reckon Michael got the leftover colours! Jam sandwiches and strawberry ice cream! YUM.

It was the best day and I think everyone really enjoyed it, even Sonya. It's lovely to think that I have shared my sweet secret with all those girls and women and that it is something really special and worth celebrating. You know I think I'm going to wear one of those beautiful red roses on my blazer on Monday and see if anyone notices!

ACKNOWLEDGMENTS

For those special spaces that helped this book come to be I will always be thankful for the cabin that Peter built, Pebble and Dash gift shop in Herne Bay, The Feminist Library in London and my old bedroom!

As to those that have encouraged me to keep at it there are many. Extra special thanks go to my sister Helen who has been a constant supporter and kept asking the dreaded question – so what's happening with the book? Same goes for Eithne Farry who had the unenviable task of reading my manuscript with her editor's hat on and having to feedback to a friend. Thank you to Laurika Bretherton for the pact we made and the friendship and inspiration that has kept me going along this path.

As for Alexandra Pope and her amazing work on Menstruality, this book hopes in a small way to get her Love your Cycle and be Powerful message out there. To all my sisters on The Women's Quest and The Red School. I have always felt your combined strength urging me on.

Thanks to even to those who went URGGH! –it's about what?

To Peter for putting up with hearing about periods for years and years and for so much more.

Thanks to Eva Megias for her wonderful job of typesetting and cover design, which made it all seem like it was finally real!

REFERENCES

Books: You just have to read..

Star Girl by Jerry Spinelli - makes you proud to be different

Are you there God , It's Margaret? By Judy Blume

I Capture the Castle by Dodie Smith - (yes 101 Dalmations writer)

Wind in the Willows by Kenneth Grahame

The Gruffalo by Julia Donaldson /Axel Schaeffer

All the Harry Potter books – so lucky if you still have them to read – by J.K.Rowling

Anne of Green Gables by Lucy Maud Montgomery.

Bilgewater by Jane Gardam – about another red head!

Amazing Grace, by Mary Hoffman and Caroline Binch

Grace for President, by Kelly DiPucchio and Leuyen Pham

Brown Girl Dreaming, by Jacqueline Woodson

Sally Lockhart Mysteries - by Phillip Pullman

The Hunger Games series by Suzanne Collins - (Katniss Everdeen is a Kali on Day 23!)

COOL WEBSITES

Museum of Menstruation – MUM for short - oh yes it really exists! – http://mum.org/

Letterbox Library – http://letterboxlibrary.com

Mooncup http://mooncup.co.uk

Young Women's Trust – http://youngwomens trust.org

The Girl Guides – they are cool really! – http://girlguiding.org.uk/

The Feminist Library - http://feministlibrary.co.uk

http://redschool.net - for the wonderful work of Alexandra Pope

FACEBOOK MUSTS

https:/facebook.comIts-Good-Being-A-Girl-1384516315170895/

https://facebook.com/FeministLibrary/?fref=ts

https://facebook.com/search/top/?q=girls %20rock%20london

https://facebook.com/search/top/?q=object

LINE SHOP: www.pebbleanddash.co.uk
Facebook: It's Good Being A Girl
Twitter: @goodbeingagirl

Spa
Invaders

'Spaceship Invaders'
An original concept by Jenny Jinks

Illustrated by Rebecca Willoway

Published by MAVERICK ARTS PUBLISHING LTD
Suite 1, Hillreed House, 54 Queen Street,
Horsham, West Sussex, RH13 5AD

+44 (0)1403 256941

A CIP catalogue record for this book is available at the British Library.

ISBN 978-1-83511-077-5

Printed in India

Maverick publishing

www.maverickbooks.co.uk

Gold

This book is rated as: Gold Band (Guided Reading)

Spaceship Invaders

By Jenny Jinks

Illustrated by Rebecca Willoway

Chapter 1

Lily kicked the ball down the long hallway and trudged after it. She was bored.

When her parents had told her they were going to be space explorers, Lily had thought life was going to be super exciting. But so far, it had just been super boring. The only places she'd explored were the corridors of the spaceship.

Lily kicked the ball extra hard. It bounced into the air and smashed into a control panel on the wall. An alarm started to blare.

BEEP! BEEP! BEEP!

"Lily, what have we told you about playing in the corridors?" sighed her dad. He pushed some buttons, and the alarm stopped.

"There's nothing else to do!" Lily moaned.

“Come on,” said Dad. “Dinner’s ready. We’ve got a surprise for you!”

Lily hoped the surprise was a proper dinner that didn’t come in a pouch.

Unfortunately not. Today’s pouch said ‘fish and chips’, but it was nothing like any fish and chips Lily had ever tasted. Space food was disgusting.

“We’re going to explore a new planet tomorrow,” Mum said. “Would you like to come with us?”

“Yes!” Lily jumped up with excitement. A new planet! Finally, something to look forward to.

Lily cared for her seeds every day. They grew surprisingly quickly. Soon, they didn't fit in her cupboard anymore. Lily found a large cleaning cupboard to put them in. But still the plants kept growing and growing. Before long, they were out of control.

Then one day, Lily went to check on the plants... but they weren't there.

Chapter 4

Lily spotted a trail of dirt leading down the corridor. She had to find them, quickly.

Suddenly, she heard a loud crash.
Lily had a very bad feeling about this.

Lily followed the noise to the kitchen and pushed the door open.

"Oh no," Lily groaned.

The Pog plants were crashing around the kitchen, pulling boxes and jars off the shelves.

Lily heard footsteps hurrying along the hall.

"What's going on?" Lily's mum asked.

"Nothing!" Lily said quickly, blocking the door.

"We heard a loud noise," Lily's dad said, frowning.

There was more crashing inside.

Lily's dad pushed the door open.

"I can explain," Lily groaned. But when she peered into the messy kitchen, the Pog plants were gone.

Lily looked around. Where were they?

They heard another crash further down the corridor. There was more mess in the dining room, but the Pog plants weren't there either.

"Has something eaten this table?" Lily's mum asked with a gasp.

"Looks like we've got some sort of alien invasion," Lily's dad said seriously. "We should prepare for battle. Lily, go back to your room."

‘Oh no,’ thought Lily. ‘This is a complete disaster!’

Lily hoped she might find the Pog plants on the way back to her room, but they had completely disappeared. She opened her door sadly, but a surprise was waiting for her...

Chapter 5

The Pog plants! They were in her cupboard, holding her backpack.

“What are you doing?” Lily asked.

They seemed to be sniffing the bag of dirt that Lily had brought back from planet Pog. Was it Lily’s imagination, or were they looking sad? Was that even possible?

"You miss your home planet, don't you?" said Lily, suddenly understanding. She patted one of the plants. "I know how you feel. You aren't supposed to live on a spaceship. I'm sorry."

Lily knew she had to rescue the Pog plants. She had to get them back home.

The problem was, how was Lily going to get two giant plants across the spaceship and into a shuttle without anyone spotting them?

Chapter 6

Lily waited until the corridor was quiet. Then she opened her bedroom door.

"Come on," she said, beckoning the plants to follow her.

They were halfway down the hall when Lily heard footsteps behind them.

She froze. What could she do? Lily shoved the Pog plants into a cupboard just in time.

“Lily, what are you doing?” asked her dad, coming round the corner. “It’s not safe for you to be out. The spaceship invaders could be anywhere!”

“I thought I could help,” Lily said.

“Leave it to us. You stay safe,” her dad said and continued on his way.

Lily breathed a sigh of relief. “Let’s go!” she said, letting the plants out of the cupboard.

Finally, Lily made it to the shuttle hatch. She was just pushing the Pog plants inside when she heard footsteps again.

"Lily, stay back!" said Lily's mum. "Those plants are the spaceship invaders."

"They're not safe," Lily's dad said.

"They're not trying to hurt us," Lily explained. "They're just homesick. I snuck them into the ship when they were just seeds, but I shouldn't have. I'm sorry. I just want to help get them back home where they belong."

"...Okay," Lily's mum said. "But we're coming with you."

Chapter 7

Lily and her parents got in the shuttle.

It was a bit of a squeeze with the giant Pog plants in there too!

They flew down to the surface of planet Pog.

Luckily the Pog plants seemed to understand what was happening. They looked calmly out of the window as their planet got nearer.

As soon as the shuttle landed, the Pog plants were desperate to get out. They pushed at the door and windows in excitement.

“Okay, okay,” Lily laughed, pulling the door open. The plants jumped out and rolled around in the dirt like excited puppies.

“Look how happy they are,” Lily’s mum said.

“They’re back where they belong,” Lily smiled sadly.

Lily's dad put an arm around her shoulder as they watched the plants walk away.

Chapter 8

That night at dinner (another disgusting pouch—this time it was meant to be sausage and mash), Lily's dad looked very serious.

"Lily, we need to talk," he said. "The Pog plants made a lot of mess."

"I know. I'm so sorry," Lily said. She knew she was about to be in big trouble.

"But they reminded us of something," her mum continued. "Maybe taking you away from your home and keeping you on a spaceship wasn't a good idea either... How would you like to go back?"

Lily looked at her parents in shock.
"Really?" asked Lily. "We can go home?"

They nodded.

Lily couldn't believe it. Tears welled in her eyes as she hugged her parents.

She looked out of the window at planet Pog below, and she almost thought she could see the Pog plants waving at her. Lily waved back. Maybe one day she would travel back through space and see them again. But for now, she was glad they were back where they were meant to be. And soon, she would be too.

The End

Book Bands for Guided Reading

The Institute of Education book banding system is a scale of colours that reflects the various levels of reading difficulty. The bands are assigned by taking into account the content, the language style, the layout and phonics. Word, phrase and sentence level work is also taken into consideration.

Maverick Early Readers are a bright, attractive range of books covering the pink to white bands. All of these books have been book banded for guided reading to the industry standard and edited by a leading educational consultant.

To view the whole Maverick Readers scheme, visit our website at www.maverickearlyreaders.com

Or scan the QR code above to view our scheme instantly!

THE ARAB EXECUTIVE

THE ARAB EXECUTIVE

Farid A. Muna

Foreword by

Kenneth Simmonds

First published 1980 by
THE MACMILLAN PRESS LTD
London and Basingstoke
Companies and representatives throughout the world

Filmset by Vantage Photosetting Co. Ltd.
Southampton and London
and printed in Hong Kong

British Library Cataloguing in Publication Data

Muna, Farid A.
The Arab executive
1. Executives – Arab countries
I. Title
301.44′47′09174927 HF5500.3.A/

ISBN 0–333–29119–0

To Simon Siksek

Contents

	Page
List of Tables and Figures	ix
Foreword by Kenneth Simmonds	xi
A Note on Transliteration	xii
Acknowledgements	xiii
1 INTRODUCTION	1
2 THE ARAB EXECUTIVE AND HIS ENVIRONMENT	5
On Being an Arab	6
The Arab as a Businessman	8
The Arab as an Executive	9
Social Structure: a Mosaic	10
Recent Political and Economic Developments	13
Emphasis on Nationalism and Tradition	14
The Creation of the State of Israel	16
The Discovery and Exploitation of Petroleum	18
The Arab Trade Union Movement	22
3 SOCIAL PRESSURES AND THE EXECUTIVE ROLE	26
Social Pressures	26
Socio-cultural Pressures	29
Pressures from the Business and Social Community	30
The Executive Role	34
Role in Community	35
Role in Organization	39
4 THE ARAB APPROACH TO DECISION MAKING	44
Decision-making Styles	44
A Decision-making Profile	47
Variables Affecting Decision Styles	53
Consultation	58

5 CONFLICT MANAGEMENT 63

6 INTERPERSONAL STYLE 71
Rituals and Customs in Conducting Business 71
Personal Ties and Connections 74
The Importance of Loyalty 78
An Open-Door Tradition 80
A Preference for 'Informality' 83

7 ATTITUDES TOWARDS TIME AND CHANGE 88
Time Orientation 88
The Value of Time 89
Time Horizons 91
The Myth of Fatalism 93
Attitudes Towards Change 98
The Context of Change 99
The Executive's Attitudes 102
Ambivalence 106

8 CONCLUSION AND IMPLICATIONS 113
The Importance of Environmental Factors 113
The Executive as a Change Agent 114
Modernization without Sacrificing Traditions 115
Implications 116
I Management Training and Development 117
II Expatriate Employees and Foreign Businessmen 120
III Future Research 121

Appendix 1: Methodology and Data Analysis 125
Appendix 2: The Interview Schedule 131

Bibliography 142
Index 149

List of Tables and Figures

TABLES

		Page
3.1	Social pressures as reported by Arab executives	28
3.2	(a) Executive role and organizational size	40
	(b) Executive role and organizational ownership	40
4.1	Comparison between decisional styles employed in this study and those of previous investigators	46
4.2	Distribution of decision styles for each decision by all Arab executives	49
4.3	Distribution of decision styles by executives from each of the six Arab countries	50
4.4	Mean score of executives from each country for all decisions	51
4.5	Mean score of executives for three categories of decisions	52
4.6	Independent variables accounting for the variance in decision-making styles	55
4.7	Distribution of responses by style for three decision categories	58
6.1	Rituals and customs in conducting business	72
6.2	Executives' preference for loyalty and efficiency: (a) employee; (b) immediate subordinate	79
6.3	The open-door tradition	81
6.4	Bypassing the hierarchy	83
7.1	Proverbs on the value of time	90
7.2	Time horizons: investment, planning, training	92
7.3	Events and factors beyond the executive's control	97
7.4	Preventive measures	97
7.5	Attitudes towards technological and social changes	103
7.6	Attitudes towards social changes, by country	103
7.7	Likelihood of occurrence: technological and social changes	105
8.1	The image of expatriates/foreign businessmen as perceived by Arab executives	121

Appendix Tables

A.1 A statistical profile of Arab executives and their organizations 126
A.2 Analysis of variance (organizational decision 6) 129

FIGURES

3.1 The executive and his environment 27
4.1 The power-sharing continuum 47
4.2 Proportion of responses for all decisions by all Arab executives 49
A.1 Pearson correlation matrix (7 decisions) 128

Foreword

Western managerial awareness of the Arab world jumped sharply with the oil boom of the early 1970s. Up to that time few international businessmen had had direct dealings with Arab executives, and the demand for more background by those anxious to capitalize on the new opportunities brought forth a torrent of writings. At the worst extreme, some texts depicted a caricature of Arab managerial behaviour as an unbounded fatalism apparently unconcerned with rational economic considerations. These alarming generalizations seemed to rest on no more substantial evidence than that Arabic speakers make frequent recourse to *'inshā' Allāh'* (God willing or if God wills). Such caricatures are not only wrong but also quite unbelievable to those from English-speaking cultures with their own common supplications of 'Goodbye' and 'Godspeed', and bold but forgotten proclamations on their coinage of 'Defender of the Faith', and 'In God We Trust'.

Dr Muna guides us away from these trite levels of observation. He has made a determined effort to describe what leading Arab executives think, feel and do within the current environment and given the social pressures placed upon them. Himself an Arab, yet equally at home in the United States and England, Dr Muna has depicted the variety and depth of differences that can exist. It is this sort of picture that the international manager needs if he is to adjust his business practices in ways that really work.

Kenneth Simmonds
Professor of International Business,
London Business School,
University of London

A Note on Transliteration

The system of transliteration of Arabic words used in most scholarly literature has been followed in this book. Familiar names, however, were not transliterated in this way; instead, they were kept in their simplified form of transliteration. Thus, for example, we have used Quran instead of Qur'ān; King Faisal instead of Fayṣal; and, of course, the simple transliterations chosen by authors and executives for their names were retained.

Acknowledgements

This book was originally written as a Ph.D. thesis at the London Business School, University of London. The valuable advice, guidance, and assistance of a great number of people made the book possible. To them all I am deeply grateful.

Two persons deserve special acknowledgements: Professor Kenneth Simmonds of the London Business School, and Mr Simon Siksek of the Middle East Industrial Relations Counselors (MEIRC). Professor Simmonds' wealth of knowledge and experience proved invaluable throughout this study. I am indebted to him for his continuous encouragement and support, and above all, for his efforts at directing my work towards the investigation of pragmatic problems. Mr Siksek, to whom the book is dedicated, encouraged me to enter this field and was always willing to take the time needed to discuss my approach and findings. I was also able to draw on his personal experiences as an Arab executive and as a leader in his field.

A number of my colleagues at the London Business School were particularly generous in extending to me needed advice and assistance. They include Drs Dennis Bumstead, Tom Poynter, and Eric Walton. Mr Michael Jefferson of Shell International, London, took a personal interest in my work and offered valuable comments.

In the field, I am indebted to the fifty-two top Arab executives whose patient and in-depth answers to a long list of questions made this study possible. To the thirteen executives who preferred to remain anonymous and to those who allowed me to mention their names herein, I offer my deepest gratitude. I sincerely hope that I will be permitted the opportunity in the future to reciprocate their exceptionally valuable help and cooperation.

Egypt:	Mr Mohamed G. Abdel-Hamid
	Dr Adel T. Gazarin
	Mr Mohamed El-Haddad
	Mr W. H. Hegazy
	Mr Yehia Omar

	Mr Hussein Reda
	Mr Youssef M. Youssef
Jordan:	Mr Raouf S. Abujaber
	Mr Tawfiq Kawar
	Mr Bassam R. Mufleh
	Mr Elia C. Nuqul
	Mr Farid Sa'd
	Mr S. K. Tell
	Dr Sobhy A. Tieby
Kuwait:	Mr Kutayba Alghanim
	Mr Abdulmalek M. Gharabally
	Mr K. A. Khalaf
	Mr Yousuf M. Al-Nisf
	Mr Fawzi Musaad Al-Saleh
	Mr Abdul Aziz M. Al-Shaya
	Mr Abdul Rahman Al-Sultan
Lebanon:	Mr Samir Hamzah
	Mr Said T. Khoury
Saudi Arabia:	Mr Omar A. Aggad
	Mr Faysal Al-Bassam
	Mr Adnan M. Khashoggi
	Sheikh Hassan Mishari
	Mr Ali I. Naimi
	Mr Khaled A. Al-Rabiah
	Mr Nasser M. Al-Saleh
	Mr Abdul Aziz Bin Ahmad Al-Sudairy
	Sheikh Abdul Majid Zahid
	Mr Abdulaziz Al-Zamil
UAE:	Mr Hussain Abdul-Rehman (Khan Saheb)
	Mr Edward Elias
	Mr Rashed M. Fakhro
	Mr Saif Ahmed Al-Ghurair
	Mr Amal Hourani
	Mr Fadhel M. Khan

Interviewing top executives in six Arab countries required the help of many friends and relatives. I am grateful to Mr Ibrahim Aghabi in Jordan; Mr Saba Abdo and his staff at Dar Al

Handasah, and Mr Adel Shoeib in Egypt; Messrs Faysal Al-Bassam, Paul J. Nance, Ibrahim and Abdullah Yunis in Saudi Arabia; and Mr Mitri Al-Muna in Kuwait.

Also my thanks go to all the expatriates as well as to the persons who participated in the pilot study. Special appreciation for the time and helpful comments kindly given by Dr Hamed Ammar, Messrs Albert Hazbun, Nayef Al-Jaabari, and Mahmud Takieddine.

My colleagues at MEIRC extended to me every help and support throughout the study. In particular, thanks are due to Mr Samih Baalbaki for his help in checking the Arabic translation of the Interview Schedule; and Mrs Leila Abiad whose typing excellence transformed my handwriting into a legible manuscript.

Finally, words simply cannot express my deep feelings of gratitude to my wife Doris and daughters Rima and Nadia. They shared with me the trials and tribulations of the return to student life.

London *Farid A. Muna*
November 1979

1 Introduction

This book is about the Arab business executive, his managerial thinking and behaviour and how these relate to his wider environment.

The Arab executive's managerial behaviour is heavily influenced by society's social structure and by the values, norms and expectations of its people. For instance, the executive's role within his community and organization is shaped to a considerable extent by the expectations of relatives, friends and employees. The top executive, by virtue of his position in the organization, sees himself as the head of a family: employees are perceived as members of that family. Society's influence is similarly reflected in the executive's distinctively Arab styles in decision making, management of conflict, and interpersonal relations.

In turn Arab executives also influence their society – they are not merely passive. There is a dynamic interrelationship between the executives and their Arab environment. The executives are continually introducing and fostering changes within their organization, community, and society. And their influence extends not only to economic and technological changes but also to changes in social values and norms. For example, Arab executives are deeply concerned with the low value and respect that people in their business community place on time. They are cognizant of the need to instil an industrial work ethic among employees and to develop their organizational discipline.

The executives recognize, however, that deep-rooted values and norms are slow to change. Their efforts at changing the environment are further hampered by the ambivalent feelings they have towards certain social changes which usually accompany modernization. They find themselves in the uneasy situation of introducing into their environment modern and scientific methods and adapting them to their new, yet traditional, work and life styles. In short, Arab executives are agents of social change in a society which itself is undergoing modernization while attempting to retain its Arab identity and character.

Indeed, the Arab executives are taking a leading part in

shaping a critical period in their history. Here is how the Arabs' history and their future potential were described by an Arab-American historian, the late Professor Philip K. Hitti. He ended the 1970 edition of his *History of the Arabs* with these words:

> Originators of the third monotheistic religion, beneficiaries of the other two, co-sharers with the West of the Greco-Roman cultural tradition, holders aloft of the torch of enlightenment throughout medieval times, generous contributors to European renaissance, the Arab-speaking peoples have taken their place among the awakened, forward marching independent nations of the modern world. *With their rich heritage and unmatched natural resources of oil, they should be able to make a significant contribution to the material and spiritual progress of mankind.* (p. 757, emphasis added)

During the 1970s the Arabs began to discover the power of their newly acquired wealth. This power together with the October 1973 war gave them a growing sense of self-confidence and achievement. Thus, if the 1970s can be characterized as their *years of awareness*, then the 1980s are likely to be their *decade of action.* A decade in which the Arabs confront the formidable task of selecting and acting upon courses of action which may contribute to their material and spiritual progress, and possibly that of mankind. The role of the Arab executive in this process is crucial; for he is in a position to influence the selection and to lead the action.

The approach used in this study is to view the Arab executive as an integral part of a business-orientated social system (his organization) which itself is inextricable from the larger social system, its social structure, and in a specific period of its history. Various contributions of social psychology, cultural anthropology, and political science have been woven into the main arguments. To that extent this study is interdisciplinary in nature.

The approach is also eclectic and empirical. It is eclectic in the sense that no attempt is made to develop and test a comprehensive conceptual framework or model, but rather to utilize various perspectives which facilitate the practical investigation of selected managerial issues. It is also based on empirical investigation of executives' attitudes and practices. The bulk of the data were collected from interviews with top Arab executives. Also a small number of expatriate managers with work experience in the Arab world were interviewed in the pilot study. The available literature on the Arab world was helpful, but very little of any substance has been published with direct reference to the Arab business executive. Finally, the author drew upon his own work experience and observations in several parts of the Arab world.

Semi-structured interviews were conducted with fifty-two top Arab executives from six countries: Egypt, Jordan, Kuwait, Lebanon, Saudi Arabia, and the United Arab Emirates (UAE).[1] The executives were either owners or top managers of business organizations ranging in size from 180 to 25,000 employees with an average size of 2480 employees. The organizations they managed were either family-owned, owned by two or more partners, or government-owned. A detailed statistical profile of the executives including their social, educational, and organizational backgrounds is presented in Appendix 1.[2]

The Arab world and its business executives do not exist in an economic or social vacuum. Interaction with non-Arab nations and individuals is inevitable and indeed indispensable. Hence, the importance to non-Arabs of understanding the Arab executive and vice versa. The issues we explore are, therefore, of concern not only to Arab executives and their Arab employees, but also to non-Arab businessmen and expatriates, to consulting and management development organizations, and to social scientists interested in international business and comparative (cross-cultural) management.

The main concern in the present work is to explore selected managerial issues. The study is clearly non-exhaustive in its coverage of topics relating to the Arab executive; also this study does not attempt to compare the Arab executive with his counterpart in non-Arab societies. Comparison is restricted to Arab countries, and references to other societies are occasionally made only to illuminate the topics under discussion. Thus the reader is left to compare the Arabs with whichever society he or she is most familiar. This study is exploratory and the single focus limits the complexity of cross-cultural comparisons.[3]

Using the analogy of a zoom lens, we varied our perspective and range of vision by first focusing on the panorama of the Arab executive's wider environment. We begin by examining the great and continuing influence which the social structure, together with the political and economic developments, have on the mind of the executives. Then we slowly 'zoom in' on the executive's role within his own community and organization.

Without losing sight of the larger social context, we shift our focus to the executive's thinking and behaviour at the individual level. We investigate the Arab executive's decision-making styles, and the extent to which he shares his decision-making power with his subordinates. Social values and norms have significant influence not only on his decision making but also on the power tactics he uses in the management of conflict.

The Arab executive's interpersonal style is characterized by a strong preference for personal and informal (rather than impersonal and formal) approaches of conducting business. This interpersonal style is used by the executive in his relationships with employees as well as with people outside his organization.

From here we move on to the executive's time orientation, and we shed doubt on the widespread view of Muslim/Arab fatalism. The Arab executive's attitudes towards the current modernization process are examined, together with the ambivalence that modernization creates in the mind of the executive. By shifting from one level of analysis to another, our aim is to sketch a portrait of the Arab executive against the background of his changing environment.

The conclusions that can be drawn from this book are set out in the final chapter. Also analysed are the implications of the findings for the training and development of Arab executives; the implications for expatriate employees and foreign businessmen; and the implications for future research.

The research methodology and statistical analyses are relegated to an appendix, as also is the full English version of the Interview Schedule. This leaves the main text less cluttered so that it may be more conveniently read.

NOTES

1. Interviews were conducted in Arabic and English. In this book only the English version of the Interview schedule appears; see Appendix 2. The Arabic translation can be found in F. A. Muna (1979), 'The Arab Executive Mind', Ph.D. thesis, University of London.
2. Appendix 1 also includes notes on the research methodology.
3. It is hoped that the inevitable cultural bias is minimized by the fact that the present author is bi-cultural (Arab and Anglo–Saxon), having studied and worked in the USA and the UK for seventeen years.

2 The Arab Executive and his Environment

> What are the social sciences all about? They ought to be about man and society and sometimes they are. They are attempts to help us understand biography and history, and the connexions of the two in a variety of social structures.
>
> C. Wright Mills (1916–62)
> *The Sociological Imagination*, p. 40

Who is an Arab executive? First, the executive is a national of one of the Arab countries which together make up the Arab world. Nationals of these countries have a common bond: a strong feeling of identity and commonality. They share the same language, religion, and history. While there are elements of diversity in these three bases of identity, the feelings of brotherhood and common destiny among nationals of Arab countries make it possible in the final analysis to refer to them as Arabs.

Second, Arab executives share the same profession: management of business organizations. Being at the top of business firms, either as owners or managers, they have been conditioned or socialized by common managerial practices and problems. Arab executives are aware of, and influenced by, a commercial and industrial tradition that dates back many centuries, and they share with each other exposure to modern business conditions through formal education and/or interaction with other Arab and Western businessmen. A Jordanian executive from Amman, for example, is likely to have more in common with a Kuwaiti or a Lebanese executive than with a Jordanian farmer.

Third, the societal and business environment in which the Arab executive lives and works has considerable impact on his attitudes and behaviour. The social structure of the Arab world has certain distinctive characteristics which dominate managerial thinking and behaviour. Furthermore, the executives are influenced by the recent political and economic developments in the Arab world, which in turn have a great effect on local and regional business conditions.

ON BEING AN ARAB

The Arab executive is first and foremost an Arab. He is a citizen of one of the twenty-two member countries of the Arab League. These countries, stretching from the Atlantic ocean in the west to the Tigris–Euphrates valley and the Arabian Gulf in the east, have a population of around 160 million people.[1] Arab executives share with each other three closely interrelated bases of identity and commonality: *language, religion,* and *history*.

The *Arabic language* has been singled out by many scholars to be the pre-eminent element in the definition of an Arab. In fact, some go as far as to define the Arabs solely on the basis of the Arabic language.[2] The significance to the Arab executive of this semitic language should not be understated; for in addition to being a key factor of Arab identity, it is the official state language and the medium of expression in daily and business life. Governmental, commercial and labour laws are issued in Arabic; and governments are increasingly insistent on the use of Arabic as the medium of negotiations, correspondence and contracts whereas a few years ago English or French would have been acceptable.

Most Arabs are well aware that for centuries Arabic was a leading language of learning, science, trade, and progressive thought.[3] They are also aware of its limitations, for colloquial Arabic, like most other languages, has suffered from a proliferation of dialects not only between different countries of the Arab world, but even between the various towns and cities of the same country. Nevertheless, classical Arabic remains the common medium of writing, publishing, and broadcasting throughout the Arab world. Finally, Arabic is the language of the Holy Quran, and it is the only language authorized for the performance of the liturgy.

Islam is a second basis for the feelings of identity and commonality. Even if the Arab executive is not a Muslim, he is living in an Islamic environment which has been influenced by Islamic traditions for 1400 years. Moreover, Islam is not simply a religion, it is a way of life.[4] Islamic teachings and laws cover the relations of man to God, men's relations with each other, as well as man's relations towards himself. The duties of man towards the community and those of the community towards man are described and prescribed by Islamic teachings. Although Islam is the stated religion in nearly all the constitutions of Arab countries, the degree of application of Islamic Sacred Law (*Sharī'a*) varies among these countries.[5] Some, for example, Saudi Arabia, still adhere strictly to the Sacred Law in many spheres of life, while others (Egypt for instance) have turned to secular laws for the administration of their economic and social affairs.

The *history* of the Arabs is another source of pride as well as inspiration for the Arab executive, as for many Arabs. If asked to define what they mean by 'the Arab world', most Arabs would include their history as a basis of this common bond. The deep impact this history has on the Arabs was well described by Albert Hourani (1962), when he wrote:

> A full definition (of what is meant by Arab nations) would include also a reference to a historic process: to a certain episode in history in which the Arabs played a leading part, which was important not only for them but for the whole world, and in virtue of which indeed they could claim to have been *something* in human history. (p. 2; Hourani's emphasis)

It was in the seventh century under the leadership of the Prophet Muhammad and his immediate successors that a unified and growing Islamic community was established.[6] The three centuries to follow were to see the Arabs reach their Golden Age under the Umayyad and the Abbasid caliphates. The slow disintegration of the Abbasid empire ended with the fall of its capital Baghdad in 1258. It was the Ottomon Turks who, in the early part of the sixteenth century, consolidated their gains over the smaller dynasties that were the remnants of the old Arab empire. The Ottomans ruled a unified Islamic empire for over 300 years.[7] Their decline was as slow as that of the earlier Arab empires and in the nineteenth century the North African provinces, including Egypt, were the first to be lost to the Ottomans. The First World War put an end to the Turkish rule; but the aftermath of the war saw the Arabs still divided and ruled this time mainly by France and Britain.[8]

During the past thirty years the Arabs have gained their independence. Today in the Arab world, the aspirations, hopes, and dreams of unity persist; but the nearest to any sort of real or permanent unity has been the creation, and most important, the survival, of the Arab League (League of Arab States). Its political achievements, however incomplete and modest, have at least served on occasions to dampen inter-Arab strife. It has also contributed to Arab cooperation in economic, technological, and cultural fields.[9]

THE ARAB AS A BUSINESSMAN

Today's Arab executive has inherited a commercial and industrial tradition that dates back many centuries. This is the case whether the Arab executive comes from the eastern part of the Arab world, the Arabian peninsula, or from the western part, North Africa. For at different periods in their history the Arabs have been, in varying intensity, involved in commerce and industry.

Ancient Arabia lay across the path of the Greek and Roman empires as they spread towards India and China. The Arabs 'were the middlemen of the southern seas, as their kinsmen, the Phoenicians, had been earlier of the Mediterranean'.[10] Commerce and industry flourished under Islam. The founder of the Islamic empire, the Prophet Muhammad, was himself a merchant for a number of years; he grew up in Mecca which was an important centre of trade.[11] The Holy Quran is rich with praise, as well as codes of conduct, for business and trade.[12]

The Arabs' leadership in industry and commerce reached its peak during the Abassid empire (AD 750–1258). The 'extensive international trade' attained was supported by 'extensive home industry and agriculture'.[13] Textiles, glass, furniture, metal, paper, and food products were the main commodities manufactured and exported. According to historians, the economic decline of the Arabs accelerated rapidly with the discovery of the Cape of Good Hope in 1498.[14] That event 'diverted the course of international trade from the Arab East and substituted the Portuguese for the Arabians and Syrians as the middlemen. The Arab lands were thus commercially bypassed'.[15] Together with the discovery of America in 1492, the Mediterranean lost its position as the 'highway of international trade'. That sea, writes the historian Hitti, had 'to wait three and a half more centuries before it could regain its position ... thanks to the opening of the Suez Canal in 1869' (Hitti, 1970, p. 728). Meanwhile, the Arabs lay dormant while the Industrial Revolution was taking place in Europe. With the West's discovery of Arab oil however and its re-discovery of the strategic position of the Arab world, there began a modern industrial and commercial era.

The old mercantile mentality which had flourished for so long still survives, but is now blended with the new industrial mentality.

THE ARAB AS AN EXECUTIVE

Today, the Arab executive directs and is responsible for the operations of a business organization engaged in one or a combination of economic activities such as manufacturing, trade, or service industries. The typical executive manages a business firm, often one that has been his family's for many years; or he heads an organization that he has recently created; or he directs an organization which was either established by government or is now government-owned.

A new type of organization which is slowly gaining prominence in the Arab world is the stock company. Some of these firms were established under joint-venture arrangements either by Arab governments or private businessmen. An example of a new joint-stock company is the Sharjah Group Company formed in 1976. This company describes itself as 'the first Arab Gulf company to have offered its shares exclusively to Arab nationals. As a result of this policy the company is now owned by some 35,000 Arab shareholders and gives us a truly Pan-Arab identity'.[16]

Only a few of these Arab companies are at present open to the public, and their shares sold on stock exchange markets in cities such as Beirut, Kuwait, or Amman. The stock exchanges are relatively new creations. The largest is now the Kuwait Stock Exchange which was formally established in the mid-1970s. Yet, despite its youth, the Kuwait Exchange (trading restricted to Kuwaitis) had in 1978 an overwhelming turnover of $5 billion in only thirty-six stocks – around 13 per cent of the total turnover in ordinary shares at the London Stock Exchange for the same period.[17]

In countries declaring themselves as socialist (such as Algeria, Egypt, Iraq and Syria), the strategic industries and services (usually large organizations) are now state-controlled. For example, the Egyptian Government owns the country's iron and steel company (24,000 employees), and the vehicle assembly company (11,000 employees).[18] Chief executives of national organizations in these countries report to the ministries of industry, finance, or trade. With very few exceptions, all other Arab governments own and run their airlines, railroads, public utilities, and their essential natural resources industries such as petroleum.

The educational background of Arab executives also varies. Some attended only high school, others graduated from universities either in the Arab world or overseas. In the Arab world, modern university education has been available since the nineteenth century. One of the oldest universities, the American University of Beirut, was founded in 1866 by American missionaries, when Lebanon was still under Ottoman rule. And while under French and British occupation, the universities of Algiers, Cairo and Damascus were established in 1879, 1908, and 1923 respectively.[19] At present, nearly all Arab countries have founded their own universities.

Executives who were educated overseas attended universities in the United States and Europe (usually Britain or France). In the present study, 50 per cent of the executives interviewed received their university degrees from the West, 35 per cent obtained their degrees from universities in the Arab world, and 15 per cent attended high school but did not obtain a university degree. The combination of education (whether at home or abroad) and the exposure to the West (through business or personal travel) has typically resulted in a bilingual Arab executive. All the executives in this study, for instance, spoke at least one foreign language, usually English or French.

SOCIAL STRUCTURE: A MOSAIC[20]

The Arab executive lives and works in a society whose social structure, with all its contrasts and diversity, has some distinctive features which have considerable impact on him. It is a social structure in which three different types of social communities co-exist and interact (tribal, rural, and urban). It is a social structure in which social and economic differentiation has begun but many remain incomplete; a social structure in which family and friendship still dominate many spheres of life.

In the Arab world today, political leaders, kings and rulers were born and brought up in three types of social communities: tribal, rural and urban.[21] Although all now reside and work in their respective capital cities, one finds, for example, that most of the state rulers in the Arabian peninsula have their roots in a tribal society; while some political leaders take pride in their village upbringing; and others were raised in cities in their respective countries. Similarly, business executives may have spent their formative years in these different communities. In our present study, for instance, 6 per cent of the fifty-two executives had a tribal background, 48 per cent came from villages, and 46 per cent from cities.

Despite the strong interdependence between these three types of communities, each has remained distinct in its demographic characteristics and economic life style. Much has been written on the stereotypes of the bedouin as a pastoral nomad; the villager as a poor peasant; and the city dweller as a worker, merchant, or administrator. These stereotypes could, however, give the misleading impression that the bedouin, villager and city dweller 'are completely different kinds of people'.[22] For while there are sharp contrasts in their life styles, there are also several socio-cultural traits and customs which they have in common.[23] For example, all three types of communities have a strong kinship structure as a basis for their social organization. Thus the clan remains the basis of tribal society, while the extended family in rural and urban communities plays the important role that the clan does in the tribe.[24] Members of all three types of communities also value loyalty to the clan or family; they value pride, manliness, and hospitality.

These are some of the values and norms to which the Arab executive and his employees were exposed during their formative years whether they were brought up in a tribal, rural, or urban milieu. The influence of these socio-cultural characteristics on managerial behaviour and the expectations they create in the minds of executives and their employees, will be discussed in greater detail as they become more relevant to the findings of this study.

At this point a closer look at the social structure of the executive's environment will be useful. By social structure we mean the patterns of relationships between members of society as these relationships manifest themselves in institutions, groups and roles.[25] The Arab executive lives in a society where family and friendship remain important and prevalent factors even in the functioning of formal institutions and groups. Consequently, we shall find that the Arab executive relies upon family and friendship ties for getting things done within his organization and society.

Societies differ in their degree of differentiation among economic, political, educational, religious, and kinship institutions. In primitive societies, on the one hand, these institutions and the functions they perform overlap considerably, that is they are largely undifferentiated. On the other hand, institutions in highly industrialized societies are highly differentiated, separated and specialized. The Arab society, not unlike many third-world societies, is only partially differentiated.[26] These societies were described by Riggs (1964, p. 38) as 'prismatic' in which the differentiation process has started but may remain incomplete indefinitely.

It is generally accepted that the importance of family/kinship ties is inversely related to the functional differentiation of society.[27] This variability and diversity could range from the undifferentiated tribe, where kinship looms large, to the highly industrialized countries where the nuclear family is the order of the day, and where this nuclear family is 'the anchoring point for most members of society'.[28]

If we view the social structure from the viewpoint of group patterns, we still find that the most distinctive feature of Arab society is the pervasiveness and importance of kinship ties in group affiliation and group interaction.[29]

As in all societies, small groups in Arab society are formed on the basis of *primordial ties* such as family, school or neighbourhood friendship, regional and religious affiliation – as well as other *competing ties* and loyalties such as political party, trade union, or profession. However, the strength of such ties, and the types of them that are important, differ from person to person, from time to time, and from society to society. In Arab society, it will be argued that it is the former *primordial ties* which are generally the more pervasive and more important. Moreover, it will be hypothesized that, as a result, the Arab executive relies heavily on highly personalized and highly informalized methods and styles in the management of his organization.[30]

It is upon these small groups that the larger organizational, professional, and governmental institutions are superimposed. Most frequently, however, the larger groups and institutions exist as 'organizational shells' or 'extraneous façades'[31] within which the smaller groups, factions, and cliques carry out their important activities.

The importance of these small groups is further augmented when their role in relation to the class structure is examined. In their excellent analysis of Middle Eastern social structure, here is how Bill and Leiden (1974) describe the effects of these groups on class structure:

> The overall social structure might best be viewed as a divided grid or creased mosiac in which the intricate web of groups is *partially* partitioned by class lines. Both group and class structures relate to one another reciprocally, and it is this reciprocity that builds coherence into the sociopolitical system. . . . *Group fissures within classes are numerous and deep enough to weaken class cohesion and to retard class consciousness. Loyalty to primordial groups such as family takes precedence over loyalty to class*'. (p. 89, emphasis added)

It is this mosiac of a social structure which constitutes the background for this study of the Arab executive. A social structure in which three communities (tribal, rural, and urban) co-exist and interact sharing several socio-cultural values and norms. In turn, these values and norms influence the behaviour and expectations of executives as well as their employees. It is also a social structure in which family and friendship ties dominate the partially differentiated formal institutions and groups.

RECENT POLITICAL AND ECONOMIC DEVELOPMENTS

Five closely interrelated developments have shaped and continue to shape current political and economic conditions in the Arab world: the increasing emphasis on nationalism and tradition; the creation of the state of Israel in Palestine; the discovery and exploitation of petroleum; the unprecedented economic boom in the region; and the establishment of Arab trade unions.

The low degrees of political stability and predictability within the Arab world have been major factors in conditioning the Arab executive's attitudes towards profit, risk, long-term investment and planning. In addition, the discovery of petroleum and the economic boom of the 1970s, while creating unprecedented business opportunities for the Arab executive, have been accompanied by severe and often peculiar business and social problems.

Emphasis on Nationalism and Tradition

Political instability in the Arab world is a result of several factors two of which are relevant to our present purposes: inter-Arab friction and the Arab–Israeli conflict. The strife between Arab countries stems to a large extent from the varieties of political and economic ideologies adopted by the various countries. In principle, every Arab country considers itself an integral part of the Arab world, and most of them state this goal in their constitutions. However, the Arabs differ on the means of achieving Arab unity and/or the political and economic systems best suited for the prospective united Arab states.

Arab nationalism, as an ideological movement, was at first concerned with issues of independence from the Ottoman Turks and later from European rule. Soon after independence the emphasis shifted to the idea of an Arab nation, and Arab unity became its goal. However, Arab countries differed sharply on economic, political and social issues. For example, some countries, such as Egypt, Syria, Iraq, and Algeria adopted a form of 'Arab socialism'.[32] Their economic and political conditions called for 'radical' changes to enhance economic and political development. Others, such as Saudi Arabia, Kuwait, Jordan, and Tunisia chose to retain their political systems and their 'free enterprise' or in some cases 'mixed' economic systems.

These ideological differences only added fuel to the existing regional and individual rivalries among Arab countries. Furthermore, the abortive attempts at political unity seemed to increase the friction between them. These inter-Arab conflicts have been affecting business conditions and activities as manifested by the occasional border closures, restrictions of trade and the absence of an effective common market. In fact, 25 per cent of the executives interviewed stated that inter-Arab conflicts, and the resultant lack of coordination and cooperation between Arab governments, represented a major problem which they face when conducting business within the Arab world.

Of special interest in this connection is the increasing prominence currently being given in various parts of the Arab world to Islamic principles and ideology. The emergence of oil as a rich and strategic commodity has brought into play local, regional, and international factors that favour adherence to the established teachings of Islam. An increasing number of Arab leaders now feel that there is no need for the Arabs to choose between 'alien' ideologies, such as capitalism and socialism, conservatism and liberalism, democracy and authoritarianism. Instead, they feel that these choices are unnecessary if only the tenets of the Islamic *Sharī'a* are applied as the guiding principles of economic, governmental, and community life.

The desire to maintain both the Arabic and Islamic identity has gained prominence not only in political circles, but also among Arab academics and businessmen. This view, for example, was expressed by several executives during the interviews when asked if they would like to 'voice an opinion' on topics related to business in the Arab world.

Since relatively little is widely known about this view, a few statements by its leading exponents will be helpful. Sheikh Ahmed Zaki Yamani, the Minister of Petroleum and Mineral Resources in Saudi Arabia, argues that the Islamic *Sharī'a* is fully implemented in his country, and is capable of meeting contemporary issues and solving them:

> . . . one ought to look at the *Sharī'a* metaphorically as an organic creature, growing, developing, and evolving; attached with a strong link of interdependence to its society, adapting to its needs, and changing with different circumstances. The *Sharī'a* must be viewed as an adequate system meeting the needs of society at any particular interval in history. However, its intrinsic value is not in this momentary adequacy, but in its capability to satisfy the requirements of an ever changing society.[33]

Sheikh Yamani goes on to conclude that Islamic countries which rely on the *Sharī'a* principles can indeed avoid the necessity of making a choice between the economic or political systems of East or West.[34] More recently, the Saudi Minister of Interior, Prince Nai'f Ibn Abdul Aziz Ibn Saud (a son of the founder of the Kingdom), stated that:

> The Islamic *Sharī'a* is the all-inclusive framework of life in the Kingdom of Saudi Arabia. It is not merely the source of law that governs criminal matters but it is also the source of all laws, regulations, orders, decrees and rules that govern all aspects of private and public life.[35]

Other top government officials from the Gulf States have expressed similar beliefs about the role Islam could play in the political, economic, and social developments of their countries. Mr Abd al-Rahman Al-Atiqi, the Kuwaiti Minister of Finance, stressed the need to re-examine certain economic precepts imported wholesale from the West in the light of the *Sharī'a* provisions:

> I would like to point to a system which we have perhaps unnecessarily ignored while being dazzled by the West's achievements, our Islamic economic system . . . Islam is not a faith that stands in the way of economic growth. We do not need to abandon our values and traditions at every obstacle we meet. Instead we are called upon to transform it into a creative power and a source of strength.[36]

Indeed, it was the late King Faisal of Saudi Arabia who set the tone for many of the rich countries in the Gulf area when he declared in 1974 that he wanted his country 'to achieve rapid economic growth and modernization without sacrificing the traditions of Islam and Arab culture'.[37]

The Creation of the State of Israel

The creation of Israel had a significant impact on the economic, political, and social aspects of life in the Middle East. While a detailed analysis of this politically loaded subject would be beyond the scope of this study, a few points will be enumerated which are particularly relevant to the Arab executive, his actions and his orientations.

1. In the past thirty years four wars were fought (1947–8, 1956, 1967, and 1973), with hundreds of skirmishes and counter-retaliations. A vast amount of wealth has been spent on men and weapons, with detrimental effects on the economies of all the warring factions. The Arab–Israeli conflict continues to be a major factor of political and economic instability in the region, especially for countries sharing borders with Israel.
2. The presence of a large Palestinian refugee population (presently about 2.5 million) has contributed directly or indirectly to several crises in the Middle East (for example Jordan in 1970 and Lebanon from 1975 to date). It is now universally recognized that the Palestinian question is the heart and crux of the Arab–Israeli conflict. The presence of such a large number of stateless refugees in several Arab countries (including the Gulf States) continues to be a potentially explosive problem for the region, with possible world-wide repercussions.
3. The creation of the state of Israel and its aftermath have added considerably to any remnants of anti-Western attitudes the Arabs may have had from past colonization. The West's support of Israel continues to alienate a large number of educated people including Arab executives who, otherwise, would prefer the West over the East if such a choice were necessary.
4. One outcome of the creation of the Israeli state was the pressure it occasionally brought to bear on the Arab states to consolidate their efforts in order to face a common foe. Most recently, however, it has created serious inter-Arab conflict and disagreement over the bases and means which should be considered for reaching a just, comprehensive, and peaceful solution to the Palestinian problem. This inter-Arab conflict tends to disrupt business plans and hinder Arab economic cooperation.
5. Finally, the Arab–Israeli conflict has prompted the Arab countries to use economic sanctions in an attempt to bring about a solution. Initially, the economic boycott was utilized. Business firms trading with and/or supporting Israel are still being boycotted – with varying degrees of success. More

recently, the Arabs have used their enormous oil and monetary resources to apply pressure on some of the major world powers in order to reach an 'equitable' solution to the Palestinian problem. While gaining improved recognition of the existence of the problem, it is not yet clear how successful this pressure will be.

The Discovery and Exploitation of Petroleum

The discovery of oil may well prove to be a major turning point in the history of the Arabs. Although oil was discovered and exploited as early as the 1920s in Iraq, and during the 1930s and 1940s in the Arabian peninsula, the greatest impact on the economic, political, and social spheres of the oil-producing countries began in the 1960s. Through nationalization of the oil companies in some countries, joint-ownership plans (participation agreements) in others, and finally through the medium of the Organization of Petroleum Exporting Countries (OPEC), the oil-rich countries are now able to reap the benefits of ownership and/or control of their oil resources.[38] Needless to say, this development continues to have wide-ranging effects on the economies both of producing and consuming countries.[39]

In the Arab world itself, the oil wealth not only transformed the oil-producing countries, but had substantial influence on the non-oil-producing countries. First, the increasing demand for manpower was met, in part, by the non-oil Arab countries. Second, the rising consumer and governmental demands for food products, manufactured goods, and services were, again, partly met by the non-oil countries. Third, the oil producers have provided their Arab neighbours with large amounts of financial aid and long-term loans, thereby stimulating their economic development and reducing their earlier dependence on non-Arab foreign aid. Fourth, because of this oil wealth and the power it commands, there occurred a shift in the political power-centres in the Arab world. The countries of the Arabian peninsula, especially Saudi Arabia, have become major economic and political powers in the Arab world. Lastly, the oil wealth has fuelled an unprecedented economic boom in the whole region. Because of its significance to Arab executives, let us take a closer look at this boom and its consequences for business conditions.

Economic boom

The unprecedented economic boom in the oil-producing countries has encouraged the establishment of welfare states able and willing to provide generous employee and public benefits. The long-term economic development and modernization plans of these countries call for massive government investments designed to provide free education, free medical care, modern forms of communication and transport; and finally, the establishment of a viable economic base on which to build manufacturing, banking, and shipping industries that are not totally dependent on petroleum resources.

These development plans are often carried out within the framework of a three-, four-, or five-year government plan. Other large-scale projects are being financed through regional cooperation. Some of the inter-Arab projects, for example, have been promoted by the Organization of Arab Petroleum Exporting Countries (OAPEC).[40] Four well-capitalized companies have been formed by OAPEC since early 1973. The Arab Maritime Petroleum Transport Company has undertaken maritime transport of oil and all related products. The Arab Shipbuilding and Repair Yard Company (established 1974) runs the largest, newly constructed, dry dock in the Gulf area designed to service tankers and ships. The Arab Petroleum Investments Corporation invests in oil refineries, petrochemical complexes, and other related industries. Finally, the newly established Arab Petroleum Services Company provides Arab states with oil exploration and other services previously handled by foreign enterprises.

Many other joint ventures have been formed in the fields of banking, investment and finance, and consumer industries. Some of these projects were undertaken in partnership with the governments and/or large corporations of the major industrialized countries.[41]

Developmental plans, however, are currently hampered in many cases by shortages of manpower, materials, and equipment. Furthermore, the necessary economic infrastructure is frequently found wanting. The manpower shortage, especially skilled and managerial, is acute. This is true not only for government agencies but also for industrial and commercial organizations. Thus, for instance, when the fifty-two Arab executives were asked to mention the problems which they presently faced, 69 per cent considered the manpower shortage to be a major problem. If we exclude the nine Egyptian executives, none of whom faced this problem, then the percentage of executives jumps to an overwhelming 84 per cent.

In those countries with a manpower shortage there is a great dependence on expatriate manpower. This condition has prevailed since the discovery of oil – despite the continuous efforts of the governments and the oil companies to recruit and train local manpower.[42] If we consider the labour law of Saudi Arabia as representative of other laws in the Gulf states, we will have a notion of the general manpower situation. The Saudi Arab Labour Regulations (Article 45) provides that the number of Saudi employees shall not be less than 75 per cent of the total number of the employer's work force. However, this ratio has been reduced by the Minister of Labour when the required technical skills or qualifications are not available in the country. The provision, therefore, is evidently intended as a goal and it has not been strictly applied during the current economic boom.[43]

Manpower shortages in other industries (that is, non-oil) seem to be as severe. Unfortunately, reliable data are not available for comparative purposes. However, even a casual observer visiting the Gulf area would readily notice the relatively large number of Indian, Pakistani, Malaysian, and recently South Korean and Filipino employees working there. Future needs and demands for expatriate manpower are likely to increase as both governmental and private enterprises expand their operations. Meanwhile, the sources of manpower from some of the non-oil Arab countries are drying up, as evidenced by the tougher restrictions these countries are imposing on their own work force in an attempt to control the manpower drain.[44]

For the Arab executive who finds himself faced with the need to recruit expatriate staff, there are at least two problems. First, he must enter what has been aptly described as a 'recruitment jungle'.[45] The competition for skilled and managerial manpower is severe and difficult; and when the desperately needed employees are recruited, the executive becomes concerned with the problem of *retaining* these employees. One Kuwaiti executive, commenting on this problem, stated that for many expatriates 'Kuwait is a mere transit lounge'. The second problem concerns the difficulties of understanding and motivating a multinational staff. In some companies in the Gulf area the number of different nationalities working together ranges between thirty and forty.[46] The manpower shortage in the Gulf area has created a 'multicultural and multinational' Arab executive.

The presence of large numbers of expatriate employees with different attitudes, behaviour, and life-styles has thus been influencing Arab executives and employees in profound ways. This phenomenon was dramatically described by a visiting American behavioural scientist as the often ignored side of the 'double-edged culture shock'.[47] This exposure to the expatriates and some of its consequences (both functional and dysfunctional) to the Arab executive is examined in more detail in Chapter 7.

The pace and the strength of the economic boom in the Arab world (especially in the oil-producing countries) accentuated several existing problems which in turn continue to have serious consequences for the Arab executive. For example, the economic infrastructure in nearly all the Arab countries constitutes a major obstacle to business efficiency. The inadequate systems and facilities for communication, transportation, public utilities, and housing were seen by 31 per cent of the executives interviewed as major obstacles. The results of intensive efforts by both the public and private sectors to alleviate these obstacles are slowly being seen. And it seems likely that the pressure will be reduced within the next 3–5 years.[48]

Another problem mentioned by 27 per cent of the executives was the inability of governmental agencies to cope with the rapidly changing economies of the region. For example, the commercial and business laws legislated were either an emulation of foreign laws enacted without careful consideration to the needs of the local environment; or were laws passed expediently to solve a short-term crisis without regard to their long-term effects, and thus partially reflecting lack of proper local or regional long-term planning. Some executives felt that many of the laws passed were not fully understood by the governmental agencies entrusted to execute them. Other executives added that these laws were frequently cancelled or reversed – thus adding considerably to the uncertainty and riskiness of conducting business.

Another closely related problem, seen by Arab executives as a major constraint on business performance, is the apparently massive inefficiency of government agencies in processing routine activities. Of the Arab executives interviewed 64 per cent mentioned the problem of government 'bureaucracy and red tape'. To combat this problem the Arab executive uses his family or friendship contacts (connections) in order to get the work done faster. This, of course, taxes his time and energy, as we shall see in Chapter 6.

Finally, the economic boom has naturally created enormous business opportunities for the nationals of the oil-producing countries. Thus, the national while employed in the larger firms usually at the middle or lower organizational levels, finds himself faced with the challenge and opportunity to participate in lucrative 'on-the-side' business ventures. The manpower shortage, the governmental restrictions discouraging non-citizens from owning small business firms, and the increased demand for goods and services, all combine to induce the national employee to act as the commercial agent, the local representative, or a provider of the 'legal umbrella' for a foreign firm. Or he may find himself engaged as a partner in a local firm, owner of a small service establishment, or active in real-estate sales and development. Clearly, these practices may have detrimental effects on organizational morale and productivity, thus increasing the burdens of middle and top management.

The Arab Trade Union Movement

With a few exceptions, no serious independent labour union movement has developed in the Arab world. In those countries where workers are permitted to organize, their unions are either deliberately created by the ruling single-party system, or they are closely controlled by the governments in power.[49] Either way, the economic and political role of labour unions has been confined to supporting the existing political system.[50]

Nevertheless, labour unions have contributed to the betterment of workers in two ways: direct and indirect. Their direct contribution was in the formation of the International Confederation of Arab Trade Unions (ICATU) in 1956; and the creation in 1965 of the Arab Labour Organization (ALO) – an agency of the Arab League fashioned after the tripartite system of the International Labour Organization (ILO). These two organizations have been instrumental in (a) prompting various Arab countries to enact new and progressive labour laws; (b) establishing centres for education and technical training; and (c) maintaining close relations of cooperation and consultation with the ILO.

Indirectly, labour unions – or rather the fear of labour unions – motivated those countries prohibiting such unions to pass highly developed labour laws, often with the cooperation and help of the ALO and ILO. In addition, the oil wealth enabled the governments of the oil-producing countries to implement generous social security (or insurance) laws, progressive retirement plans, employee home-ownership schemes and various other employee benefit programmes. These have reduced the economic incentive for workers to organize.

In summary then, recent political and economic developments have a great and continuing influence on the mind of the Arab executive. The internal ideological conflicts, coupled with the external political events, are bound to increase the unpredictability and instability of the region, and hence the uncertainty of business conditions. The executive's time horizons and attitudes toward risk, profit, and other business-related activities will reflect these uncertainties. Additionally, the pace of the economic boom and the problems stemming from the inadequate economic and organizational infrastructures are burdening the Arab executive with social as well as business problems which are peculiar to that region of the world.

NOTES

1. United Nations, *Demographic Yearbook* (1978).
2. See Nuseibeh (1956), *The Ideas of Arab Nationalism*; Berger (1962), *The Arab World Today*; and Jabra (1971), 'Arab Language and Culture'.
3. Hitti (1970), *History of the Arabs*, p. 4.
4. Hitti (1971a), *Islam: A Way of Life*; van Nieuwenhuijze (1971), *Sociology of the Middle East*, among many others.
5. The sources of Islamic Sacred Law (*Sharī'a*) are the Holy Quran; the *Sunna* (the practices and traditions of Prophet Muhammad); *Ijmā'* (the consensus of Muslim jurists); and *Qiyās* (analogical deductions).
6. For a short history of the Arabs, see Hitti (1971b), *The Arabs: A Short History*; and Nutting (1964), *The Arabs*. For a long and detailed history, see Hitti (1970), *History of the Arabs*.
7. With the exception of Morroco.
8. Italy occupied Libya for about thirty years; Spain occupied southern Morocco and the Sahara for about forty years.
9. MacDonald (1965), *The League of Arab States*, pp. 284-6.
10. Hitti (1970), p. 44.

11. Lewis (1970), *The Arabs in History*, pp. 34-5.
12. Rodinson (1974), *Islam and Capitalism*, pp. 12-19 and *passim.*
13. Hitti (1970), pp. 343-9.
14. Lewis (1970), pp. 157-8; see also Hitti (1970), pp. 728-9.
15. Hitti (1970), p. 728.
16. Sharjah Group Company *Annual Report*, 1977. For a recent article on this company, see *International Management*, vol. 33, No. 9 (September 1978), pp. 62-4. Several companies were formed by OAPEC (Organization of Arab Petroleum Exporting Countries) in the mid-1970s; they are discussed in the last section of this chapter.
17. *The Financial Times* (London: 26 February 1979), p. 18. Turnover in ordinary shares in 1978 totalled £19.2 billion (around $39 billion); source: *Financial Statistics*, Central Statistical Office (London: HMSO, March 1979) p. 134.
18. For articles on these two companies see *International Management*, vol. 33, Nos. 7 and 9 (July and September 1978).
19. This excludes Islamic universities, some of which are many centuries old. The oldest, Al-Azhar University in Cairo, was established in AD 970. It now has a faculty of commerce. For details on dates and number of students, see *The World of Learning, 1978-79*, vols. 1 and 2 (London: Europa Publications, 1978).
20. The term mosaic was coined by Carleton S. Coon, in reference to the Middle East; see his book *Caravan: The Story of the Middle East* (rev. edn, 1958).
21. This typology is used by many scholars from various disciplines; see Berger (1962); van Nieuwenhuijze (1971); and Gulick (1976), *The Middle East: An Anthropological Perspective.*
22. Gulick (1976), pp. 54-61.
23. *Ibid.*, p. 61.
24. Tomeh (1970), 'Reference-group Supports Among Middle Eastern College Students', pp. 156-65; Prothro and Diab (1974), *Changing Family Patterns in the Arab East*, pp. 70-3; and Gulick (1976), pp. 42-6.
25. The concept of social structure is used widely in social sciences and with a variety of meanings. The above definition draws on works by Radcliffe-Brown, (1940), 'On Social Structure', pp. 1-12; Blau, (1976), 'Parameters of Social Structure', pp. 315-35; and Stinchcombe (1965), 'Social Structure and Organizations', pp. 142-93.
26. Riggs (1964), *Administration in Developing Countries*; Eisenstadt (1964), 'Social Change, Differentiation, and Evolution'; and Farsoun (1970), 'Family Structure and Society in Modern Lebanon'.
27. Moore (1969), 'Social Structure and Behaviour', p. 306; see also Goldthorpe (1975), *The Sociology of the Third World*, pp. 128-44.
28. Moore (1969), p. 306.
29. Eisenstadt (1964); Farsoun (1970); Melikian and Diab (1974), 'Stability and Change in Group Affiliations of University Students in the Arab Middle East'; and Gulick (1976).
30. See Chapter 6 for development of these points.
31. Bill and Leiden (1974), *The Middle East, Politics and Power*, pp. 60-1.
32. Sharabi (1966), *Nationalism and Revolution in The Arab World.*

33. Yamani (1972) 'Islamic Law and Contemporary Issues', p. 53.
34. *Ibid.*, p. 81.
35. *Al-Bilād* (Riyadh), 15 October, 1976, p. 5. From an address by H.H. Prince Nai'f to a regional conference on the application of the principle of *Sharī'a*, 9-13 October, 1976, Riyadh.
36. *Middle East Economic Survey* 'Atiqi on Investment in Arab World', 7 November, 1977, pp. i-vi.
37. MEIRC, S.A. (1977) 'A Summary Analysis of the Labour Movement in the Middle East and North Africa', January 1977, p. 4. This issue will be examined in more detail when we discuss social change and modernization in Chapter 7.
38. Sampson (1975), *The Seven Sisters.* OPEC membership in 1979 included seven Arab countries: Algeria, Iraq, Kuwait, Libya, Qatar, Saudi Arabia, and United Arab Emirates; and six non-Arab countries: Ecuador, Gabon, Indonesia, Iran, Nigeria, and Venezuela.
39. For a discussion on the economics of Arab oil, see Casadio (1976), *The Economic Challenge of the Arabs.*
40. OAPEC was established in 1968 and now includes: Algeria, Bahrain, Egypt, Iraq, Kuwait, Libya, Qatar, Saudi Arabia, Syria, and United Arab Emirates.
41. Casadio (1976), pp. 119-25.
42. For an excellent analysis of the origins of the manpower shortage, see Badre and Siksek (1960), *Manpower and Oil in Arab Countries.*
43. MEIRC, S.A. (1976c), 'Labour and Social Insurance Regulations: Saudi Arabia'.
44. A private discussion with the Jordanian Minister of Labour, Amman, Jordan, June 1977. In addition, Lebanon and Egypt have passed similar restrictions aimed at the regulations of employment policies covering their nationals working in neighbouring countries.
45. MEIRC, S.A. (1978), 'A Summary Analysis of the Labour Movement in the Middle East and North Africa', p. 12.
46. *Ibid.*, p. 12.
47. A private discussion with Dr H. C. Hayward, March 1976.
48. *The Financial Times*, 'Arab Transport' (London: 18 December, 1978).
49. In the Gulf area, the labour laws of Saudi Arabia, Qatar, United Arab Emirates, and Oman do not permit the formation of labour unions. In Bahrain, the law permits the formation of unions but, so far, none has been formed.
50. Hazen and Mughisuddin (1975), *Middle Eastern Subcultures*, pp. 143-8.

3 Social Pressures and the Executive Role

All the world's a stage,
And all the men and women merely players;
They have their exits and entrances;
And one man in his time plays many parts.
W. Shakespeare (1564–1616)
As You Like It, II, vii, 139

Social pressures impinge on the Arab executive's attitudes and behaviour. These pressures impose on his time, energy, and performance. In the first part of this chapter we examine the nature and extent of these pressures. In the second part we 'zoom in' and focus more closely on the Arab executive at the micro-level by examining his role in his community as well as in his organization.

SOCIAL PRESSURES

The Arab executive is viewed as a person who is at the helm of an organization which, in turn, is perceived as a business-oriented social system embedded in the larger systems of community and society. Viewed from this perspective, we may regard the executive as both a *target* and an *agent* of social influence and change.

One helpful way of conceptualizing the executive's environment is depicted in Figure 3.1. The political and economic sectors of the environment were briefly examined in the preceding chapter, and the major business-related problems were also highlighted. In this section our focus is on the social pressures stemming from the wider systems of community and society. Of course, one must bear in mind that the conceptual separation shown in Figure 3.1 is only meant to simplify social reality and aid in its analysis.

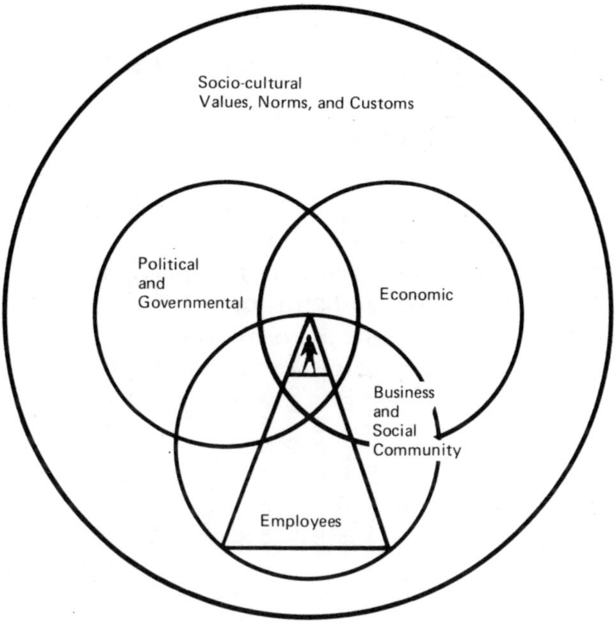

FIG. 3.1 The executive and his environment

The term social pressure refers here to the expectations, demands, or constraints which society places on its members. These pressures can be seen as the price of membership which individuals must pay to belong to a social system. In turn, these expectations, demands, and constraints originate from, and are shaped by, the socio-cultural values, norms, and customs. As in all societies, these values, norms, and customs (often summed up by the term culture) have their roots in a long history of traditions, in religion, and past and present philosophical, political, or economic ideologies.

A large number of social pressures were mentioned by the fifty-two Arab executives. However, only those mentioned by three or more executives are summarized in Table 3.1. Although closely interrelated, these pressures are categorized into those that stem from the wider society (socio-cultural) and those pressures from the executives' immediate business and social communities. We discuss very briefly each of these pressures, leaving until later an explanation of how they influence the executives' managerial and interpersonal styles.

TABLE 3.1 Social pressures as reported by Arab executives (N=52)

Socio-cultural		*Business and social community*	
Type	*Frequency of mention**	*Type*	*Frequency of mention**
1. Low value of time	19	1. Fusion of business, social, and personal life	18
2. Lack of industrial mentality	10	2. Reputation in community	17
3. Restrictions on women	9	3. Top-man syndrome	11
4. Individualistic approach to work	6	4. Social visits at the office	10
5. Dislike of manual work	4	5. High expectations for success	5
6. Marketing constraints	3	6. Nepotism	3
7. The week-end problem	3		

* It must be pointed out that the frequency of mention shown in this table is a conservative estimate of social pressures as felt by Arab executives. This is because open-ended questions were utilized and therefore the above responses were *volunteered* by the executives. Now that these pressures have been identified, future research on this subject will do well to use more structured questions.

Socio-cultural Pressures

Low value of time

Nineteen Arab executives voiced concern over the low value which their fellow countrymen place on time. The examples given by the executives range from lack of punctuality in time schedules and appointments; procrastination and 'tomorrow' *(buqra)* attitude; to a general lack of respect for time. Moreover, this seems to apply to many people: from employees and clients, to government officials. Interestingly, these nineteen executives were nationals of all six Arab countries, and were almost equally distributed among these countries. There will be a fuller discussion of this serious problem in Chapter 7 when we examine the executives' own attitudes towards time.

Lack of industrial mentality

Closely related to the above, this attribute was seen by ten executives as a constraint on their performance. This attribute is exemplified by the lack of industrial discipline in such things as aversion to systems and procedures, lack of organization (especially delegation), and a non-professional attitude toward business. Again, the ten executives were nationals of all six Arab countries.

Restrictions on women

Nine executives considered the societal restrictions on women – especially their exclusion from the work arena – as a constraint on their organizational performance. Five out of the nine executives were from Saudi Arabia; two were Lebanese executives who were referring to their extensive business operations in Saudi Arabia; and two were Jordanian executives who had women on their payroll but complained that it was difficult to include them in the social activities of their companies. Although women in the other four Arab countries are, comparatively speaking, far from being liberated, none of the executives from these other countries considered the present level of women's involvement in business as a serious problem.[1]

Individualistic approach to work

Six executives (from five countries) felt that Arab employees are individualistic as exemplified by a preference to work alone rather than in a team; and by the tendency to take sole credit for good deeds and to pass the blame to others, or to circumstances, when things go wrong.

Dislike of manual work

Three Saudi Arab executives and one UAE executive expressed displeasure regarding the dislike of manual work by the nationals of their respective countries. These executives felt that 'it is a shame that our young men demand only clerical and administrative work'.

Marketing constraints

Three executives felt that societal values and norms restrict certain types of advertising or marketing. For example, one executive in the consumer industry complained that he cannot advertise certain women's garments and articles in many parts of the Arab world. Another executive felt that door-to-door selling and mail advertising may take years before it is acceptable. The third executive pointed out that the Arab consumer (including the industrial buyer) often bases his buying decision on the personality of the salesman rather than the quality of the product being sold, and/or after-sales service offered.

The week-end problem

For those executives whose business is highly interrelated with western companies, there exists the problem of two week-ends in which communications are difficult for $3\frac{1}{2}$ to 4 days out of each week. The week-end for Arab companies is usually Thursday afternoon and Friday, meanwhile the western firms observe Saturday and Sunday as their week-end. Only three Arab executives mentioned this as a practical problem which they face, but if the volume of business with foreign companies increases it is likely that this problem will be felt by more Arab executives, as well as the foreign businessman.

Pressures from the Business and Social Community

Fusion of business, social and personal life

This heading refers to the inability of executives to separate business affairs from social or personal life. As one executive put it: 'In the West one may be able to compartmentalize his business life, his social life, and his personal life, but it is not easy in the Arab world . . . they are often one and the same.' This was a problem for eighteen Arab executives from all six countries. Both employees and outsiders (clients, suppliers and government officials) would call on them at home and on week-ends to handle business problems. Also, many of their social affairs are meant to enhance the business. These executives felt *compelled* to accept this sort of pressure in order to remain successful.[2] Only a minority of four executives indicated that they have been able to escape this pressure by making it well known to employees and outsiders that evenings and week-ends 'belong to me and my family'. The remainder of the executives did not seem to see this pressure as a problem – for, either they encourage this practice, or they willingly accept it as part of their work even though it taxes their time, energy, and family life.

Reputation in community

The executives were asked to name those people whom they take into consideration when making personal decisions; in short, people whose opinion and approval matter. Twenty-eight executives said that what mattered was the opinion of family members, close friends and/or employees. This was an expected response since the reference groups and 'significant others' to most persons usually are a small circle of family, friends and work groups: those people whom one knows personally and is affiliated with.

What is interesting, however, is that as many as seventeen executives mentioned the 'larger' community as their reference group, or those whose judgement and approval matter. This community includes those people whom one knows personally as well as those people one does not know. Here, these executives repeatedly mentioned the word reputation – often family reputation. They felt that this reputation is at stake if one did not conform to the community's norms and expectations. Indeed, three of these executives said that when travelling (within Europe) they are able to relax and 'let their hair down'. One executive said: 'I don't care what people think or say when I am in London, for example.' In short, these seventeen executives (from five Arab countries) felt that the community is exerting a pressure on them to which they must *conform*. Perhaps some are conforming to the social pressure because they consider it correct and right (that is they have internalized the community's values and norms); others may be conforming because they feel that the cost of membership in the community is not too high. It is not our purpose here to determine the reasons for conformity, but it is interesting, nevertheless, that several executives voluntarily stated that they do lead a different life-style when they are in an alien country.

Of the remaining executives, four said they 'did not care what people would think or say'. Three others preferred not to express their views on that question.

Top-man syndrome

The top-man syndrome refers to the insistence by clients, suppliers, and government officials on dealing only with the head of the organization. Eleven executives (from five countries) considered this an unnecessary burden on their time and energy.

There are two aspects to this problem. First, there is the feeling among outsiders (clients, suppliers, and so on) that only the top man of an organization can get things done: their trust and confidence is often in the person rather than in the organization. As one president of a large company (over 10,000 employees) put it: 'They [clients] insist on my presence during the negotiations. . . . They are offended if I am not personally involved. . . . I am unable to delegate these things to my specialized subordinates.' Another executive complained: 'People with a problem come here and demand to see me; they start from the top instead of starting from where the problem eventually gets solved.'

The second aspect concerns the executive's inability to escape from his many ceremonial duties such as invitations to social events, conventions, and various other ceremonies. Although these executives accept their role as formal representatives of their organization,[3] it is the *excessive* pressure on their time which troubled them.

Social visits at the office

Ten Arab executives (from four countries) were annoyed by the custom of close friends who would drop in to the office for non-business chats over coffee or tea. This phenomenon is closely related to some of the items discussed above such as value of time and the fusion of business, social and personal life. It is difficult for the busy and over-burdened executive to discourage such custom since it stems from the strong societal norm of hospitality.[4] There were a few executives who actively discouraged this custom, but as one executive said: 'It takes time before we can change these deeply-rooted habits.' Another executive from the Gulf area – who incidentally considered himself a maverick not only in breaking this custom but also with his management style – admitted to having two offices in the same city, mostly to escape from such visitations by friends and colleagues. In some respects, those executives who slowly and carefully discourage these customs can be considered as agents of change in their respective countries. More will be said about this role shortly.

High expectations for success

Five executives, three from Kuwait and two from Saudi Arabia, felt that they were under great pressure from friends, colleagues, and government officials who expect them to succeed in any new venture they undertake. One Kuwaiti executive said: 'After receiving our university education we came back with no work experience . . . we had no models to follow . . . we were the pioneers and the older generation could not advise us and yet their expectations were always high.' A Saudi executive stated that government officials often approve industrial projects and the formation of new companies in which he is involved expecting – or rather taking for granted – a successful outcome. This type of pressure was well described by a Lebanese executive who works closely with executives from the Gulf area: 'These men took charge of large companies when they were still young and with little, if any, on-the-job training. . . . The pressure on them is high. . . . it is really unfair to them.'

Nepotism

The struggle against nepotism was reported by only three executives – two Lebanese and one Jordanian. One executive indicated that many of his relatives are 'angry at him', because of the self-imposed regulation prohibiting nepotism in his organization. But he quickly added that his help to his close-knit extended family takes the form of financial assistance and educational grants. The rest of the executives seemed willing to accept this strong socio-cultural pressure to hire relatives, although four of them considered it a potential burden since they had ultimately to accept the final responsibility if the relatives' performances were poor.

Two main observations are possible when we analyse the social pressures enumerated above. First, there are both similarities and differences among the six Arab countries in terms of the social pressures felt by the executives of these countries. Thus, for instance, executives from all countries complained about the low value of time; lack of industrial mentality and the fusion of business, social and personal life; while, on the other hand, restrictions on women, dislike of manual work, and the high expectations for success were more keenly felt by executives from the Gulf area.

A brief word on women's status in the Arab world. Although restrictions on women differ vastly from one country to another, the trend towards female emancipation has accelerated in most Arab countries, possibly at a relatively faster rate than was the case for Western women some fifty years ago. In Kuwait, for example, one finds women employed in business organizations and government agencies. Indeed, one of the largest Kuwaiti contracting companies is headed by a Kuwaiti woman.[5] We shall examine the executives' attitudes towards women in business later on in Chapter 7.

Second, the Arab executives facing these social pressures can be viewed both as targets and agents of social influence. We have seen that some of them are actively discouraging those socio-cultural values and norms which they regard as an unnecessary burden on their time, energy, and performance. Examples were provided in which a few executives attempted to minimize the following social pressures: fusion of business, social and personal life; social visitations at the office; and nepotism. The majority of executives, however, seemed either willing to accept these pressures as a price of membership in society, or did not consider these pressures as burdensome.

THE EXECUTIVE ROLE

The examination of social pressures in the preceding section leads us to the important question of what specific behaviour is expected by those people around the Arab executive, by virtue of his position in the community and in his organization? In short, what role is the Arab executive expected to play in his immediate community and in his organization? Let us first examine his role in the community.

Role in Community

For the Arab executive, the community consists mainly of his extended family, friends, business associates, and government officials. From each of these groups the executive is aware of a set of expected activities; a role which he feels obligated to carry out. And with each role there is usually a pattern of reciprocal obligations and claims.

The essence of reciprocity is the give-and-take characteristic in which people are often mutually dependent on one another. In this section, we shall emphasize the executive's obligations, the 'giving' aspect, while the 'taking' aspect will be examined in Chapter 6. First, we will consider the executive's role with his extended family.

We pointed out in the preceding chapter the important part that the extended family plays in the rural and urban communities of the Arab world. Recent studies indicate that the extended family has maintained its importance in spite of the economic development and modernization process now taking place in the region.[6] Prothro and Diab (1974) conclude that 'even though the extended family is not living in one household, it is nevertheless a strong social psychological reality'.[7]

In view of these findings, the executives were asked to describe their relations with their extended family. Based on these descriptions, their answers were coded into three categories: extremely strong, strong to moderate, and weak.[8] Not surprising for the Arab world, relations with the extended family were extremely strong for 67 per cent of the executives, 27 per cent described them as strong to moderate, and only 6 per cent said that they were weak. It must be re-emphasized that although the extended family is often physically scattered, family ties and relations are still strong. Thus, a few executives mentioned that although their relatives are living in many parts of the world, yet they maintain strong family ties (correspondence, visitations, financial assistance, and so on). Modern living and working conditions have, as expected, physically separated the extended family; but it seems, at least so far, that the psychological bonds remain strong.

The patriarchal family system is still the basis of Arab society.[9] Research studies on group affiliation of Arab students at the American University of Beirut showed, in 1958, that the family had a clear preference over other loyalties such as the nation, political party, or religion. When the study was repeated in 1971 there was a slight decline in religious affiliations but the family still came first.[10]

It is interesting, for instance, that when Arabs meet their countrymen for the first time, they usually attempt to establish each other's family identity. In the West, on the other hand, it appears that the initial conversation revolves around a person's occupation or profession. In Japan, introductions are made with reference to one's organization or company rather than profession.

The importance of the family becomes more apparent when we investigate the responses of the fifty-two Arab executives to the open-ended question about the expectations of their extended family. Thirty-nine executives (75 per cent) mentioned that their extended family demand and receive from them all sorts of help and assistance. Some of the more frequently mentioned examples include:

(a) consultation on personal problems or family decisions;
(b) employment in his organization or other organizations with which he is associated;
(c) contacts or pressure on government agencies or other institutions (that is to act as the intermediary);
(d) family visitations and/or maintaining family contacts and ties;
(e) financial assistance and loans.

Some executives, when asked to give additional examples, replied: 'All kinds of help is expected . . . all kinds that the mind can imagine.' In fact, four of the thirty-nine executives described their role as the 'leader of the family', or the 'head of the family', and one even described himself as the 'godfather' of his extended family. Needless to say, these demanding roles add to the executive's existing responsibilities and burdens, and are especially taxing on his time.

Of the remaining executives, six viewed their role as limited to maintaining contact through visits, correspondence, and the telephone; or as one executive put it 'a need to maintain roots'. Finally, seven executives felt that there were very little or no expectations from their extended family.

The executive's role toward his friends, business associates, and government officials is also distinguished by the prevalence of reciprocal obligations and claims. Let us briefly examine the nature of these obligations. When asked to enumerate the expectations which the community held towards them and to describe their role in their community, forty-nine executives were able to describe a variety of expectations. Only three executives felt that they had no role to play in the community, and that the community had no expectations of them by virtue of their positions. The replies given by the forty-nine executives were wide-ranging but described quite similar patterns. The most frequently mentioned examples were:

(a) *Social responsibility.* Under this general title the following expectations were mentioned: efficient management of one's organization; development of the industry in which the executive is engaged (innovation and being kept up-to-date); and the recruitment and training of local national employees. The executive is also expected to give opinion and guidance to friends, associates, and government officials. In short, the executive is expected to be an active member and a responsible leader in his community.

(b) *Contribution to the national interest.* This heading refers to the expectations (especially by government officials) of contributions to the national economic plans of the country. Many executives felt a commitment to achieve, in the national interest, such aims as economic progress, modernization and industrialization.

(c) *Financial assistance to community.* Executives were expected to extend financial help to those friends and associates who are in trouble, and also to support financially social activities in the community, including charitable groups.

(d) *Intermediary role.* The intermediary role refers to the executive's use of family and friendship ties (and of course his position) to expedite, advance, or influence the course of events in favour of other relatives and friends. In the Arab world, one speaks of having 'connections' or 'contacts' in order to get things done faster or as desired.[11] Here, the executive is usually at both the giving and receiving ends of this reciprocal activity. (His own extensive use of this method will be examined in Chapter 6.)

(e) *Link between organization and community.* Executives saw themselves as the crucial link between their organization and its community. This role includes public relations activities such as enhancement of company reputation and standing, and official representation of the organization in the community. This role is akin to Mintzberg's (1973, p. 56) 'spokesman', 'liaison', and 'figurehead' roles. Of course, these are the roles which provide unique opportunities to the effective executive who turns these obligations to his advantage.

It is quite likely that most of the above activities are performed by chief executives from all parts of the world. However, the significance lies in the important nuances such activities have in various societies. Note, for example, that for the Arab executive there is the lack of political affiliation or activities; the lack of organized pressure from labour unions or consumer groups; and the heavy emphasis on the executive's intermediary role.

So far we have perhaps overstressed one aspect of the executive's role in his community; namely the concomitant obligations of that role. Let us briefly examine the other side of the coin. The top executive of an organization, while discharging some of the above-mentioned obligations, is in a unique position to act as his organization's *radar* scanning the environment for vital information, pertinent events and trends, business opportunities, and so on. The ability to do this is similar to what has been called the 'helicopter view', or the ability 'to see the forest from the trees'. It was referred to by some as the *conceptual* ability of top management as contrasted with the interpersonal and technical skills of middle and lower managerial levels.[12] Similarly, Katz and Kahn advocate that organizational leaders must adopt the external perspective (or system perspective) in order to avoid stagnation or failure:

> External perspective is in part a *sensitivity* to environmental demands, to the requirements that organizations must meet in

> order to maintain a state of equilibrium with its environment. In part external perspective involves a *sensitivity* to environmental opportunities, to the possibilities of achieving a more advantageous relationship with the environment. Finally external perspective requires *sensitivity* to trends and changes in the environment, which is characteristically in a state of movement both with respect to the demands it makes on organizations and the opportunities it affords to them. (Emphasis added.)[13]

This 'sensitivity' to processes in the environment, along with the ability to foresee how the organization fits within that environment, are executive-level skills. These skills can be learned and achieved by the executive if he is willing to cultivate the obligations and the opportunities provided by his role in the community.

Role in Organization

It was mentioned earlier that the family is one of the dominating social institutions in Arab society. We also referred to the strength of the extended family. The question that comes to mind is whether executives and their employees bring with them to the work organization any of these strong values and norms? In order to explore this topic we asked the Arab executives how they viewed their role in the organization? And what they perceived as the main expectations which their employees held towards them? Responding to these open-ended questions, the executives gave the following answers. Twenty-three executives (44 per cent) described themselves as the *chief executive* of their respective organizations. These executives used a variety of terms to describe this chief executive role. Here are some examples: the leader; the 'motor' of the company; the decision maker; the person who is responsible for the profitability and growth of the company; and various other functions and duties relating to the 'good management' of the organization. In most cases these twenty-three executives also mentioned that their employees expect good wages, good working conditions, promotion, training, and help in personal and family matters. For convenience, this role will be referred to as the *chief executive role*.

What is interesting, however, are the responses of the other twenty-nine executives (56 per cent). These executives perceived their organization as a *family*, and they described their roles using familial terms. Thus, of the twenty-nine executives, eleven saw their role as the 'head of a family'; eleven more described their role as a 'father'; six used the term 'elder brother'; and one saw himself as the 'godfather' of his organization. In contrast to the *chief executive role* let us refer to this role as the *family role.*

Immediately, one would suspect that the executives who saw themselves in the family role are in charge of smaller organizations, or they are possibly the heads of family-owned organizations. In short, is the *family role* related to size or type of ownership of the organization? Looking at the findings, as shown in Tables 3.2 (a and b), the answers to these questions are unmistakably in the negative.

TABLE 3.2(a) Executive role and organizational size*

	Family	*Chief executive*	*Total*
Small (180–499)	10	8	18
Medium (500–999)	7	7	14
Large (over 1000)	12	8	20
Total	29	23	52

$\chi^2 = 0.4$; not significant.
*Size=number of employees.

TABLE 3.2(b) Executive role and organizational ownership

	Family	*Chief executive*	*Total*
Family-owned	12	8	20
Partnership	9	11	20
Government-owned	8	4	12
Total	29	23	52

$\chi^2 = 1.68$; not significant

Using the chi-squared (χ^2) test, we can ascertain that there are no statistically significant relationships between executive role and organizational size or type of ownership. Similar tests were used to see whether or not family role is related to the executive's age, or his education. Again, no significant relationships were found. It is interesting to note, however, that the younger executives were more likely to describe their role as the 'elder brother', while the older executives would use the terms 'father' or 'head of family'.

An explanation of the phenomenon of *family role* can be found, in part, when we examine how the Arab executives perceive their employees' expectations. Other than the usual demands for increased wages, better working conditions, promotions, and so on, the executives felt obligated to help employees with their personal and family problems (both financial and emotional). Employees' expectations, as seen by the executives, included 'kind and humane treatment', 'care', 'respect', 'control', and 'guidance'. These were some of the terms used by the executives; the examples of help to employees ranged from assistance with governmental agencies (getting a passport, a visa, or even cancelling a traffic violation); advice about housing problems or a divorce; to providing guidance regarding the children's education or future.

A classical self-fulfilling prophecy seems to be at work here: employees' expectations (and behaviour) towards the executive reinforces his perception of his role as a 'father'. Alternatively, the executive's behaviour towards his employees is paternal and this reinforces the employees' perceived role as members of a family. Either way, it seems that both parties' expectations of one another coincide. Let us briefly look at the employees' attitudes on this matter. Although employees were not included in this study, there are some research findings which supplement and support the present study. Research studies by MEIRC, S.A. were carried out in three oil companies operating in three Gulf countries.[14] The main results of these studies indicate that the Arab employees interviewed (N=205) had three expectations of what they considered as a 'good' manager. First, employees expected to be 'treated well' by their manager and their organization. For the employees, a good manager would treat his employees in a considerate and humane manner. He would be interested and willing to provide good services and facilities as well as 'care and guidance' to their personal problems, on and off the job. This is closely related to the expectations as seen by the executive, which is to play the father role. Second, employees expected to be 'paid well' in terms of higher salary levels and improved employee benefits. Third, the employees expected their skills to be 'used well' in their present jobs, and they expected to be trained (in and out of the company) in new skills in order to enhance their future careers.

Unfortunately, the MEIRC studies are the only ones available which shed some light on the expectations of Arab employees. Although these studies covered employees in a specific industry (oil) and region (Gulf area), their findings are relevant and lend support to our investigation of the Arab executive's role in his organization.

In this chapter we began by examining the nature of the social pressures as felt by Arab executives. We discovered that these pressures act as constraints on the executives' behaviour, attitudes, and time. However, we found that these pressures vary from one country to another, and that the reaction of the executives to the social pressures also varied. Thus, while most of the executives accepted many of the socio-cultural values, norms, and customs (thus, being targets of social influence); a small number of executives were attempting to change those values, norms, and customs which they considered as burdensome (thus, acting as agents of social change).

In the second part of the chapter, we investigated the roles of the Arab executive in his community and in his organization. We drew attention to the strength and importance of the executive's relations with his extended family. An attempt was made to differentiate between the obligations and opportunities afforded to the executive, especially by his role in the community. Finally, when examining the executive's role within his organization, it was found that the majority of Arab executives viewed their organization as a family unit. They described their role in familial terms such as father or elder brother. It seems that the executives' expectations coincide with those of the employees in the form of a self-fulfilling prophecy.

NOTES

1. The Arab executives' attitudes towards working women will be examined in more detail in Chapter 7.
2. This group included both the owner/partner and the non-owner executive.
3. This role of a formal representative is termed by Mintzberg the 'fig-

urehead' role. As he points out, it is very likely that executives utilize this role to maintain strong links (informational and friendship) with other businessmen and government officials; Mintzberg (1973), *The Nature of Managerial Work*, pp. 58–60, 126–7.

4. On hospitality of Middle Eastern people, see Antoun (1965), 'Conservatism and Change in the Village Community', p. 7; Gulick (1976), *The Middle East: An Anthropological Perspective*, p. 46.
5. This executive was the subject of the cover article in a business magazine, *Alam Attijarat*, February 1978, pp. 26–7. For further articles on this executive and on women's status in Kuwait, see *The Times* (London: 12 June, 1978), p. iv.
6. Tomeh (1970), 'Reference-Group Supports Among Middle Eastern College Students', pp. 156–65; Prothro and Diab (1974), *Changing Family Patterns in the Arab East*, pp. 70–3; Farsoun (1970), 'Family Structure and Society in Modern Lebanon', pp. 257–307.
7. Prothro and Diab (1974), p. 70.
8. The three categories were based upon the intensity of contact and commitment to extended family. It includes, for example, visitation to and time spent with relatives; emotional and financial support; and other miscellaneous help and support.
9. It is interesting to note in this respect that the middle name for most Arabs consists of their father's name, see Gulick (1976), pp. 39–42, 215–21.
10 Melikian and Diab, (1959), 'Group Affiliations of University Students in the Arab Middle East', pp. 145–59; Melikian and Diab (1974), 'Stability and Change in Group Affiliations of University Students in the Arab Middle East', pp. 13–21; and Melikian (1977), 'The Modal Personality of Saudi College Students', pp. 166–209.
11. Farsoun (1970), pp. 269–70. Farsoun describes the intermediary role as follows: 'The term *wastah* is colloquial Arabic for an "intermediary" a go-between, or the process of employing an intermediary or go-between, "a process of mediation" in almost any and all types of activity' (p. 269).
12. Mann (1964), 'Toward an Understanding of the Leadership Role in Formal Organizations'.
13. Katz and Kahn (1978), *Social Psychology of Organizations*, p. 504.
14. MEIRC, S.A. (1975), "Job Attitude Survey of Saudi and Kuwaiti Employees'; MEIRC, S.A., (1976a), 'Jcb Attitude Survey of Omani National Staff'; and MEIRC, S.A. (1976b), 'Das Island Attitude and Motivation Survey'.

4 The Arab Approach to Decision Making

> Consult them in affairs of the moment, then, when thou hast taken a decision, put thy trust in God.
>
> The Holy Quran, III, 159.

In the preceding chapter we have focused on the Arab executive as a target of social influence and control. We delineated the extent to which social pressures act as constraints on his behaviour, energy and time. Our attention in the present chapter will be on the executive as an organizational leader, viewing him as the prime agent of influence and control within his own organization. The ability as well as the capacity to exert influence and maintain control over the actions of others is one of the more common definitions of the power concept,[1] and it is this definition which is used here. In this chapter, we shall be looking at the Arab executive's use of that power in a very important reality of organizational life: decision making.

DECISION-MAKING STYLES

The literature in the field of decision making is immense. The often-made statement that decision making is *the* organizational activity[2] has motivated researchers from a variety of social science disciplines to its study.

From scholars of organizational behaviour came an abundance of literature on leadership and leadership styles – which often incorporated and/or discussed the decision-making process.[3] One facet of this highly complex phenomenon is the executive's choice about how much and in what ways to involve subordinates in decision making.[4]

In the present study we are interested in the extent to which the Arab executive shares his power of decision making with his subordinates under various situations involving different types of business decisions. We are also interested to find what effects, if any, would socio-cultural, economic, and political factors have on the decision-making styles of the Arab executive. For instance, would factors such as the following have any influence on how 'autocratic' or 'democratic' the Arab executive is when making decisions: the prevalence of paternalistic and familial social patterns; the absence of Western-styled democratic systems; the recent economic boom; and the manpower shortage.

In short, our aims here are (a) to draw a profile of the decision-making styles of executives from the six Arab countries; (b) to analyse the similarities among, and the differences between, these executives; (c) to isolate those variables which provide the best explanation of the variation in decision-making styles; and (d) to provide support for the recent empirical research which emphasizes that decision-making styles are dependent on the interaction between social-structural, situational, and personal variables (often termed situational or contingency approach).[5]

The conceptual framework and the methods used in this study of decision-making styles reflect borrowing from several research studies dating back forty years. Table 4.1 summarizes the relationships between this author's approach and those used in prior investigations. As can be clearly seen, the latest two studies (Heller, 1971; Vroom and Yetton, 1973) had a substantial influence on the present approach.

Decision-making style is defined and measured by a four-point equal interval scale reflecting the various degrees of power sharing between the executive and his subordinate(s).[6] The power-sharing continuum is illustrated in Figure 4.1. An almost similar continuum was used by Heller (1971) which he called the influence-power-sharing continuum (IPC). The only difference between the two continua is that ours does not include Heller's style 2 (own decision *with* explanation – see Table 4.1). It was felt that Heller's style 2 cannot be considered a distinct style, but rather an elaboration on his style 1 (own decision *without* explanation); to explain or to 'sell' the decision to subordinates is not likely to change either the power wielded by the executive or the influence exerted by his subordinates on the outcome of a decision he had already made. In other respects, however, we share Heller's inclusion of delegation as an extension to the conventional decision-making styles. It highlights an

TABLE 4.1 Comparison between decisional styles employed in this study and those of previous investigators. (Adapted with modification from Vroom and Yetton, 1973.)

Lewin, Lippitt and White (1939)	*Maier (1955)*	*Tannenbaum and Schmidt (1958)*			*Likert (1967)*		*Heiler (1971)*		*Vroom and Yetton (1973)*		*Muna (present study)*
Autocratic leadership	Autocratic management	Manager makes decision and announces it	Manager sells decision	Manager presents ideas and invites questions	Exploitive authoritative (System 1)	Benevolent authoritative (System 2)	Own decision without detailed explanation (Style 1)	Own decision with detailed explanation (Style 2)	Manager makes decision himself (A1)	Manager makes decision, obtaining necessary information from subordinate (A11)	Executive makes decisions without consulting subordinate(s), but may consult superiors, partners or outsiders (Style 1)
	Consultative management	Manager presents tentative decisions, subject to changes	Manager presents problems, gets suggestions, makes decision		Consultative (System 3)		Prior consultation with subordinate(s) (Style 3)		Manager shares problem with subordinate, makes own decision (C1)	Manager shares problem with group, makes own decision (C11)	Prior consultation with subordinate(s) (Style 2)
Democratic leadership	Group discussion	Manager defines limits, asks group to make decision	Manager permits group to make decisions within prescribed limits		Participative group (System 4)		Joint decision-making with subordinate(s) (Style 4)		Manager and subordinate together arrive at mutually agreeable decision (G1)	Manager (acting like a chairman) and group discuss, evaluate, and make a group decision (G11)	Joint decision-making with subordinate(s) (Style 3)
Laissez-faire leadership							Delegation of decisions to subordinate(s) (Style 5)		Delegation of decisions to subordinate (D1)		Delegation of decisions to subordinate(s) (Style 4)

important, even crucial, managerial responsibility with potentially great benefits to the organization, the manager, and the subordinate. For delegation can serve not only as a motivator to employees (satisfying ego and self-actualization needs), but could also be an excellent managerial training technique. Furthermore, the ability to delegate is an indispensable tool to the executive which, if used properly, could possibly lead to a better management of his own time – especially so for the Arab executive, as will be pointed out throughout this study.

Again, we share Heller's aversion to the use of the term participation in studies on decision making. Indeed, participation is a value-laden concept, reflecting a normative standpoint often with a positive value attributed to it. The term also lacks precision and thus would be difficult to measure. Finally, if the term participation has emotional implications in the West, it is even more so in the Arab world where participation sometimes has the wider connotation of joint-ownership (often government ownership), especially in the oil industry.

A DECISION-MAKING PROFILE

Let us now turn to the results obtained from interviews with the fifty-two executives from six Arab countries. In the decision-making section of the semi-structured interviews, each executive was presented with a description of four alternative decision styles (see Figure 4.1). Each was then given seven decisions and

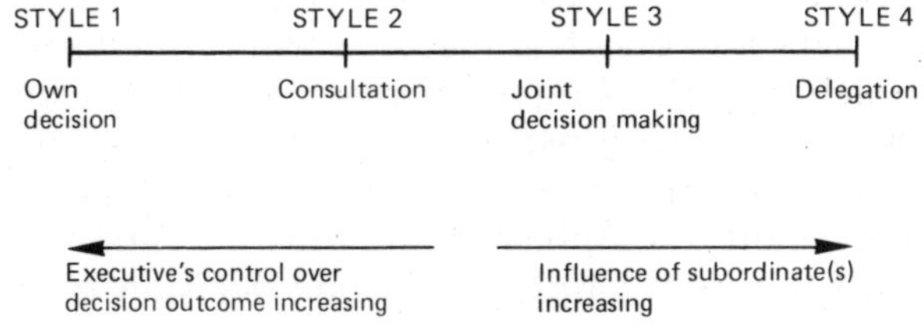

FIG. 4.1 The power-sharing continuum

was asked to describe which of the alternatives he would normally use to arrive at the decision. The author would then code each decision – often after a few minutes of discussion and probing. This procedure minimized response bias. The four alternatives (styles) were:

I. the decision is made for you, no consultation or discussion with subordinate(s);
II. prior consultation with subordinate(s); he/they may or may not influence your final decision;
III. you and your subordinate(s) *together* analyse problems and come to a decision – subordinates have as much influence as you have on the final decision (majority decision);
IV. ask subordinate(s) to make decision on his/their own.

The seven decisions were:

1. The decision to promote one of the employees directly supervised by one of your subordinates;[7]
2. the decision to discipline one of the employees directly supervised by one of your subordinates;
3. the decision to terminate the services of one of the employees directly supervised by one of your subordinates;
4. the decision to reduce the total work force by 20 per cent;
5. the decision to increase the work force in a subordinate's department/division;
6. the decision to introduce a new product, or enter a new market, or take on a new project, or expand existing work facilities (whichever is applicable);
7. the decision to alter/modify the formal organization chart (changes in job and/or responsibilities, re-organization) in your subordinate's department/division.

Two approaches were used to analyse the data; each with its own advantages and disadvantages, as will be seen shortly. The first approach uses the frequency distribution of responses for each of the seven decisions; or it can use the responses of the executives from each of the six countries for all decisions. This approach is meant to emphasize and draw attention to the fact that executives rarely employ only one decision-making style irrespective of the type and nature of the decision. Indeed, executives vary their style in accordance with the problem at hand, as common sense suggests.

Table 4.2 and Figure 4.2 present the results using frequency distribution of reponses by style broken down for each decision and for the total of all decisions. It is clear from Table 4.2 that the four decision styles were utilized on nearly all decisions. There were three exceptions: Style 3 (joint decision making)

TABLE 4.2 Distribution of decision styles for each decision by all Arab executives (N=52) (expressed as percentages)

Decision	*Style 1* *Own decision*	*Style 2* *Consultation*	*Style 3* *Joint decision*	*Style 4* *Delegation*	*Total*
1	8	60	19	13	100
2	10	58	15	17	100
3	10	71	10	9	100
4	51	40	9	—	100
5	8	54	29	9	100
6	52	48	—	—	100
7	19	52	10	19	100
All decisions	22	55	13	10	100

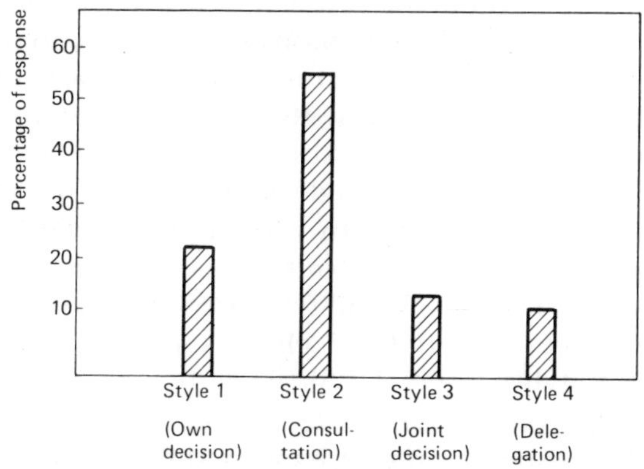

FIG. 4.2 Proportion of responses for all decisions by all Arab executives (N=52)

was not employed for decision 6, and Style 4 (delegation) was never utilized for either decision 4 or 6. It is worth noting that both decisions 4 and 6 involved major decisions for the organization.

It is also clear from Table 4.2 and Figure 4.2 that Style 2, consultation, was predominantly preferred by Arab executives for this specific set of decisions. Obviously, a different set of problems is likely to produce a different profile. But consultation, as will be seen later, seems to be the preferred style for Arab executives.

TABLE 4.3 Distribution of decision styles by executives from each of the six Arab countries (N=52) (for all decisions) (expressed as percentages)

Country	*Style 1* *Own decision*	*Style 2* *Consultation*	*Style 3* *Joint decision*	*Style 4* *Delegation*	*Total*
Egypt	35	55	10	—	100
Jordan	32	55	6	7	100
Lebanon	9	66	21	4	100
Kuwait	23	47	8	22	100
Saudi Arabia	17	44	27	12	100
UAE	10	71	2	17	100
All countries	22	55	13	10	100

Using the same approach as above, Table 4.3 shows how the executives from *each* country responded to the seven decisions. This table provides a good description of responses by executives from the various countries. It shows the extent of differences and similarities: it is interesting, for example, to note that none of the Egyptian executives delegated any of the seven decisions. Instead, the Egyptian executives showed a strong preference for only two of the four styles (90 per cent of their responses were for Styles 1 and 2). In comparison, the Saudi Arabian executives varied their choices slightly more evenly among the four styles.

A second approach makes use of the power-sharing continuum and the assumption that its four styles are separated by equal intervals. This assumption allows us to use the mean scores (arithmetic averages) and, more importantly, to analyse the variances among these scores. One potential disadvantage of this approach is that it can give a misleading impression that there is one 'average' decision style. This is not so. As we have cautioned from the beginning of this chapter, managers do employ various styles for different problems and situations.

The following values were assigned to components of the power-sharing continuum (see Figure 4.1): Style 1 (own decision) = 10; Style 2 (consultation) = 20; Style 3 (joint decision making) = 30; and Style 4 (delegation) = 40. Thus, a high score implies that an executive allows his subordinate(s) to share his decision-making power thereby increasing the influence of his subordinate(s) on the outcome of the decision. Conversely, a low score implies a lower degree of power sharing and, consequently, more executive control over the outcome of the decision. Let us first look at the mean scores of executives from *each* country for all seven decisions. The results are presented in Table 4.4. Examining the mean scores in this table tells us that, *in general*, the Egyptian and Jordanian executives interviewed involved their subordinates in decision making to a lesser extent than executives from the other countries. A simple one-way analysis of variance resulted in an F (5,46) equal to 3.48 ($p < 0.01$) indicating that the mean scores of the executives from the six countries are indeed significantly different. This indicates that it will be fruitful to extend the analysis in two ways.

TABLE 4.4 Mean score of executives from each country for all decisions

Country	*Mean*	*N*
Egypt	17.6	9
Jordan	18.8	10
Lebanon	21.9	8
Kuwait	23.6	9
Saudi Arabia	23.3	10
UAE	22.5	6
All countries	21.2	52

First, the seven decisions are broken down into three categories. The first category includes decisions 1, 2, and 3, the second includes decisions 4, 5, and 7, and the third includes only decision 6. Statistically,[8] this grouping of decisions showed the highest intercorrelations between the decisions within each category. Conceptually, the breaking down of the seven decisions into three categories follows common sense. Thus, the first category of decisions (1, 2, and 3) relate to personnel problems of subordinates two levels removed from the executive; mainly, the promotion, discipline, and termination of service of an employee who is directly supervised by one of his subordinates. Decisions 4, 5, and 7 contain departmental/divisional problems: substantial reduction of the work force across all departments/divisions; increasing the work force in a subordinate's department/division; and a re-organization of a subordinate's department/division. Finally, decision 6 is an organizational decision with potential serious consequences for the whole organization. It involves a major and a long-term venture requiring large financial outlays or risk taking.

Second, the analysis must be extended to include the other independent variables which may have an influence on the decision process (the dependent variable). Data were collected on a variety of socio-psychological variables such as the size, age, nature, and ownership of the organization; the age, education, social background, status, and country of the executive. The intent here is to ascertain how much of the variance in decision styles can be explained, and to which socio-psychological variable(s) it can be attributed.

TABLE 4.5 Mean score of executives for three categories of decisions

Country	*Three personnel decisions (1, 2 and 3) (Mean)*	*Three departmental decisons (4, 5 and 7) (Mean)*	*One organizational decision (6) (Mean)*	*N*
Egypt	20.0	15.6	14.4	9
Jordan	19.5	19.2	14.0	10
Lebanon	24.6	20.4	18.8	8
Kuwait	27.8	22.1	12.2	9
Saudi Arabia	25.0	24.4	14.0	10
UAE	23.3	23.1	16.7	6
All countries	23.3	21.1	14.8	52

Let us first examine the responses of the executives from each of the six Arab countries for the three categories of decisions, as shown in Table 4.5. From this table it is clear that the executives interviewed involved their subordinates more in personnel-related decisions than in the organizational decisions. In fact, all the mean scores of executives from each country were consistently decreasing as we moved from personnel to departmental to organizational decisions. This finding corroborates Heller's (1971) conclusions that managers tend to be less autocratic when dealing with problems related to the employees of their subordinates, and more autocratic when facing the more important organizational-level decisions.

This variation in decision-making styles also lends some support to Vroom's general conclusion that 'it makes more sense to talk about participative and autocratic situations than it does to talk about participative and autocratic managers'.[9] Although the situational variables in the Vroom–Yetton model focus on a different set of problem attributes than those used here, nevertheless, the same principle is shared.

Also from Table 4.5, it will be noted that the mean scores of Egyptian and Jordanian executives (on personnel and departmental decisions) are generally lower than the scores of the executives from the other countries. This could be easily misinterpreted if we attribute the lower score solely to the nationality of the executives. To avoid this misinterpretation, we must quickly introduce the effects of the other independent sociopsychological variables listed earlier. These other independent variables may indeed be more closely associated and correlated to decision-making style than the country variable. The questions, therefore, are: which variables are most closely related to the decision-making styles of the fifty-two executives? And to what extent do these variables account for the variance in their decision-making styles?

Since some of the independent variables (country, age, and education of executive, size of company and so on) are interrelated, several spurious relationships may exist which will distort the analysis. However, the multiple regression method helps us to overcome this problem. It controls for any spurious effects and it isolates only those variables which contribute substantially to the variation in decision-making styles. Details of the statistical steps and results are presented in Appendix 1.

VARIABLES AFFECTING DECISION STYLES

It is now possible to discuss the findings for each of the three categories of decisions. Table 4.6 presents a summary of the results. Let us start with the personnel decisions 1, 2, and 3. Multiple regression analyses indicate that three independent variables had significant contributions to the variation in personnel decision-making styles. The three variables are: the age of the executive, his education, and the size of his organization. These three variables taken together account for 22 per cent of the variance in decision style. That is, given these three variables, one can explain 22 per cent of the variation in personnel decision styles.

Taken independently, each of these variables is related to decision styles in some way or another. Thus, the data indicate that the older the Arab executives are, the more autocratic they tend to be – sharing less of their decision-making power with their subordinates. One possible explanation could be that older Arab executives, recognizing that the 'Arab respect for age' syndrome increases their position and referent power, are not as concerned about their subordinates' acceptance of the decision as their younger counterparts. In essence, the older executives can 'afford' to be more autocratic.[10]

The data also show that executives without a university education tend to share more of their power with subordinates when compared to university-educated executives. One can only speculate that those executives without a university education are more likely to rely on experienced specialists, thereby involving these specialists more in the decision-making process. Finally, there seems to be a relationship between the size of the organization and decision styles related to personnel matters. The larger the organization the more likely that its top executive will involve his subordinates with the personnel decisions. This finding was not an unexpected one, as common sense would indicate.

Turning to departmental decisions 4, 5, and 7, Table 4.6 shows that there are two sets of variables explaining the variation in decision styles. One set of variables included only individual attributes, while the other set contained organizational attributes. Therefore, a proportion of the variance in departmental decision styles could be explained using either individual or organizational variables.

The individual variables refer to the executive's occupational status (owner-executive or non-owner executive); his educational background; and his age. These variables taken together accounted for 42 per cent of the variance in departmental decision styles.

Again, if taken independently, each was highly related to decision style. The individual variable accounting for the greatest proportion of the variance is the executive's occupational

TABLE 4.6 Independent variables accounting for the variance in decision-making style. (Three decision categories.)

Personnel decisions 1, 2 and 3		*Departmental decisions 4, 5 and 7*		*Organizational decision 6*	
		(A)			
Variable	*Direction**	*Variable*	*Direction**	*Variable*	*Direction**
Age of executive	(−)	Non-owner/partner executive	(−)	Lebanon	(+)
No university education	(+)	Arab university education	(−)	No university education	(+)
Size of organization	(+)	Age of executive	(−)		
$R^2=22\%$†		$R^2-42\%$†		$R^2=20\%$†	
		(B)			
		Family-owned organization	(+)		
		Egypt	(−)		
		Saudi Arabia	(+)		
		$R^2=43\%$†			

* The (+) or (−) under direction indicates whether the variable is positively or negatively related to the score of decision style.

† R^2 is the square of the multiple correlation coefficient, adjusted for the number of independent variables in the equation and the number of cases. It is a more conservative estimate of variance explained, especially when the sample size is small.

status. Non-owner/partner executives, as might be expected, shared less of their decision-making power with subordinates than executives who owned or partly owned the organization. The non-owner executive probably had to consult or persuade his own superiors (government ministries or a board of directors) before arriving at the final decision, especially since the decisions involved important departmental changes.

Educational background was also found to be related to decision style. The data indicated that the executives who obtained university degrees from an Arab university were likely to be more autocratic than (a) executives without a university degree; or (b) executives who received degrees from Western universities; or (c) executives who received degrees from both Arab and Western universities.[11] It will be interesting to compare the average scores of the executives (for decisions 4, 5, and 7) broken down by level and type of education. It will be recalled, from Table 4.5, that the average score for all executives was 21 for the departmental decisions. The following are the scores moving from the most to the least autocratic: executives with Arab degrees scored 17; those with both Arab and Western degrees scored 20; those with only Western degrees scored 22; and executives without a university degree scored 26.

Lastly, executive age, as in the previous category of decisions, was again negatively related to power sharing; the older executives showed less power sharing than the younger ones.

As mentioned above, the variation in style for departmental decisions 4, 5, and 7 could also be explained by a set of organizational variables (called by some contextual or sociological variables). Three of these variables jointly accounted for 43 per cent of the variance in decision styles. The three variables are: type of organizational ownership; Egypt; and Saudi Arabia. Let us take a closer look at each. Executives from family-owned organizations involved their subordinates in departmental decision making to a greater extent than their counterparts working in government-owned organizations, or in organizations owned by two or more partners.

Executives from Egypt shared less of their decision-making power with their subordinates than executives from the other five countries. Their average score on the power-sharing continuum was significantly lower at 15 when compared to a score of 22 for all the other executives ($p < 0.01$). One probable explanation is that the business sector in Egypt is highly influenced by the pervasiveness of government rules, regulations, and controls.[12] In fact, during the author's visit to Egypt (while conducting the interviews), the Egyptian Prime Minister in office at that time delivered a speech to several hundred top executives. In his speech the Prime Minister voiced his government's concern about its own restrictive rules and regulations, and he promised the executives that, in line with Egypt's new open-door policy, government restrictions on the internal and external affairs of all companies will be relaxed.[13]

Finally, the executives from Saudi Arabia showed more power sharing in departmental decisions than the executives from the other five countries. A plausible reason might be the heavy reliance by top Saudi executives on highly specialized expatriate and/or other Arab managers. These specialized managers are given more freedom in departmental affairs, thus allowing the Saudi executives to concentrate their time and energy on the more urgent business problems and opportunities so common in a fast-moving economy.

The third and final decision category contains organizational decision 6. Here, as with the previous categories, multiple regression analysis isolated two variables which taken together accounted for 20 per cent of the variance in decision style. The two variables are: Lebanon as compared to the other countries; and executives without university education as compared with executives with a university degree.

The Lebanese executives had an average (mean) of 19 on decision 6 as compared to an average of 14 for all other executives ($p < 0.01$). One can only speculate that, as a result of the 1975–6 Civil War and its aftermath, several of the Lebanese executives interviewed who were doing business outside Lebanon (often from branch offices located outside Lebanon), were more geographically decentralized. Decision 6 is a major organization decision involving large financial outlays and/or high risk; the Lebanese executives interviewed were more likely than not to consult their top subordinates who were in charge of the various geographical centres.

Lastly, executives without university education had significantly higher scores on the power-sharing continuum than their university-educated counterparts. Again, this may reflect their utilization of business specialists – in finance, marketing, or production – whose advice on decision 6 would be essential.

Before proceeding to the next section, it is worth looking again at the frequency distribution of the total responses for the three decision categories discussed above. Table 4.7 summarizes this distribution (this table is a reduction of Table 4.2, shown earlier in this chapter). The table highlights two major results. First, as we move from personnel to departmental to organizational decisions, we notice lesser power-sharing (more autocratic) behaviour from the fifty-two executives. As already indicated, this shows that the importance of the decisions to the organization (a situational variable) is closely related to decision style.[14] The second finding concerns the pervasiveness and dominance of Style 2, consultation, among Arab executives. Consultation has a special meaning for Arabs, and especially so for Arab executives, as we have just seen. Let us take a closer look at this phenomenon.

TABLE 4.7 Distribution of responses by style for three decision categories (N=52) (percentages)

Decision category	*Style 1* *Own decision*	*Style 2* *Consultation*	*Style 3* *Joint decision*	*Style 4* *Delegation*
Personnel (Decisions 1, 2, and 3)	9	63	15	13
Departmental (Decisions 4, 5, and 7)	25	49	16	10
Organizational (Decison 6)	52	48	—	—
Weighted average	22	55	13	10

CONSULTATION

There are strong historical roots for consultation in the Arab world, and particularly in the Arabian peninsula where tribal leaders have practised consultation for millennia. It is a norm which is still practised by the present-day rulers of countries in the peninsula. Senior members of the ruling families, or the community, are consulted on matters of importance. The final decision, however, is always made by the leader who may or may not adhere to the advice of his senior men.

Added impetus for the consultation practice was provided by Islam. One finds that consultation is actively encouraged by the Holy Quran and the *Ḥadīth* (the *Ḥadīth* consists of the acts and sayings of Prophet Muhammad and early Islam).

Consultation is mentioned several times in the Quran and the *Ḥadīth*. In fact, one of the 114 *Sūras* (chapters) of the Holy Quran is entitled *Shūrā*, that is Consultation. In this *Sūra*, it is revealed that those who conduct their affairs by consultation are among the ones upon whom God's mercy and heavenly rewards will be bestowed (XLII, pp. 36–9).

It is interesting to note that the importance of consultation was emphasized by several executives during the interviews. For example, three executives quoted different verses from the Quran on consultation; significantly, these quotations were volunteered in free response (that is without direct prompting). Similarly, four other executives mentioned consultation when asked which personal traits or characteristics have contributed to their success. Finally, we have seen that 55 per cent of the total responses on decisions 1 to 7 were for Style 2, consultation.

What are the reasons for the prevalence of consultative behaviour among Arab executives? Who is being consulted, and when? Here are some of the reasons and conjectures, made possible through extended discussions with a few of the executives whose time, fortunately for us, permitted such a luxury in what otherwise would be a hectic schedule. Briefly, these are some answers to the above questions:

1. There are strong expectations among senior managers, partners, and even some friends and relatives to be consulted on organizational or daily issues. One executive described it as 'a tradition, a custom . . . there are always some people whose opinion you must seek, or else they will be hurt and angry'. The same executive reminded the author that this 'custom' applies not only in business organizations, but at the higher levels of family, clan, tribe, or nation.
2. Consultation, for some Arabs, seems to be an effective 'human relations' technique. It is used for several occasions and situations: (a) to avoid potential conflict between an executive and his subordinate; (b) to please, to placate, or to

win over persons who might be potential obstacles to one's ideas or actions; and (c) to provide the person being consulted with a 'face-saving' mechanism which enables him to reply, 'Yes, I was consulted on . . . ', if he was ever asked.

3. There is, of course, the conventional use of consultation during which necessary information is gathered, or genuine guidance and advice is sought.
4. Finally, it must be stressed that only a few 'selected' people are generally consulted. This seems to be the case whether we are referring to a business organization, family, tribe, or nation. Understandably, there is no hard and fast rule for specifying who these selected few are; it is dictated by the situation and the circumstances.

Up to this point we have said relatively little about joint decision making (Style 3). It will be recalled that Style 3 received an average of 13 per cent of the total responses on all seven decisions. An immediate question which comes to mind is why such a low score? One possible reply would be to attribute this low score to the societal context. Thus, in none of the countries included in this study do we find a prevalence of truly democratic practices such as elections, majority rule, and so on. If that is the case, why should one expect a change in the beliefs, attitudes, or behaviour of both executives and their employees once they start working in a business-oriented social system (organization) which is part of the larger societal system? Most persons (including executives and subordinates) would bring to the business organization those same values and attitudes they have been forming ever since childhood.

Another argument of equal relevance would be that Arab executives generally seemed to dislike committee or group meetings. Consequently, on those decisions concerning more than one subordinate, the executives seem to prefer individual-to-individual consultation with each subordinate thereby, *de facto*, avoiding majority decisions. Indeed, Arab executives have a strong preference for personalized and informal methods of conducting interpersonal business affairs – as will be discussed at length in Chapter 6.

Finally, a brief word about delegation (Style 4). This style, receiving the lowest score (10 per cent of total responses), seems to be under-utilized especially if we keep in mind that the fifty-two executives we interviewed were top executives in their respective companies. It is generally believed that the higher in the hierarchy a manager's position is, the more likely he is to delegate non-policy decisions – especially if his organization is large and long-established. Our findings indicate that age of company was not related to style, and that size of company was related to style for only three out of seven decisions.[15]

As mentioned earlier in this chapter, delegation has several benefits to the organization, the top executive, and the subordinate. If delegation is indeed under-utilized, the consequences for the growth and development of the above-mentioned parties could be detrimental indeed.

NOTES

1. Weber (1947), *The Theory of Social and Economic Organization*; Dahl (1957), 'The concept of Power'; French and Raven (1959), 'The Bases of Social Power'; and Cartwright (1965), 'Influence, Leadership, and Control'.
2. Barnard (1938), *The Functions of the Executive*; Simon (1957), *Administrative Behaviour.*
3. For a recent review, see Vroom (1976), 'Leadership', pp. 1527–51.
4. A distinction is made in this study between leadership styles and the styles of decision making. A leader, in whatever type of organization, has a large number of tasks and roles besides that of a decision maker, see Mintzberg (1973). Hence, the term decision-making style is preferred here to the traditionally used term of leadership style.
5. For a leading exponent of the leadership contingency approach see Fiedler (1967), *A Theory of Leadership Effectiveness.*
6. The equal interval assumption is discussed in Appendix 1.
7. Decisions 1, 3, and 5 were adopted, with modifications, from Heller's (1971) questionnaire.
8. Details of the statistical tests and analysis are presented in Appendix 1. Only the final results are reported here with minimal discussion of the statistical methods employed.
9. Vroom (1976), p. 1545.
10. Vroom and Jago showed that managers are more 'participative' on problems requiring subordinate acceptance than on problems that did not, see Vroom and Jago (1974), 'Decision Making as a Social Process', p. 760.
11. Western-founded universities, such as the American University of Beirut (AUB), are referred to in the present study as Arab universities. The curricula are taught in both Arabic and English; and the education took place in an Arab environment.
12. It is widely recognized that the Egyptian bureaucracy and its methods of

managing the public sector have been among the serious obstacles to Egyptian industrial efficiency and progress. See Mabro and Radwan (1976), *The Industrialization of Egypt, 1939–1973*, p. 96.

13. *Al-Ahrām*, 15 January, 1978 (p. 1). In Egypt, all companies are severely restricted in their employment practices. Additionally, government-owned companies are required to obtain government approval even for minor departmental changes.
14. This finding provides further support to the contingency approach recently popular among management and organizational scholars.
15. The average company size in our study was around 2500 employees, while the average company age was 27 years.

5 Conflict Management

> I apply not my sword where my lash suffices, nor my lash where my tongue is enough. And even if there be one hair binding me to my fellowmen, I do not let it break: when they pull I loosen, and if they loosen I pull.
>
> Caliph Mu'āwiyah AD 661–680.

The main interest in this chapter is on conflict between the Arab executive and his immediate subordinate during or after the decision-making process. Specifically, we are interested in the extent of such conflict, and how the Arab executive uses his power to manage it. In general, the Arab executive experiences relatively low opposition from his immediate subordinates. The executive reduces the frequency of conflict either by 'authoritarian' behaviour and/or by frequent consultation with his subordinates. Furthermore, the Arab executive prefers to avoid open confrontation whenever conflict occurs. This is done either through the mediation efforts of a third party or by complete avoidance of the issue in conflict.

There is a wealth of literature on conflict by scholars from a wide variety of disciplines. It covers many types of conflict at many levels, from the international, social, organizational, departmental, to conflict between individuals.[1] There is, however, little available literature on how Arab executives handle conflict in organizational contexts. One would expect that Arab executives would be influenced by societal values and norms in managing conflicts within their organizations. This is what we set out to explore in this chapter.

It is important to note that our concern here is deliberately limited to dyadic conflict along the vertical dimension of a hierarchy (executive and his subordinate) and our interest is on one of the parties to the conflict only – the executive. Lastly, the conflict is over an episode involving a business decision.

Dyadic conflict (conflict between two persons or two social units) is defined as a process in which the actions of one person tend to prevent or force some outcome against the resistance of another person.[2] Thus, an executive may impose a decision against the resistance of his subordinate, or he may intentionally block a decision favoured by the subordinate.

We have already seen in the preceding chapter the extent to which Arab executives retain or share their decision-making power. It was found that, on average, the Arab executive chose to limit his subordinate's influence on decision outcomes. Indeed, the executives chose Style 1 (own decision) and Style 2 (consultation) an overwhelming 77 per cent of the time; both styles tend to limit subordinate's influence. A few questions immediately come to mind: what about opposition or resistance from subordinates, if any, when they do not agree with the decision? How is it handled? And what are the executive's reactions to proposals submitted by his subordinate if he does not favour these proposals?

To answer these questions, the executives were presented with hypothetical incidents in which two types of conflict situations were present. Conflict situation *Type 1* is when the hypothetical issues are favoured by the executive, but opposed by the subordinate. *Type 2* is the reverse: the issues are opposed by the executive, but favoured by the subordinate. Each executive was given two incidents and was asked to describe how he would handle the conflict situations Type 1 and Type 2. One of the incidents involved a personnel-related conflict: a disagreement between the executive and his immediate subordinate about the promotion of a key employee working for the latter; while the other incident was at the organizational level: a disagreement between the executive and his immediate subordinate about an expansion plan (or a new product/project) which involves the department/division of the subordinate. The executives were familiar with the incidents since both were an extension of the decision-making section of the interview to which they had just responded.[3]

Furthermore, each executive was asked to provide a proverb or a saying which guided or influenced his thinking when facing the sort of conflict described above. This approach was designed to add depth to our understanding of the executive's conflict management techniques.

Let us now turn to the results of the interviews. We shall first present a brief summary of the overall findings. Later, we shall discuss the implications of these findings for conflict management. There were five major findings:

1. *Insufficient opposition from subordinates.* Five Arab executives complained that, in general, there was insufficient resistance or opposition from their immediate subordinate(s). They felt that the frequency and magnitude of resistance and opposition were undesirably low. In short, they wished more of their subordinates would act as genuine devil's advocates from time to time. This, of course, would be benefical as long as the devil's advocate role is not institutionalized or systematized, in which case it may become useless.[4]
2. *Open confrontation is taboo.* When irreconcilable positions were reached, neither executive nor subordinate allowed it to develop into direct or open confrontation. Values and norms dictate the use of a third party to convey the message of rejection. The role of a third person (a mediator) in Arab society is crucial in conflict management.[5] Open confrontation is also avoided by the use of other indirect methods to communicate one's position, such as non-verbal behaviour, deliberate procrastination, or even a complete avoidance of the issue.
3. *Consultation reduces conflict.* Seven executives believed that the frequency of conflict was substantially reduced because the immediate subordinate was often consulted, and his opinion taken into account. If the subordinate's advice and opinions are occasionally incorporated into the decision, then to that extent consultation will tend to reduce conflict. If, on the other hand, consultation turns into a ritual where the executive is repeatedly asking for opinions and advice, but then always making decisions contrary to such advice, then conflict might be exacerbated and long-term relationships will suffer.
4. *Reliance on position power.*[6] With the above comments in mind, it was found that for Type 1 situations (executive favours, subordinate opposes) the power tactic most favoured by fifteen executives was 'pulling rank' or going ahead with a decision in spite of subordinate's opposition.

   For Type 2 situations (executive opposes, subordinate favours) the power tactic most often used was non-decision making. Twelve executives used such phrases as 'freeze it', 'keep it pending', and 'give it time to die', to describe their non-decision-making tactics.

   Finally, many of the executives preferred not to differentiate between Types 1 and 2 conflicts and stated that they would initially attempt to convince the subordinate of their viewpoint by reasoning with him, using knowledge or information only they possess, or will attempt to persuade the subordinate using their 'diplomacy' and 'personal touch'. Failing all that, the executives will resort to their formal authority and power, as described above.

5. *Importance of issues does not change tactics.* The importance of the issues (personnel *vs.* organizational) was related to the likelihood of conflict occurrence. For example, many executives indicated that it is unlikely that conflict will occur over the personnel issue, but may occur over the organizational one.

   However, when asked to assume that conflict did happen on the hypothetical personnel issue, an interesting reaction took place. The executives would use the same firm tactics they used for the organizational conflict. This indicates that the importance of the issues at stake is not as relevant as the fact that opposition did occur (albeit, hypothetically). One would expect milder tactics (such as persuasion, bargaining and the like) to be employed; instead, the same tactics as reported above were most commonly used. One is reminded of the several research studies showing that conflicting action (opposition from subordinates) evokes similar reactions (pulling rank or non-decision by executives).[7] Role expectations (such as boss has the final word), clearly influenced the executive's behaviour.

The above five findings, if taken separately, are clear and do not need further elaboration. However, if we examine the first finding (insufficient opposition from subordinates) in relation to the other four, then a contradiction becomes apparent.

One way of explaining the phenomenon would be to take an increasingly popular view which states that, in general, certain kinds of conflicts are not only inevitable but also desirable (functional) to the conflicting parties if effectively managed.[8] This broad statement invites further questions, such as: what level or magnitude of conflict?; how do we effectively manage it?; and so on. These questions are appropriate and necessary, but are beyond the scope of this chapter. However, using this perspective and keeping these questions in mind provides us with a frame of reference, a context, to discuss the findings. Viewed in this context, the five findings can be translated into two observations: (a) the frequency and magnitude of opposition leading to conflict is low – as reported by a number of executives and as observed by the interviewer; (b) Arab executives tend to handle these conflicts in such a manner as to discourage future opposition. What we have here is a classic dilemma – or even ambivalence. A desire for some opposition from subordinates, and a concomitant fear of losing control and influence (power) if the executive yields to the opposition.

Let us look at the first element of this ambivalence: insufficient opposition. The reasons given by some executives for the low occurrence of conflict support the notion that power is often wielded in the following manner:

Executive's preferences
↓
Subordinate's anticipation of executive's future reactions
↓
Subordinate's response (in our case, compliance)

(With feedback loops, of course)

Here is how one executive described it: 'The subordinate gets to know his boss so well he can "read his mind" – he is so eager to please his boss that he is unlikely to think of or engage in activities which may displease the boss. The result . . . no opposition.'

This type of executive power is creating subordinate compliance[9] which probably is at an unhealthy level. If a reasonable amount of conflict and opposition does lead to creativity and positive stimulation[10] then subordinate's over-compliance could indeed be unhealthy. (Bearing in mind that we are discussing subordinates at a high managerial level reporting directly to top executives.)

The question, then, becomes: what is a reasonable amount of conflict? Again, it is beyond our present scope: it must be noted, however, that future research on this question must include the norms, expectations, and attitudes towards authority and conflict prevalent in the countries being studied.[11] Nevertheless, the fact remains that a few executives did express their desire for more opposition (devil's advocate role, as some put it).

The other side of the ambivalence equation is the fear of losing power if conflict is encouraged. One Egyptian executive summarized it well: 'If a leader, whether on the national or organizational level, does not suppress opposition, then people (including my employees) would think he is weak, thereby losing respect.'

The solution to this dilemma, *if a solution is desired*, is entirely in the hands of the executive. Two of the several choices he has are: (a) to change the attitudes and predisposition of his employees towards authority, conflict, and power. This is a difficult and a very slow process, but not impossible; and (b) to modify role expectations and/or organizational structure with the aim of creating manageable conflict. This would be done through creation of devil's advocate roles, suggestion box, and other devices to encourage opposition – designed to fit the needs and the climate of the organization at that stage of its growth and development.

The above findings were based on responses from executives who were asked to describe their hypothetical behaviour.[12] However, as mentioned earlier, another approach was used which assessed the executive's values and beliefs about dyadic conflict. This was accomplished by asking each executive to provide a proverb or a saying (in either Arabic or English) which guides or influences his thinking when facing this type of conflict (see Interview Schedule, Appendix 2). The proverbs/sayings told by the executives added further support to the earlier findings.

Twenty-four of the fifty-two executives gave a total of eighteen proverbs/sayings (*all in Arabic*). Here is a translation of three proverbs (proverbs mentioned by more than one executive):

1. Four executives mentioned this proverb: 'Time is a problem-solver', or 'Time solves problems'.
2. Three executives recited this Quranic verse: 'Consult them in affairs of the moment, then, when thou hast taken a decision, put thy trust in God' (III, 159).[13]
3. Two executives referred to the famous words in Arab history attributed to the founder of the Umayyad Caliphate, Mu'āwiyah (AD 661–80). The Caliph Mu'āwiyah, known for his political finesse, was reported to have declared: 'I apply

not my sword where my lash suffices, nor my lash where my tongue is enough. And even if there be one hair binding me to my fellowmen, I do not let it break: when they pull I loosen, and if they loosen I pull'.[14]

The other fifteeen proverbs conveyed various messages most of which can be summarized in a few advisory sentences: be reasonable; avoid extremes; avoid confrontation; be co-operative; and finally, there are many things that an executive ('apex of pyramid') sees, or hears, that cannot and should not be seen, or heard, by the subordinates.

A moment of reflection will show that the values reflected by these proverbs do not contradict the executives' responses as summarized earlier. In fact, they add support to them. Thus, we have the proverb, 'Time is a problem-solver', relating directly to non-decision-making tactics; the Quranic verse associated with the use of consultation to reduce potential conflict; and finally Mu'āwiyah's political finesse of being 'diplomatic but firm', and avoiding head-on confrontation or the risk of 'breaking the hair' which binds the executive to his subordinates.

In this chapter, we have seen that Arab executives, in general, experience relatively low opposition and resistance (low in frequency and magnitude) from their immediate subordinates. This could be partly attributable to their consultative style, as demonstrated in the preceding chapter; but it can also be attributed to the societal values and norms which shun open confrontation and encourage rather authoritarian behaviour on the executive's part. We have also examined the dilemma facing those executives who would like to see increased 'constructive' resistance from their immediate subordinates – bearing in mind that these subordinates are top-level managers. Finally, we were able to look at some of the power tactics, as well as the thoughts behind these tactics, which Arab executives use in managing conflict.

NOTES

1. For reviews and analyses of recent literature on conflict see Thomas (1976), 'Conflict and Conflict Management', pp. 889–935; Nightingale (1976), 'Conflict and Conflict Resolution', pp. 141–64; and Katz and Kahn (1978), *Social Psychology of Organizations*, pp. 612–51.

2. From Katz and Kahn (1978), p. 613.
3. Details of the incidents and the conflict situation are shown in Appendix 2, which contains the complete Interview Schedule.
4. See Thomas and Bennis (Eds.) (1972), *Management of Change and Conflict*, pp. 17–19.
5. Ayoub (1965), 'Conflict Resolution and Social Reorganization in a Lebanese Village', pp. 11–17. Also see Farsoun (1970), 'Family Structure and Society in Modern Lebanon', pp. 257–307.
6. As opposed to other bases of power; reward, coercive, referent, and expert power, to use French and Raven's (1959) typology. A sixth base of power, information power, is usually added by many others.
7. Katz and Kahn (1978); Thomas (1976); Thomas and Walton (1971) 'Conflict-handling Behaviour in Interdepartmental Relations'.
8. Coser (1956), *The Functions of Social Conflict*; Hall (1971), 'Decisions, Decisions, Decisions'; and Katz and Kahn (1978).
9. Even if we wish to use one of Kelman's (1958) other categorizations (compliance, identification, or internalization), the end result for our purposes is the same – minimum opposition from subordinates.
10. Katz and Kahn (1978), p. 641.
11. For example, Melikian found that there is 'a general willingness among Saudi college students to accept the authority of a "boss" and to esteem it . . . this acceptance and esteem of authority are accompanied by a willingness to be in that position themselves'. See Melikian (1977), 'The Modal Personality of Saudi College Students', p. 180.
12. Aided by quasi-participant observation by the author during the periods of waiting for and conducting the interviews.
13. Ali, *The Holy Qur'ān: Text, Translation and Commentary* (1975).
14. As quoted in Hitti (1970), *History of the Arabs*, p. 197.

6 Interpersonal Style

> Men's natures are alike; it is their habits that carry them far apart.
>
> Confucius, 551–479 BC

The most distinctive feature of the Arab executive's interpersonal style is his strong preference for a *personal* or person-oriented approach in his managerial activities. In fact, he has a strong aversion to *impersonal* relationships. This, as we shall see shortly, stems largely from the strength of the executive's primordial (family and friendship) ties, as well as from the characteristics of his society's social structure.

This personal approach is a dominant feature in four important behavioural aspects of interpersonal relationships. The four aspects, to be discussed separately in this chapter, are:

1. the use of rituals and customs in conducting business;
2. the use of personal ties and connections;
3. the importance of employee loyalty;
4. the open-door tradition.

A natural consequence of this heavy emphasis on the personal approach is the executive's preference for 'informality' both in the structure of his organization and in his own style of dealing with people. We will be examining this preference for 'informality' in the last section of this chapter.

It must be added at this point that it is these aspects of interpersonal relations which are at once noticed by expatriates and foreign businessmen; and are often the cause of their initial sense of bewilderment or frustration when working with the Arab executive.

RITUALS AND CUSTOMS IN CONDUCTING BUSINESS

When starting a business discussion, the Arab executive will invariably engage in social talk and amenities with his guest for what may seem a long time. The guest is first offered coffee, tea, or soft drinks. Then for a period ranging from 2 to 15 minutes,[1] the executive and his guest would talk about several topics of interest to both parties provided it is *not* the subject of the business at hand. It is generally regarded as 'impolite' or even 'shocking' to start immediately with the business discussion.

Thus, it was not considered unusual to ask the Arab executives whether they engage in this ritual, and how they felt about it. Their responses, as reported in Table 6.1, confirm the prevalence of this ritual. Fifty-one executives (98 per cent) stated that they normally engage in this business practice. Of those, forty-two executives considered it beneficial while the other nine executives felt that it was mostly a waste of time. Only one executive stated that he does not perform or even encourage such practice, viewing it as a total waste of time.

TABLE 6.1 Rituals and customs in conducting business (*N=52)*

Response	*Number of executives*	*With whom?*	*Why?*
Yes, and it is a beneficial custom	42	Employees and outsiders=10 Outsiders only=32	Know guest on personal basis Evaluate person and establish trust Cement relations (if guest is known) 'Break the ice' – relax – put at ease
Yes, but it is a waste of time	9	Outsiders only=9 (mostly with Arabs)	Must do it . . . it is an expected custom Hospitality and tradition
No, it is a waste of time	1	—	Waste of time

What is perhaps more interesting are the reasons given by the forty-two executives who considered this custom beneficial. These reasons include: getting to know the guest on a person-to-person basis; to evaluate the person; to establish trust in the person; to cement relations (if parties already know each other); and finally to 'break the ice' and put the parties involved at ease.

It is also interesting that the nine executives, while considering this ritual as a waste of time, felt obligated to perform it because it was expected, mostly by other Arabs. Tradition and the norms of hospitality prescribed this sort of behaviour. Furthermore, these executives did not employ this practice with their subordinates but only with outsiders such as clients, suppliers, government officials, and other visitors. The nine executives come from all six countries; they had various social and educational backgrounds; were in different brackets; and were from various types of organizations.

The above business ritual seems to be a universal one. Desmond Morris calls it 'grooming talk'. This is how Morris describes the practice during 'formal business encounters':

> Here its expression (grooming talk) is almost entirely confined to the opening and closing moments. *Instead of waning slowly*, as at the dinner party, *it is suppressed rapidly, after a few polite, initial exchanges.* It reappears again, as before, in the closing moments of the meeting, once the anticipated moment of parting has been signalled in some way. Because of the strong urge to perform grooming talk, business groups are usually forced to heighten the formalization of their meetings in some way, in order to suppress it. (Emphasis added)[2]

However, the duration and purpose of the opening period of social talk differ from society to society. It has been pointed out long ago, by Hall and Whyte, that for Anglo-Saxons, and especially North Americans, the acquaintance and discussion time in business tends to be comparatively short and impersonal.[3] The American businessman, for example, regards acquaintance and discussion periods as opportunities in which he tries to make his point 'quickly, efficiently, and neatly'. Businessmen from many other countries, on the other hand, do not look favourably upon such quick business meetings or what Hall and Whyte call 'the "hit-and-run" school of business behaviour'. Businessmen from various countries not only act differently during the opening period of business discussion, they also do so for varying reasons.

For the Arab executives the use of this business practice can be distinguished in two important ways. First, the reasons given by forty-two executives for engaging in this practice seem to be more *person-oriented* than role- or task-oriented. Executives used such terms as 'person-to-person', 'personalized', and 'personal approach' as contrasted to impersonal, when describing their reasons for engaging in these rituals. Second, these rituals were characterized by their seemingly prolonged duration. This is demonstrated by the responses of the other ten executives who considered the practice a waste if time. It is also demonstrated by the estimated range of 2 to 15 minutes as given by some executives. In brief, the Arab executive tends to dislike *impersonal* and *transient* relationships when conducting business. Here is how one European expatriate working in the Gulf area summarized it: 'You rarely walk into an Arab's office and start by discussing a business problem. After you socialize a bit, you bring out the subject in an "incidentally" or "by the way" manner, even though the problem at hand is an important one . . . in the long-run you will be more effective doing it this way.'[4] It seems that the majority of Arab executives would agree with these remarks, especially when *outside* business visitors are involved.

PERSONAL TIES AND CONNECTIONS

The use of personal (family and friendship) ties and connections is not only widespread, but is also an important and necessary means of doing business. This approach is in direct contrast with the reliance upon official, institutional, or formal business channels for conducting business affairs. In the Arab world the use of such personal ties and connections is evident in a wide range of activities. Typical examples that were provided by the executive include; (a) expediting and getting a work-permit, a passport or a visa, and generally bypassing or expediting most governmental formalities and paperwork; (b) obtaining referrals or employment; and (c) knowing about, negotiating, and eventually securing a multi-million dollar business contract.

An explanation for the above phenomenon can be found in our earlier discussions of the social structure and of the executive role (Chapters 2 and 3). In both chapters we examined the nature and the strength of primordial ties based on family and friendship. For the Arab executive, there is a powerful incentive to use personal (family and friendship) ties instead of institutional or formal channels in getting things done. This is partly due to the inefficiency, and sometimes the absence, on institutional systems and procedures; and partly due to the importance of family and friendship ties which are usually more powerful than institutional rules and procedures. This combination of institutional inefficiency and the strength of family and friendship ties leaves the executive without a viable alternative. Time and effort will be minimized if the executive uses his personal ties and connections in lieu of the formal channels. Of course, this sort of activity will, as in a vicious spiral, only increase the inefficiency of the formal systems – at least for those who have weaker ties or connections.

Furthermore, as we have seen in Chapter 3, the executive is under strong social pressures and expectations to play the intermediary role.[5] By virtue of his high position in the community and in the organization, he is expected to wield his power to influence the course of events in favour of relatives and friends. The intermediary role is, however, characterized by its reciprocal nature. In Chapter 3 we emphasized the 'giving' aspect of this reciprocity; we shall now turn to the 'taking' aspect and examine the Arab executive's attitudes on this subject.

The fifty-two executives were asked the following question: 'In your community, to what extent do people rely on family ties, friendships or other means of influence to get things done, or done faster?' All the executives, except one who preferred not to answer, indicated that this practice occurs to a great extent. Their replies varied from 'considerable', and 'very great', up to 'an enormous extent'; with some saying that it is 'the rule rather than the exception' or it is the 'custom'. It is very likely that some of these executives were unconsciously using their experiences in or with the major industrialized countries as a criterion for judgement, while others were explicitly comparing their circumstances with these countries. Not that industrialized countries are immune from this business practice, but the incidence and preponderance of such practices are probably lower.

When asked whether this business practice is a help or a hindrance to them in performing their duties, thirty-three (65 per cent) of the executives indicated that it is a help. Twelve (23 per cent) of the executives felt that it is both a help and a hindrance, and the remaining six (12 per cent) executives considered it a hindrance to their performance. A typical example of how this practice was seen as helpful, is when personal ties are used to 'save time and trouble' in dealing with the formalities of other organizations (especially government agencies). Several of these executives in describing this practice commented that it is a 'necessary evil', saying that it is 'sad' and 'unfortunate' but one must 'play by the rules of the game'. For those executives who considered the use of personal ties as both a help and a hindrance, this practice is a 'double-edged weapon'. Along with the benefits there are usually concomitant obligations; we have already seen in Chapter 3 that the executive's time and energy is taxed partly because of these obligations. Additionally, an executive may be 'influenced' to hire or promote an incompetent employee, thus adding to the burdens of that executive.

Finally, there were six executives who considered this practice a hindrance; they felt that it is an unfortunate form of 'favouritism' in which 'who you know' counts more than 'what you know'. This of course can be detrimental to executives who do not have powerful connections as well as to those who do. As one executive pointed out: 'Because of my organization's dependence on my personal connections, efficiency and performance often suffer whenever I am on a holiday, an extended business trip, or for any other reason which takes me out of the country.'

It is clear that having and using personal ties and connections are a necessity for doing business. It is also clear that the underlying principles of this practice are reciprocity and the *quid pro quo* of business and social exchange.[6] The question that immediately arises is how do foreign organizations and businessmen fit in this framework? If the foreign organization does not have the necessary ties or connections, it is very likely that a national (local) agent or middleman would have to be used.

The use of agents or middlemen evokes the topic of commissions and bribery: a very delicate and controversial topic. To start with, it seems that bribery and other corrupt practices are world-wide phenomena. Reports of corruption involving individuals and organizations are common in the leading industrialized countries. On the individual level, for example, these reports cover corrupt practices by a variety of people including police commissioners, elected and non-elected politicians and so on. On the organizational level, there was an upsurge recently in reports of corruption by organizations engaged in business, especially in overseas business.[7] The six Arab countries included in this study are no exception. It is not the intention here, however, to raise questions regarding the extent and magnitude of corrupt practices in the Arab world *vis-à-vis* other countries; what functions/purpose, if any, these practices serve; what value standards we use to judge the immorality or morality of these practices. These and other questions are beyond the scope of this study.[8]

The pertinent question for present purposes is: what are the relationships between personal ties/connections and middlemen/agents. To the Arab business mind, using personal ties and connections, because of their reciprocal nature, means using up old 'credits' or accumulating new 'liabilities' depending on one's 'balance sheet' of reciprocal transactions. Either way, there is usually a value attached to the use of personal connections which is not always an economic value. Now, when a foreign organization employs an agent or a middleman to act on its behalf, the agent/middleman will incur several costs, one of which might be the cost of capital; his personal ties/connections 'capital'. For these services the agent/middleman feels entitled to a commission. Thus, while there is one line between commissions and bribery for the Westerner doing business in the Arab world, the dividing line may be drawn differently for the Arab middleman. The line of demarcation to the Arab is a clear one. He may or may not use a portion of his commission for bribery; but for him the commission represents a fee for services rendered. This is how one Arab businessman differentiated between corruption and commission:

> If one offers money to a government to influence it, that is corruption. But if someone receives money for services rendered afterwards, that is a commission.[9]

When asked about the closely related subject of giving and taking gifts, most of the Arab executives interviewed indicated that token gifts are 'normal' and 'acceptable'. They placed token gifts in the same category as other acts of hospitality such as business entertainment and/or receiving business guests at the airport.[10] They explained that such gifts when exchanged by businessmen are considered as mementoes of friendship and association. If, however, they are heavily one-sided, or greatly unequal in value, or given with the purpose of inducing favourable treatment, then such 'gifts' may become bribery.

In brief, bribery and the use of personal ties and connections have roots not only in the social structure and its institutions, but are also influenced by the value system of that society. Fayerweather viewed it as a societal decision involving the society's value system.

> The choice is between an irregular and personalized method of administration and a systematized and impersonal approach. In the United States there is tremendous emphasis on regularizing and systematizing life in the interests of efficiency and maximum productivity. By contrast, in many foreign countries these objectives receive far less weight and, given the individualistic approach to life along with the low pay of government workers, the exchange of bribes for special treatment does not meet with the same disapproval.[11]

It is worthwhile to reiterate here that while many of the executives viewed with disfavour the use of personal ties and connections, it is often their only viable alternative. As we have pointed out, both society's values and its formal institutions strongly encourage the use of these 'irregular and personalized' methods of doing business.

THE IMPORTANCE OF LOYALTY

We have seen in the preceding chapters that loyalty and trust are of paramount importance in Arab society. When the three types of Arab communities (tribal, rural and urban) were examined, it was pointed out that loyalty is a highly valued personality trait which is considered essential to the solidarity of tribes, clans and families. Additionally, there are strong societal norms and expectations which regard nepotism as natural and acceptable. Finally, we have seen that the majority of Arab executives view their organizations as family units, often assuming a paternal role in them.

In view of the above findings, we set out to investigate the attitudes of Arab executives towards employee loyalty. To what extent do executives value employee loyalty within their organizations? Is employee loyalty more highly valued than, for instance, employee efficiency? The executives were asked to rank the importance of loyalty and efficiency. The following questions were asked:

1. 'The ideal employee would be, among other things, both loyal and efficient. But unfortunately this does not always occur. In such cases, then, which would you prefer – to have *employees* in your company who are (a) more loyal to the company, *or* (b) more efficient on the job?'
2. 'What about your preference concerning your own immediate subordinate – would you prefer your *immediate subordinate* to be (a) more loyal to you, *or* (b) more efficient in his work?'

TABLE 6.2 Executives' preference for loyalty and efficiency

	(a) Employee		*(b) Immediate Subordinate*	
	Loyalty	*Efficiency*	*Loyalty*	*Efficiency*
Number	35	17	37	15
Percentage	67	33	71	29

The results show that executives valued loyalty more highly than efficiency for both employees in general, Table 6.2(a), and for their immediate subordinates, Table 6.2(b). Before we discuss the implications of these findings, let us briefly examine the relationship between the executives' responses and other organizational or individual variables. As mentioned earlier in Chapter 4, data were collected on a variety of variables such as country, size, age, nature of business and ownership of the organization; the age, occupational status, educational and social background of the executive.

Starting with Table 6.2(a) and using χ^2 tests, we find that executives' responses are significantly related to only one of the above variables: educational background. Executives with exposure to Western university education (N=26) were equally divided (50 per cent) between employee loyalty and efficiency. While 85 per cent of the executives without exposure to Western university education (N=26) preferred loyalty to efficiency (χ^2=7.08; df=1; p<0.01). Those executives who were exposed to Western education did so by obtaining either their undergraduate, graduate, or postgraduate (Ph.D.) degrees from Western universities; while the executives without exposure to Western education either had no university degrees or held degrees from Arab universities. It seems that some of the Western-educated executives have been influenced by Western educational curricula as well as by Western norms, both of which emphasize efficiency at the organizational level.

Turning to Table 6.2(b), we find that the executives' preferences between loyalty and efficiency of their *immediate subordinate* are also significantly related to only one variable: the executive's occupational status, that is whether he is an owner/partner or a non-owner/partner. Of those executives who owned or partly owned their organizations ($N=29$), 86 per cent preferred loyalty of immediate subordinate over efficiency; while 52 per cent of the non-owners ($N=23$) felt that way ($\chi^2=7.35$; df=1; $p<0.01$). In this case, where immediate subordinates are concerned, the executives' ownership stake in the organization overshadows any influence which Western exposure and education may have had on their attitudes towards efficiency and loyalty.

Tables 6.2 (a and b) show that over two-thirds of Arab executives rank loyalty higher than efficiency for all levels of employees. The attributes of loyalty and efficiency as used in this section are meant to serve as indicators of person-orientation and task-orientation respectively. Thus loyalty with its connotation of trust and faithfulness emphasizes the person more than the task; while efficiency with its connotation of capability and competence puts more emphasis on the task and the ability to get the work done. The implication for personnel selection can be summarized by this typical statement mentioned by some of the executives: 'If the employee is loyal we can always train him and improve his efficiency.' In short, the attitude of 'loyalty first, efficiency second' within organizations seems to be in accordance with the larger societal values of group loyalty, nepotism, and paternalism.

AN OPEN-DOOR TRADITION

Another deeply-rooted tradition that found its way into today's Arab organizations is the open-door policy. In some countries in the Arabian peninsula it is still possible for any national to walk into the sheikh's, ruler's, or king's *majlis* (assembly or visiting room) where the visitor can either pay his respects, or request a favour, or submit a grievance.[12] While it is easier for the ruler to control the frequency and timing of his *majlis* meetings, the Arab executive will probably find it harder to do so with his employees.

How widespread is this open-door tradition? Table 6.3 summarizes the responses of the executives concerning this tradition. It must be noted that many of the executives who believed in the unconditional open-door policy (75 per cent of all executives), hastily added that their employees come to them with two different types of problems or requests. The first type consists of work-related problems or requests in which case the executive, having listened to the problems, will usually refer the employee back to his immediate manager or supervisor. The second type is when the employee has a personal problem or request. Here, the executive may either refer the employee to the personnel department or he may himself get involved, depending on the nature of the problem or request. We have seen earlier in Chapter 3, that handling the personal problems of employees is an accepted and expected part of the executive's role. The open-door tradition facilitates the playing of that role. Viewed in this context, the open-door tradition is an integral part of the 'unwritten' or 'informal' organizational structure.

TABLE 6.3 The open-door tradition

Level of employees who can meet the executive	*Number*	*Percentage*
1. Any level of the company, without going through hierarchy	39	75
2. Any level, provided they go through proper hierarchy	9	17
3. Managerial level only	3	6
4. Immediate subordinates only	1	2
Total	52	100

There were, however, thirteen executives (25 per cent) who were trying to discourage the open-door tradition, most of whom insisted that their employees must go through the established chain of command; a conditional open-door policy (see Table 6.3). A relevant question here would be whether there is any relationship between the open-door tradition and the other variables especially, as one would suspect, the size of the organization, the country, or the social and educational background of the executive? Surprisingly, the executives' responses were not related to any organizational or individual variables. What these thirteen executives shared in common was a desire to break away, within their respective organizations, from a tradition which they perceived as an unnecessary imposition on their energy and time. To that extent, these executives can be regarded as agents of social change, whether or not they are aware of the consequences of their actions.

It would be interesting to see how often Arab executives bypass their subordinates when issuing instructions to employees at the middle or lower levels.

It is clear from Table 6.4 that the executives were more careful about bypassing the hierarchy. Again, as with the preceding responses, there were no significant relationships between the executives' responses and the various variables. It is noteworthy, however, that most of the thirteen executives who favoured either conditional open-door or closed-door policies were relatively consistent in their attitudes towards bypassing the hierarchy. Eight of the thirteen said that they 'seldom' break the chain of command, and the remaining five indicated that they do so 'occasionally'. The executives were aware of the inevitable dilemma they face when deciding whether or not to break the chain of command. On the one hand, if they choose not to bypass subordinates they will encounter two disadvantages. The first is the loss of valuable time when the matters under consideration are urgent. The second disadvantage concerns communication; the ways in which communication can become distorted when flowing up and down the hierarchical levels are well known. On the other hand, if the executives decide to break the chain of command they will again face two disadvantages. One is the detrimental effects on the morale and effectiveness of their middle managers who are being bypassed. The other disadvantage is the bad example and precedent which actions of this kind could create for employees. One executive described it well when he said: 'We are having a hard time as it is getting our employees accustomed to organization charts and job descriptions. What will happen if I go around breaking these rules?' The solution to this dilemma rests with each executive who has to weigh the advantages and disadvantages of each alternative, taking into account the situational factors that led to the dilemma in the first place.

TABLE 6.4 Bypassing the hierarchy.

'How often do you personally give instructions to employees at the middle or lower levels without going through their immediate supervisors?'

	Number	*Percentage*
Very often	5	10
Occasionally	25	48
Seldom	22	42
Total	52	100

A PREFERENCE FOR 'INFORMALITY'

We have seen in the preceding sections that Arab executives tend to be more person-oriented that role- or task-oriented. They engage in prolonged rituals when starting a business discussion; they use personal ties and connections extensively; they value loyalty over efficiency; and they adhere to the open-door tradition. This strong emphasis on personal relations and the human side of business may seem incompatible with the rationale of formal organizational structures, rules and systems. In other words, the personal relationships within an organization often take precedence over formal structures, rules and procedures, and so on. The formal systems, being very fluid and elastic, are often used as tentative guidelines to action if and when necessary or convenient.

The above situation is best illustrated if seen through Western eyes. To an expatriate manager who has never worked in an Arab organization, the first few months at his new assignment may be traumatic. This is not so much due to the expected culture shock, but more to the manner in which his new organization functions. One such expatriate was given upon arrival an elaborate set of manuals which included company policies and procedures, job descriptions, and organization charts. Being in a relatively large public company (around 2500 employees), the expatriate expected that the formal rules and regulations would be applied most of the time. His comments were:

> I can now say that rules and regulations are being applied about 20% of the time. Not that they are not suitable for this type of firm; the problem is that we have too many exceptions around here: exceptions because of friendship, exceptions for relatives, exceptions because of convenience, etc. . . .

A similar phenomenon was observed by Riggs when studying public administration organizations.[13] He noted that in societies where partial differentiation has taken place (that is developing countries), there is great discrepancy between the formally prescribed laws and procedures and the actual behaviour of government officials. A study of Saudi Arabian bureaucracy, using the conceptual model developed by Riggs, has added further support to this observation.[14] To a non-Arab, such situations as described above will seem chaotic and unorganized. The expatriate (and to some extend the researcher) is bewildered at the discrepancy between organizational rules and procedures and the actual behaviour of top and middle level managers. Another expatriate who joined a large Arab organization at the vice-presidential level described his initial experience as follows:

> After the first three months I was convinced that the company was run in the most chaotic way imaginable; nothing like I ever experienced in my 20 years of work experience in the United States. But, now after nine months, I must admit these fellows are sharp, shrewd and efficient. . . . What they have is organized chaos and if you can adjust to that, it's a great place to work.

What are the Arab executive's views on this topic? Once again the executive is in a dilemma on this matter. He recognizes the benefits of formal rules and procedures especially as his firm increases in size and complexity: a well-organized firm has a better chance of increased productivity and effectiveness. But he is constantly faced with overwhelming pressures to use impersonal and irregular ways and means of getting business done, both in and out of the organization. He strives for more formalization, often by emulating those formal organizational methods used by non-Arab companies or those prescribed by non-Arab management textbooks. However, these more formalized structures and methods are necessarily impersonal and universalistic[15] and as we have seen earlier, society's values and its institutions do not encourage the use of such impersonal methods.

Of course, Arab executives do use and adhere to formal rules and regulations whenever possible or legally required. But the majority of them seemed to favour keeping formal methods to the *minimum* required by legal, accounting, contractual and other necessary procedures. They also favoured keeping to a minimum the formality of interpersonal relations, stating that with informality a 'personal' and a 'humane' management approach is more possible; an approach which they seem to value highly, and which is consistent with both the executive's and the employee's perception of their organization as a family unit.

What is particularly interesting is the Arab executive's informality in decision making. We have already seen that the executives prefer the consultative style of decision making. This consultation is usually carried out on a person-to-person basis whereby group meetings are strongly avoided. Moreover, decisions are often made in an informal and unstructured manner, as one European expatriate discovered early on in his career with a large oil company in the UAE:

> It took me several months to realize that what looked and sounded like social talk and playing around was in fact the most preferred mode for Arab managers to discuss business, solve problems, or make decisions.

Another indication that Arab executives prefer informality and the personal approach to business can be seen from their views about expatriates and/or foreign businessmen. When asked to mention the characteristics of expatriates/foreign businessmen which they strongly disliked, nine executives mentioned the formal and impersonal notion of 'business is business' which they felt was carried too far by expatriates/foreign businessmen.[16] In a society where the personalized approach is prevalent, it is not surprising that what is normally considered professional business behaviour was seen as highly rigid and impersonal. This is not to say that Arab executives do not believe in the notion of 'business is business', it is only that they feel business should be conducted in a personalized and friendly atmosphere – even though this may require 'a lot of play-acting', as one of the executives put it.

In conclusion, the discussion presented in this chapter points to a strong preference by the Arab executive for a person-oriented approach to interpersonal relations. This was evident not only when the executive was dealing with people from outside his organization, but also with his employees. In turn this approach led to its corollary: a preference for 'informality'. This type of behaviour is partly shaped by social structural factors and partly by the prevailing customs and value orientations. It is significant to note, however, that there were some executives who consciously or unconsciously were striving for more impersonality and formality in conducting business. This suggests that the differences in approaches may well be reflections of the social changes now taking place in the Arab world: a topic we shall focus on in the next chapter.

NOTES

1. This range of 2 to 15 minutes is based on estimates given by sixteen executives from the six Arab countries. The average time for this ritual was 5.7 minutes and the mode was 5 minutes.
2. Morris (1967), *The Naked Ape*, p. 180.
3. Hall and Whyte, 'Intercultural Communication', pp. 5–12.
4. Six expatriates were interviewed and their opinions were solicited regarding Arab executives.
5. The importance of the intermediary role in Egyptian civil service was described over twenty years ago by Berger (1957), in *Bureaucracy and Society in Modern Egypt*. For the importance of this role in Lebanon, see Farsoun (1970), 'Family Structure and Society in Modern Lebanon', pp. 270, 281–5.
6. For an excellent analysis of social exchange, see Homans (1961), *Social Behavior*; or Blau (1964), *Exchange and Power in Social Life*.
7. See for example, 'Bribery, Corruption, or Necessary Fees and Charges?' *Multinational Business* 3 (1975), pp. 1–17; Jacoby *et al.* (1977), *Bribery*

and Extortion in World Business. For a vivid account of bribery in the arms industry, see Sampson (1977), *The Arms Bazaar.*

8. For an excellent collection of articles and studies on these questions, and on world-wide corruption, see Heidenheimer (1971), *Political Corruption: Readings in Comparative Analysis,* especially Part 4 on Corruption and Modernization, pp. 479–578.
9. As quoted in Sampson (1977), p. 189.
10. Business guests in the Arab world are often treated in the same individualized manner as would heads of state visiting other countries – but of course on a lesser scale and without the paraphernalia.
11. Fayerweather (1960), *Management of International Operations,* p. 27.
12. Hobday (1978), *Saudi Arabia Today,* pp. 67–8. It was at one such *majlis* where the late King Faisal was assassinated in March 1975.
13. Riggs (1964), *Administration in Developing Countries.*
14. Al-Awaji (1971), 'Bureaucracy and Society in Saudi Arabia', Ph.D. diss., University of Virginia.
15. Universalistic as contrasted to particularistic; the classic examples of the latter are nepotism and other forms of favouritism; see Parsons (1966), *Societies: Evolutionary and Comparative Perspectives.*
16. These views were in response to an open-ended question which also asked executives to mention the characteristics which they *admire* most about expatriates/foreign businessmen. The responses to both these questions will be examined in the next two chapters.

7 Attitudes Towards Time and Change

Time present and time past
Are both perhaps present in time future
And time future contained in time past.
T.S. Eliot, 1888–1965
'Burnt Norton', *Four Quartets*

A study of the Arab executive would be incomplete and inadequate without examining his attitudes towards time and change. For these are two crucial elements of the business mind which, in turn, have significant bearing on managerial behaviour and practices, including business activities at the international level.

In the first part of this chapter, the time orientation of the Arab executive will be examined. Here we focus on the value the executive places on time, his time horizons; and his attitudes towards the future. The second part will investigate the executive's views on the technological and social changes which are now permeating his organization and his society. Finally, the last part will examine the socio-psychological consequences to the executive of these recent changes, particularly the recent rush towards economic development and modernization.

TIME ORIENTATION

Because of its importance to the understanding of human nature and behaviour, the time orientation of man has interested social scientists especially in their endeavour to understand human behaviour in societies other than their own.[1] In the following sections our interest goes further than presenting a description of the executive's time orientation, for we shall also attempt to identify the environmental and social structural factors which are at present influencing the executive's time orientation. Viewed from this perspective, time orientation ceases to be a mere static cultural trait or value pattern, instead it will be viewed both as a product of early socialization and enculturation as well as a product of an ever-changing social structure.

The Value of Time

One of the Arab executive's gravest problems is the low value placed on time by many of his countrymen. Executives were deeply concerned and irritated by the lack of appreciation towards time shown by people with whom they come in contact. The seriousness of this problem was perhaps best expressed by the motto of a large firm in the UAE. Above and across the main entrance of its building there is written in huge letters the following: 'WASTE EVERYTHING EXCEPT TIME'.

We have already seen in Chapter 3 that Arab executives considered procrastination and the low value placed on time as a major problem in their society. In fact this problem was the most frequently mentioned and was seen as such by nineteen executives (see Chapter 3, Table 3.1). The executives' profound concern with the value of time is also reflected in their responses to the following question: 'what are some of the characteristics of the expatriates employed here (if no expatriates, then foreign businessmen) which you admire most?' The admired characteristic which again was the most frequently mentioned (eighteen executives mentioned it) is the expatriate's punctuality and respect for time.

In view of the above, it was not suprising to find that executives placed a very high value on time; at least when asked to provide proverbs or sayings that would best represent their views and attitudes towards time. The results are presented in Table 7.1. Clearly, the executives value time highly. However, cognizant of the fact that the above responses are only views and attitudes and as such are not necessarily indicative of actual behaviour, the author attempted to uncover the precise meaning which executives attach to these proverbs. In other words, could this high value placed on time possibly be an overreaction to the widespread general indifference and apathy towards time? Or is it an aspiration and a goal on the part of the executives for more appreciation of time? Where do executives draw the line when they say 'time is money'? The discussions and the probing that took place indicate that the degree and extent to which time is valued may differ from other non-Arab societies. Thus while time is highly valued by Arab executives there seem to be several other competing factors which often take precedence over time. For example, one executive said: 'It is unethical to say to an unexpected guest or visitor: "Sorry I've an appointment or urgent work".' Similarly, it is difficult for the executive to shorten a guest's visit even though the executive's work load justifies doing so. In such cases, both the norms of hospitality and deference to others preclude time-saving actions. Other competing factors are friendship and personal ties. Here, again, executives were aware that while time is spent in seemingly non-productive activities, they viewed time thus spent as an investment in friendships and personal ties – both highly valued elements – whether or not future benefits are forthcoming. Finally, a few executives indicated that while they believe that 'time is money' or 'gold', one must temper this attitude whenever human relations and personal problems are involved. It was a Saudi executive, with extensive exposure to US management and personnel, who succinctly summarized the views of many Arab executives: 'While Arabs, unfortunately, have little respect for time, the Americans go to the other extreme ... there must be a happy medium'.

TABLE 7.1 Proverbs on the value of time

	Proverb	*Frequency of mention**	
1	Time is gold (translated from Arabic)	14	} 24
2	Time is money (mentioned in English)	10	
3	Time is like a double-edged sword, it could either benefit or harm you (translated from Arabic)	8	
4	Don't postpone today's work till tomorrow (translated from Arabic); which is similar to the English: 'Never put off till tomorrow what may be done today'.	6	
5	Time is a problem solver (translated from Arabic)	4	

*A total of eleven proverbs were mentioned; the six proverbs which do not appear above were mentioned only once.

Let us very briefly summarize the probable pressures and reasons which inhibit a better utilization of time in the Arab world. Some of the following may in other societies be considered as easily avoidable constraints on time but are seen by

Arab executives as either necessary or uncontrollable:

1. The inadequacy of the economic and organizational infrastructures was discussed in Chapter 2. Here, delays and waste of time are often a result of the non-existence and/or poor utilization of such items as transportation, housing facilities, communication channels, technology, and human resources, or efficient government agencies.
2. A range of social pressures and constraints impose on the executive's time. They include: fusion of business, social, and personal life; top-man syndrome; and social visits at the office (see Table 3.1, Chapter 3).
3. The executive's role in the community and the organization, as we have seen in Chapter 3, resulted in heavy time commitments and obligations to the extended family, friends, and employees.
4. The low level of delegation by executives, as was discovered in Chapter 4, is an obstacle to good management of time. Here the onus is on the executives themselves. Clearly delegating more of the operating-level decisions will, *inter alia*, relieve the over-burdened executive and speed up the decision-making process.
5. The executives' person-oriented interpersonal style, discussed in Chapter 6, was partly imposing on their time; especially with executives who use the Arab rituals and customs while conducting business, and with those who believe in the open-door tradition.

These constraints could have detrimental effects on attempts to manage one's time. It must be pointed out, however, that throughout this study an effort was made to highlight those few executives who were actively resisting the social and structural constraints on their time, energy, and behaviour. Those executives were, on several occasions, termed agents of change. The main point is this: the executive may indeed have a choice. Clearly, it is not an easy choice; the price of non-conformity may be too high for some executives.

Time Horizons

How far into the future do Arab executives attempt to glimpse or predict? And to what extent do political and economic factors influence their time horizons? These questions become even more crucial if we keep in mind the instability and unpredictability of political and economic conditions in the Arab world. There are strong indications that executives, given these adverse conditions, nevertheless project their business plans well into the future. In order to find out the extent to which they do that, the executives were asked to indicate their time horizon on three preselected business activities: capital investment; company-wide planning; and managerial training and development. Their responses were recorded on the time scale shown in Table 7.2. Additionally, comments on these activities were solicited from executives whenever their time permitted. The responses and some of the comments will be briefly outlined here, while the implications of these results will be discussed in the following section.

TABLE 7.2 Time horizons: investment, planning, training

Time period (years)	*Payback on capital investment*	*Company-wide planning*	*Managerial training and development*
Under 1	1	7	14
1– 2	2	18	16
3– 5	30	25	19
6–10	14	2	3
Over 10	1	–	–
Total	48*	52	52

* Four executives preferred not to respond, stating that their expectations on payback periods varied greatly depending on the nature and circumstances of individual projects.

The most interesting comments were related to company-wide planning. For in addition to the unstable and uncertain political and economic conditions (discussed in Chapter 2), the dearth of data and information was seen as a main obstacle to corporate planning. Business-related information and data in the Arab world are scarce resources; and if available they are, in the words of one executive, 'often inadequate, unreliable, and conflicting'. Under such conditions, the necessity to review and revise corporate plans on an annual basis becomes obvious, as many executives seem to be doing. Finally, since governmental expenditures have the greatest impact on the national economies, several executives utilize the three-, four-, or five-year economic development plans for their own corporate planning. Of course, executives in the government-owned organizations (there were twelve such executives) coordinate their long-term planning with the government's own 3–5-year development plan.

Only a brief comment is necessary on managerial training and development. At the one end of the scale (under 1 year), short training programmes are being utilized, ranging in duration from 1 week to several months. At the other extreme (3–10 years), executives from some organizations stated that 'a whole second generation of top men is at present being groomed for future leadership'; while other executives mentioned that their organizations pay for the university education of prospective managers.

The results on capital investment horizons demonstrate that Arab executives have generally the same time horizons as businessmen in some industrialized countries, as indicated by the following quotation:

> Surveys among businessmen almost invariably reveal that for judgements about the desirability of individual projects and for choices among projects the shortness of the payback period is a much more popular criterion than the other analytical criteria. . . . Some of these surveys disclose, indeed, that a surprising number of businesses set arbitrary payback period cutoffs, such as three, four, or five years, beyond which they will not go in making investments in new facilities.[2]

Table 7.2 shows that there were three organizations with payback periods of 2 years or less, and one organization with a period of over 10 years. The former organizations were all small (less than 500 employees) contracting companies, while the latter was a shipping firm whose capital investments are greater in magnitude and have longer economic lives.

The Myth of Fatalism

There is a widespread view which asserts that Arabs are fatalistic, and that this fatalism is in direct contrast with the spirit of activity and initiative said to be characteristic of Anglo-Saxons and Europeans. Furthermore, this view attributes this fatalistic indifference to the teachings of Islam.[3]

The aim of this section is not to engage in a delicate and philosophical debate concerning the relationships between the revelational religions (Judaism, Christianity, and Islam) and fatalism – a topic beyond the scope of this book. Instead, our aim is to highlight the findings of this study which cast serious doubt on the above view held mostly by Western social scientists. More specifically, there are two objections to this view:

1. That the degree of fatalism in the Arab world – and there are degrees of fatalism – must not be attributed solely to Islam without taking into account all other socio-economic and political factors. Moreover, that there are within Islamic teachings as many precepts exhorting initiative, activity, and reasoning as there are precepts which encourage fatalism.
2. That, as a corollary to the above, any generalization which implies that *most* Arabs (Muslim or non-Muslim) are fatalistic, regardless of their socio-economic and educational background, is academically irresponsible and misleading.

Let us now turn to the first point. The view which attributes fatalism to Islam is not a new one. Rodinson (1974) writes:

> This view is, as is well known, one of the most widespread held about Islam in Europe, and has even acquired the status of an established truth, a dogma for the European collective mind, well expressed in Leibniz's expression *fatum mahumetanum*. It was developed by innumerable European writers in the eighteenth and nineteenth centuries. . . . It is still frequently repeated in our own time. And yet it is highly questionable. (p. 109)

The interest in the relationship between Islam and fatalism gained prominence when scholars attempted to explain the decline and prolonged stagnation of the Arab empire and Islamic civilization. In the majority of these investigations Islam – as a religion and a civilization – was being compared to Christian or European civilization *without* taking into account the historical, political, socio-economic, or geophysical factors.[4] Under these circumstances, that is, ahistorical and non-specific analyses, 'it was perhaps inevitable that Islam itself should emerge as the fundamental reason why the East has not developed in the same way as the West'.[5] It was in this type of analysis that the alleged fatalism was ascribed to Islamic teachings and hence was held responsible for the general stagnation.

To confound matters, the social scientists studying this topic focused their attention mostly on the rural areas of the Islamic countries, generalizing from there to all Muslims. To quote Rodinson (1974) again:

> The examples of 'Muslim fatalism' that have probably been most often quoted by European writers were taken above all from the under-developed *rural areas* of the Islamic world. G. Destanne de Bernis has shown in a very scholarly way, using mathematical methods and with a close and deep knowledge of the Tunisian *country life*, that, if the peasants of the Muslim countries are indeed fatalistic, this is not at all an irrational attitude on their part, but represents a just estimation of the enormous, and discouraging, weight of the chancy factors that condition the success of their efforts. (p. 113, emphasis added)

With regard to Islamic precepts exhorting initiative, activity and reasoning, it would be relatively easy to quote verses from the Quran and the *Ḥadīth* in order to illustrate Islam's rationalist and activist teachings.[6] It would be equally easy to quote verses which can be interpreted as fatalistic.[7] For our present purpose, it suffices to report what some Arab executives had to say on this topic. Three of the executives reminded the author of a saying from the *Ḥadīth* which in effect admonishes man first to think and plan ahead, then put his trust in God. Another executive quoted the following verse from the Quran: 'Verily never will God change the condition of a people until they change it themselves.'[8] The fifth executive stated his belief that 'Man's trust in God or belief in God's will does not necessarily mean a curb on human will . . . man must strive to do his best and if he acts rightly God will be with him; I don't believe that this leads to passive resignation.'

Indeed, past and present Islamic achievements (which are in harmony with Islamic teachings) demonstrate the use of long-range planning and a desire to understand and control nature or the environment. These include, to name a few examples, empire building in the past and economic development today; the utilization of technological, scientific, and medical know-how; and the advancement of knowledge through education and research. None of these indicates a belief that man cannot or should not shape his future. And yet these are the goals and aspirations of many devout Muslim nations and/or individuals.

Let us now consider the second point, namely, the insinuation that most Arabs are fatalistic. This usually stems from the argument we have just discussed alleging that Islam encourages fatalism. By association, since 90–95 per cent of Arabs are Muslims, it is erroneously implied that most Arabs are fatalistic. This may well have been the case many decades ago when poverty and ignorance were widespread, especially in the rural areas of the Arab world. Today, modern agricultural technology and methods are widely used; bedouins and peasants seek medical attention (even if abroad);[9] agricultural cooperatives and banks are widespread, and so on. Again, none of these activities suggest a belief that man should not seek self-betterment or should not influence future events. However, it is perhaps the frequent use by Arabs of the phrase *inshā'Allāh* (God willing or if God wills) which alarms expatriates and foreign visitors. But instead of interpreting it as a sign of resignation and inactivity, one must consider it a sign of religiousness and/or religious custom which most often it is. One is reminded of the phrase 'In God We Trust' which appears on US coin and note currencies; or the Christian Lord's Prayer: 'Give us this day our daily bread'; or the expression of shock and sadness upon the untimely death of Pope John Paul I in September 1978 as expressed in these quotations: 'God has willed it, as painful as His will is', or 'The Ways of the Lord are disconcerting to our human perspective'.[10]

Turning to the Arab executive's attitudes toward this subject, we find that he is not only future-orientated but also takes as many preventive measures against undesirable events as it is technologically and economically feasible. We have already seen in the preceding section that his time horizons extend to 10 years on capital investment, company-wide planning, and managerial training and development. The most common (mode) time period for these business activities being 3–5 years.

TABLE 7.3 Events and factors beyond the executive's control. (In open response.)

Event	*Frequency of mention**
Adverse political and economic conditions (national and international)	33
Government rules and regulations (unstable or restrictive)	21
World currency fluctuation (especially in the dollar)	9
Manpower and labour shortage	7
Climatic conditions or natural disasters	6
Inflation	5
Delays with imported materials (at sending and receiving ends)	4

* Shows only events mentioned by three or more executives

Further data from the interviews strongly support the claim that Arab executives are not fatalistic. The executives were asked to mention the events and factors that have an effect on their business, but over which they have little control. Table 7.3 summarizes their responses. The seven items mentioned in Table 7.3 are self-explanatory except the first and most frequently mentioned one.[11] Executives combined political and economic events at both the national and international levels. The most prominent examples were: world-wide recession and market conditions; regional and internal wars and border closures; and local economic instability and uncertainty. The executives were also asked whether they take steps or measures to prevent undesirable events from occuring in the course of doing business. Their responses are shown in Table 7.4.[12]

TABLE 7.4 Preventive measures. (In open response.)

Measures	*Frequency of mention**
Contingency planning (plan ahead)	30†
Safety	27
Preventive maintenance	18
Insurance (on plant and/or personnel)	13
Maintaining good labour and employee relations	6

* Shows only measures mentioned by three or more executives.
† Includes six executives who specifically mentioned spare parts planning.

Finally, executives were asked if they carry life insurance and if not, why not. Twenty-nine executives (56 per cent) have life insurance, while the other twenty-three (44 per cent) did not. The reasons given by those who did not have life insurance are interesting and worth looking into. Of the twenty-three executives, sixteen said they did not need life insurance because of their individual or family wealth and financial security; and five of those sixteen stated that in the past they had insurance but could not see a need for it now. Of the remaining seven executives, four said they did not feel that they need life insurance since their countries' (Kuwait and Saudi Arabia) social security systems, as well as their company's pension and benefit plans, are very generous and thus adequate. The other three executives simply stated that they do not believe in its financial benefits or its usefulness, without elaborating further.[13]

In brief, the data we have presented indicate that Arab executives are far from being fatalistic: they are future-oriented, rational in their planning and deliberation, and they attempt to control and prevent adverse future events.

From our brief exploration of this important issue, it would seem that the myth of fatalism, at least among businessmen, must now be laid to rest. Any future investigation of this topic should not only seek objectively to assess the degree and extent of fatalism, but also take into account the relevant historical and contextual variables. In this way, we can not only compare the degrees of fatalism within a given society, but we can also compare fatalism across different societies.

ATTITUDES TOWARDS CHANGE

In the remainder of this chapter, we focus on the Arab executive's attitudes and reactions to social and technological change. The understanding of these attitudes and reactions is of great importance since the executive himself is a target of change; and as we have seen throughout this study, he could also be an agent of change. It is equally important, however, that we discuss the executive's attitudes and reactions to change within a specific background: that of change and modernization at the national level. The next few pages will thus provide a context for the following discussions.

The Context of Change

There is no doubt that many changes are taking place in the Arab world. In Chapter 2 we discussed at the macro-level several major events which are still influencing every aspect of life in the region. Clearly, the pace and intensity of these changes differ from one country to another. Moreover, internal as well as external developments and forces are inducing the changes since none of the countries is in complete isolation.

There are, however, two types of change.[14] Stated simply, one type refers to the minor, and in the short run, insignificant changes that are continuously occurring *within* society and its social structure. When such changes occur, the structure and the values and norms of society do not change substantially. A good example would be the introduction of modern technology to replace the old. The use of modern communication and information systems (telephone, telex, computers and so on) by governmental, military, or business organizations are changes in methods but not in basic structures. Examples of such changes abound: changes in national dress, diet, housing, entertainment, or medical practices. However, these changes are taking place *within* the social structure, and may not be cumulative or sufficient to induce lasting structural or normative changes.

The second type of change involves fundamental and substantive shifts in a society's social structure, its institutions, or in its values and norms. This type of change may take place either gradually, as a result of the cumulative effects of the minor changes discussed above; or more abruptly as a reaction to crises and major historical events. Either way, the form and functions of the social structure or some of its institutions change dramatically. Again, the change may well be in one or more of its political, military, religious, economic, or family institutions. Specific examples of such fundamental changes include: major shifts in power centres or in societal values which could result from political or social revolutions; the discovery and exploitation of natural resources, such as oil, in a previously impoverished country; a shift from the extended family to a nuclear one; and generally, a greater degree of differentiation in the political, economic, or social systems of a society.

The Arab world is experiencing *both* types of change; but

perhaps more of the first than the second. While changes are overwhelming in countries like Kuwait, Saudi Arabia, and the UAE, fuelled by the rapid increase in wealth; the social structure and most of its institutions have not changed drastically. Modernization and industrialization are taking place but within, more or less, the same traditional, political, religious, economic, or social systems.

It would be absurd, of course, to suggest that there is no conflict or tension between the old and the modern. It would be equally absurd, however, to argue that the old and the modern are diametrically opposed and hence completely incompatible; or to suggest that the evolutionary path to modernization must inevitably lead to a Western type of modernity.[15] This school of thought, referred to as the convergence school, measured societies on Western modernity indices which included (depending on the social scientist's field of interest) such items as literacy, fatalism, empathy, media participation, urbanization, political participation, division of labour, and the like. Nearly all the work done by adherents of this school theorized that 'modernizing' societies go from the 'traditional' stage through an intermediate 'transitional' stage on their way to more or less a Western 'modern' stage. And that in this modernization process the incompatible traditional values and institutions will ultimately disappear.

However, reality and systematic studies have not fully borne out these theories or their assumptions.[16] Riggs, among many others, has shown that the modern and the traditional can and do coexist in what he called the 'prismatic society' which is neither traditional nor Western-type modern,[17] and that the resultant partially differentiated society may be a viable alternative. Others have shown that tradition and modernity can be mutually reinforcing rather than in conflict, as has been found in field studies from Lebanon, Nigeria, and Indonesia.[18] A case study of Saudi Arabia supports these important findings:

> In conclusion, we find that modernization proceeds in degrees and stages. It does not have a uniform impact on the total structure of traditional societies. Whether it proceeds at first on the economic, the social, or the political level is determined by the national goals of the country concerned, given the limitations set by internal and external forces. *Moderniza-*

> *tion does not necessarily entail destruction of traditional structures, but rather it allows for 'wide margins' of coexistence between traditional and modern forms.* On the other hand, tradition does not constitute a uniform, static system that is *antagonistic* to modernity. Tradition was found to have a significant degree of flexibility and diversity to *accommodate* modern patterns.[19] (Emphasis added)

Critical evaluations of the convergence school have been many,[20] and their criticisms fairly consistent: mainly that these studies ignore the viable mixture of traditional and modern elements as often found in contemporary societies, and that 'the mixture of the two types is too situational and historical to be consistent with the evolutionary theory which posits them as opposites'.[21] The author of the study on Saudi Arabia reached the same conclusion:

> Modernization is thus a continuing process in which the cultural and historical experience, and the national goals of the country concerned interfere to set their 'choice' of the margins of co-existence between tradition and modernity.[22]

It is perhaps with such thoughts in mind that the late King Faisal of Saudi Arabia declared in 1974 that he wanted his country 'to achieve economic growth and modernization without sacrificing the traditions of Islam and Arab culture'. He may have at that time set the tone for the Gulf states, but recent events in Egypt, Pakistan, and especially Iran, seem to indicate that Islam is also asserting its identity in other Muslim countries.[23] History and systematic studies have shown that modernization can be achieved under the tutelage of a variety of competing political, economic, or religious ideologies and systems. Indeed, modernization does not inevitably have to be of the Western type. Let us take, for example, the following countries and ask ourselves what must be included in a traditional/modern index for comparative purposes: USA, Japan, USSR, Italy, and Sweden. There is a great variety in their political, economic, social, and religious ideologies and systems. What is most common among them is the extensive usage of science and advanced technology for the production of goods and services.

In brief, it seems that a country could achieve economic

progress and could become modern in some but not all aspects of human activity. That is it could become neo-traditionalist: new and modern in form and style but not in substance or essence.[24]

The Executive's Attitudes

Now that the background has been set, let us turn to the Arab executive and examine his attitudes toward the technological and social changes which are now occurring within his milieu. Changes which he has some control over and hence could either promote or discourage, at least, within his organization and family. The executives were asked to express their attitudes towards three such changes:

1. an increase in the introduction of sophisticated scientific systems and equipment (computers, latest machinery, etc.) to business when and where applicable;
2. women holding high managerial positions in business firms;
3. the newer generation to gain more freedom and independence from family, customs, religion and traditions (for example, a move from the extended family to the nuclear one, and so on).

For convenience, let us abbreviate the wording of these changes and refer to them henceforth as follows:

1. advanced technology;
2. women in management;
3. freedom from family and traditions.

The responses, in their aggregate form, are summarized in Table 7.5. It is clear at once that Arab executives have a 'thirst' for technology; in fact some of these who only 'favoured' rather than 'strongly favoured' advanced technology admitted that they may well have been 'oversold' on its applicability. Nevertheless, introducing technological changes (where applicable) into Arab organizations is unlikely to meet resistance.

The second change, women in management, was also welcomed. In Chapter 3 we briefly discussed the societal restrictions on women, especially in Saudi Arabia and to a much lesser

TABLE 7.5 Attitudes towards technological and social changes (Percentages) (N=52)

Response	*Advanced technology*	*Women in management*	*Freedom from family and traditions*
Strongly favour	62	15	6
Favour	38	58	23
Oppose	—	21	40
Strongly oppose	—	6	31
Total	100	100	100

extent in Jordan. It was also stated that the trend towards female emancipation has accelerated in most Arab countries, possibly at a relatively faster rate than was the case for Western women some 50 years ago. It would be useful to take a closer look at the data. Table 7.6 shows, by country, the executives' attitudes towards women in management as well as the interesting responses on freedom from family and traditions.

TABLE 7.6 Attitudes towards social changes, by country (Percentages and mean scores)

	Women in management			*Freedom from family and traditions*			
Country	*Percentage*		*Mean*	*Percentage*		*Mean*	*N*
	Favour	*Oppose*	*score**	*Favour*	*Oppose*	*score**	
Jordan	90	10	3.1	40	60	2.4	10
Lebanon	63	37	2.5	63	37	2.7	8
Saudi Arabia	90	10	3.1	40	60	2.1	10
Kuwait	78	22	3.1	11	89	1.8	9
Egypt	44	56	2.4	11	89	1.6	9
UAE	67	33	2.5	—	100	1.5	6
Total	73	27	2.8	29	71	2.0	52

* The mean score is based on a four-point scale: 1=strongly oppose; 2=oppose; 3=favour; and 4=strongly favour. Thus, the higher the score the more favourable the attitude.

There are two noteworthy observations as suggested by the data. First, in regard to attitudes towards women in management, it seems that executives from those countries with lesser restrictions on women (Egypt and Lebanon) are least favourable to having women in managerial positions. This attitude is similar to the prevailing Western attitudes towards women 10 or 15 years ago. Although Egyptian women, especially in the urban areas, are holding high positions in politics, education, medicine, and social welfare, discrimination in industry and business continues. On the other hand, executives from the other four countries seem to be reacting strongly in response to what they see as the slower-than-desired process of women's emancipation in their respective countries.

The second observation relates to the reversal of attitudes from favouring women in management to opposing freedom from family and traditions. We must find out how many executives were involved in this attitude reversal; we can then look for possible explanations. Of the fifty-two executives:

(i) Fourteen executives (27 per cent) favoured both changes.
(ii) Thirteen executives (25 per cent) opposed both changes.
(iii) One executive (2 per cent) opposed women in management *but* favoured freedom from family and traditions.
(iv) Twenty-four executives (46 per cent) favoured women in management *but* opposed freedom from family and traditions.

Our primary interest is in those executives in (iii) and (iv) above. The one executive (in (iii)) is an Egyptian who, while favouring freedom from family and traditions, was opposed to women in management, an attitude not different from the one prevalent in the West not so long ago. Of the twenty-four executives (in (iv) above), twenty are from the same four countries (Jordan, Kuwait, Saudi Arabia and UAE) in which only recently did women's emancipation become an issue. The remaining four executives were from Egypt. One possible explanation for this seemingly ambivalent attitude is the belief that while more rights and opportunities for women is desirable, it is neither desirable nor inevitable for family ties and traditions to be weakened.[25] In other words, women's emancipation (especially in the management of business) is not seen as incompatible with the maintenance of strong family ties and/or customs, religion and traditions. In short, as one executive put it: 'there is no need to go to the other extreme'.

Finally, it is worth noting that two executives from the Gulf area, after responding to the question on women in management, took the opportunity to comment on the subject of women's employment at all levels. Some pointed out that the acute manpower shortage in the Gulf area will be slightly alleviated if they utilize some of the 'womanpower surplus'. Of course, this has serious consequences for most of the Arab countries where the economically active population averages a low 26 per cent of the total population.[26]

What is the likelihood of each of the three changes occurring in the next 5–10 years? The executives' responses to this question are summarized in Table 7.7.

TABLE 7.7 Likelihood of occurrence: technological and social changes (Percentages) (N=52)

Response	*Advanced technology*	*Women in management*	*Freedom from family and traditions*
Very likely	63	17	10
Likely	37	40	67
Not likely	—	31	19
Highly unlikely	—	12	4
Total	100	100	100

Notice that while all three changes were seen by executives as likely to occur, the executives were opposed to only one of them; namely, freedom from family and tradition (see Table 7.5). A closer look at this incongruence reveals the following:

(i) Thirteen executives (25 per cent) favoured freedom from family and traditions, *and* believed it is likely to occur in the next 5–10 years.

(ii) Two executives (4 per cent) favoured *but* believed it is unlikely to occur.

(iii) Ten executives (19 per cent) opposed *and* believed it is unlikely to occur.

(iv) Twenty-seven executives (52 per cent) opposed *but* believed it is likely to occur.

Again, our interest is in the twenty-seven executives in (iv) above.[27] Further probing as to why they opposed the change and/or why they thought it was likely to happen brought three types of replies. First, there were those who felt that the new generation has already gained considerable freedom to which they were opposed. In these cases there already exists a generation gap. The second group felt that while they favour freedom in some customs and traditions, they oppose freedom in others – such as family or religion or vice versa. Clearly the question put to them was too general, thus suggesting the need to be more specific on this point in future research. Finally, the third group felt that while they favour a gradual change in these spheres of life, they wondered 'where does one draw the line?' Most were in effect saying it is 'unfortunate' but nevertheless likely that such a social change will occur *in the next 5–10 years.*

Our discussion of the executives' attitudes towards these three changes brings us back to the topic of 'convergence', and to the question of whether modernization will result in a 'mixture' of modern and traditional institutions and values. While political and social forces and events will mostly determine the outcome of such 'mixture', the executive's role in this process must not be understated, for he is still in a position to influence the composition and the ingredients which make up this 'mixture' of modern and traditional. However, the typical executive has ambivalent feelings towards modernization; a desire to avoid some of the negative consequences which might accompany economic development and modernization.

AMBIVALENCE

Modernization, perceived as a process whereby the old and the new ways of life mix and coexist, will invariably result in tension between the modern and the traditional. This tension is often manifested by ambivalent attitudes and emotions, especially by those persons most exposed to both modern and traditional. One such person is the Arab executive. He is torn between the old and the new; determined to introduce into his life and into his environment modern and scientific methods and adapt them to his modified, yet fundamentally traditional, work and life styles.

What is ambivalence? And how does it feel to have ambivalent attitudes, emotions, or behaviour? In its general sense, ambivalence means the coexistence in one person of opposing emotional attitudes towards the same object, or the simultaneous operation in the mind of two irreconcilable wishes. Examples of ambivalence abound, the many dilemmas and paradoxes of social life make ambivalence a more common phenomenon than is generally thought.[28] The classic example is of love and hate towards the same object, person, or situation (as in marriage, bringing up children, or even cigarette smoking). Other examples of ambivalence, whose sources are in the person's professional status and role, would include the ambivalence felt by physicians who were trained, and thus expected, to show sympathy as well as detachment towards patients; or the ambivalence of the scientists who feel obliged to publish quickly and to avoid rushing into print; to value humility as well as to take pride in originality.[29]

Yet the ambivalence felt by the Arab executive comes from an additional and different source: his exposure to the West. Of course, it was well before the executives in this study were born that the Arab world as a whole was reopened to the West. But the recent exposure of most executives has been considerable. Their educational backgrounds and the nature of their work made this exposure possible. For example 50 per cent of the executives received their first and/or second degree from Western universities. Another 20 per cent were educated at Western-styled universities (mostly at the American University of Beirut, but some at the American University of Cairo). These executives as well as all the others were also exposed to the West through one or more of the following: (a) extensive business and/or holiday travel in the industrialized countries; (b) short and intermediate (up to 1 year) training courses in the West; and (c) working closely with Western expatriates and businessmen.

The ambivalent feelings and attitudes of the executives are not unlike those felt by foreign students or immigrants who go to the West.[30] They see and experience the best and the worst of Western social order. They love the West for its many good features and they hate it for its many bad ones. When they return home, as in the case of foreign students, they begin to love even more than before their society's good points, but they start to hate the newly discovered bad ones. Most of them realize that a great deal has to be learnt now from the West, just as Europeans did from the Arabs a few centuries ago.

The solution for many of the executives is to adopt as many as possible of the West's good points which do not conflict with their own or society's values and norms. Whatever cannot be adopted is often adapted to fit in with the cherished traditional ways. At the same time, these executives attempt to discourage or curtail local habits and customs which they feel are hindering 'progress'. In one sense, the executives are searching for, and attempting to shape, the 'right mixture' of modernity and tradition. Again, they may or may not be in a position to influence deeply those in power or the larger social system. But many feel they could influence their immediate community including their organization and family.

What specific indications have led us to believe that Arab executives are ambivalent towards the old and the new? First, we shall briefly examine the types and sources of ambivalence within the executives' society. Later we will examine their feelings toward the West and especially the Western expatriates and businessmen.

The typical Arab executive we talked with is a proud person: he is proud of his nation and its people, and proud of his organization and its achievements. But invariably this executive is very aware of the weaknesses in his nation and its people. At times those interviewed would be depressed about the present conditions, and at times angry, but most of the time hopeful and desirous to rectify and improve the weak points. Most of these weaknesses have been examined within their contexts in the preceding chapters. It will be sufficient, therefore, to list the main ones, with a few words on the desired changes in each:

1. *Inter-Arab strife*: rectification of this may result in greater cooperation among Arab countries; political and economic stability; and a large common market with all its implications of growth and profits for executives.
2. *Low value of time*: any improvement would lead to better utilization of valuable (and often scarce) human resources. (This and the next point are especially relevant to governmental agencies).
3. *Lack of industrial mentality*: intensive industrial training and education may develop the desperately needed industrial

discipline and organizational skills among the work force and middle management.

4. *Extremes in 'informality' and 'personalism'*: the key phrase is striking a 'happy medium' between the extremes of the Arab style of 'informality' and 'personalism' in interpersonal relations, on the one hand, and the Western formal and impersonal style on the other. The likely outcome of such moderation will be improved efficiency while still retaining effectiveness in human relations.

Turning to the Arab executives' opinions of expatriates and/or foreign businessmen, we find not surprisingly that the characteristics which Arabs admire are the same ones they would like to see learned by their own people. The following are the characteristics most admired by the executives (figures in parentheses are frequencies of mention).

1. High value and respect for time (18)
2. Productivity and hard work (15)
3. Technical know-how and competence (10)
4. Organized and systematic approach to work (10)
5. Dedication and conscientiousness to work (9)
6. Discipline (5)
7. Accuracy and precision (5)

These, then, are the business-related characteristics which executives long for and which they miss most in their people. Yet these characteristics can be learned and acquired by employees and managers without giving up cherished values and institutions such as friendship, religion, family and the like. Clearly these characteristics have to be inculcated through life-time education (socialization): starting from childhood, in schools and universities, throughout work careers, to retirement. However, from the executives' viewpoint, training and education are never too late. Indeed, a few of the executives cited Japan as an example of a country in which the industrial mentality was instilled without drastic changes to its customs or traditions. While Arab and Japanese societies differ in many aspects and their circumstances are vastly different, Japan is nevertheless a reference 'model' to the Arab executive's mind of how modernization can be achieved in their own society while still retaining its distinctive Arab identity and character.

When the executives were asked to mention the characteristics of expatriates or foreign businessmen which they strongly dislike, there were two such characteristics which pertain to our topic.[31] The first relates to treatment of employees. Eleven executives strongly disliked the expatriates' manner of treating local employees, using the following terms to describe it: 'ruthless', 'treat like machines', 'inhumane', and 'easy resort to firing'. It is not difficult to understand the reasons for such resentment if we take into account on the one hand the expatriates' strong preoccupation with efficiency and productivity, and on the other hand the executives' paternalistic (and often emotional) management style. The second strongly disliked characteristic concerns what was seen by executives as the extremism in the 'business is business' approach. This approach was considered by nine Arab executives as too dry and impersonal for their part of the world.[32]

Once again, the crucial questions here are whether or not the industrial mentality could be acquired without sacrificing the desirable elements of Arab personality (such as hospitality, friendship, family-orientation, religiousness and so on)? Is the typical executive being realistic in holding these hopes and aspirations? Finally, at the macro-level, will societies and their institutions be able to maintain a 'mixture' of the traditional and modern? Clearly there are no easy answers to these questions. Yet they are the burning questions in the minds of all persons associated with change in the Arab world: politicians, businessmen, academics, and the like. Their own personal exposure to the West, and the subsequent changes in their own personality, have led many of them to believe that a mixture of the traditional and modern is indeed feasible.

NOTES

1. Hall, (1959), *The Silent Language*; Kluckhohn and Strodtbeck (1961), *Variations in Value Orientations*; McClelland (1961), *The Achieving Society*; Farmer and Richman (1965), *Comparative Management and Economic Progress*; and Robock, Simmonds, and Zwick (1977), *International Business and Multinational Enterprises*.
2. Kent (1969), *Corporate Financial Management*, p. 293.
3. See Patai (1973), *The Arab Mind*, pp. 147-50, 310. For critiques of this view see Rodinson (1974), *Islam and Capitalism*, English edn, chapter 4.

Also see Naim (1978), 'Towards a Demystification of Arab Social Reality', pp. 48-62.

4. Owen (1976), 'Islam and Capitalism: A Critique of Rodinson', p. 86. See also Mansfield (1976), *The Arabs*, pp. 95-105, for an analysis of the conditions of peasants.
5. Owen (1976), p. 86.
6. See Rodinson (1974), chapter 4, for a large number of such quotes.
7. See Patai (1973), p. 148, for a large number of quotes.
8. *The Quran*, Sūra XIII: 11 (A. Y. Ali's translation).
9. Compare this behaviour to the Christian Scientists' attitudes toward medical treatment.
10. *Time Magazine*, Europe Edition, 9 October, 1978, p. 8.
11. Similar to the finding of Y. Sayigh that political conditions constituted the greatest unknown facing the entrepreneurs which he surveyed in Lebanon in the early 1960s; Sayigh (1962), *Entrepreneurs of Lebanon*, p. 117.
12. It is interesting to note (Table 7.4) that six executives viewed good labour and employee relations as a preventive measure.
13. A strict interpretation of the Quran would result in condemnation of insurance; and in the Arab world only Saudi Arabia interprets it thus. However, insurance companies can operate in Saudi Arabia if they are registered elsewhere. *The Times*, 'Easy marriage of pragmatism and principle', a special report on *Insurance in the Arab World*, 27 November, 1978, p. II.
14. Radcliffe-Brown (1957), *A Natural Science of Society*, p. 87, as quoted in Nisbet (1972), *Social Change*, pp. 14-15. The first type of change is called 'readjustment change'; the second 'change of type'.
15. As has been suggested by many writers on modernization; see, for example, Lerner (1958), *The Passing of Traditional Society*; Kerr *et al.* (1960), *Industrialism and Industrial Man*; Levy (1965), *Modernization and the Structure of Societies*; Parsons (1966), *Societies: Evolutionary and Comparative Perspectives*; and Inkeles and Smith (1974), *Becoming Modern*.
16. Eisenstadt (1977), 'Convergence and Divergence of Modern and Modernizing Societies', p. 4; and Lauer (1971), 'The Scientific Legitimation of Fallacy', pp. 881-9.
17. Riggs (1964), *Administration in Developing Countries: The Theory of Prismatic Society*; and Riggs (1966), *Thailand: The Modernization of Traditional Polity*.
18. On Lebanon, see Khalaf and Shwayri (1966), 'Family Firms and Industrial Development'; and Farsoun (1970), 'Family Structure and Society in Modern Lebanon'. On Nigeria, see Ogionwo (1969), 'The Adoption of Technological Innovations in Nigeria', Ph.D. Thesis, University of Leeds; and Onyemelukwe (1973), *Men and Management in Contemporary Africa*. On Indonesia, see Geertz (1963), *Peddlers and Princes*.
19. Shaker (1972), 'Modernization of the Developing Nations: The Case of Saudi Arabia', Ph.D. diss., Purdue University, p. 383.
20. For criticisms of the 'convergence' school, see Desai (ed.), (1971), *Modernization of Underdeveloped Societies*, 2 vols, Eisenstadt (1973), *Tradition, Change, and Modernity*; Eisenstadt (1977); and Coser (1975), 'Structure and Conflict'.

21. Gusfield (1978), 'Review Essay', p. 446.
22. Shaker (1972) p. 383.
23. 'The Assertion of Islam', a leading article by *The Times* newspaper, London, 16 November, 1978. In Egypt, there has been a strong resurgence of Muslim fundamentalism, particularly among university students, young people, and labour union leaders. In fact, the labour union leaders have recently submitted to the Egyptian government a labour manifesto whereby the Constitution and the Islamic *Sharī'a* shall be the main sources of the law. See *Al-Ummāl* (Cairo), published by the General Federation of Egyptian Trade Unions, 17 July 1978, pp. 7-8.
24. Here, neo-traditionalist suggests a new form rather than a revival of the old; it is used as in 'neo-colonialism' rather than in 'neo-classical'.
25. See Prothro and Diab (1974), *Changing Family Patterns in the Arab East*, pp. 206-7.
26. Compared with 46 per cent in the major industrialized nations (Source: UN, *Yearbook of Labour Statistics*, 1977). The lower percentage is, of course, due to several reasons, one of which is the low employment of women. Another reason is the high percentage (44 per cent) of population under 15 years of age, compared with 25 per cent in five major industrial countries. (Source: *Ibid.*)
27. The twenty-seven executives were from all six countries. No significant relationship was found between their attitudes on this social change and their age, social or educational background.
28. For an excellent discussion of ambivalence and how it is built into normative structures, see Merton (1976), *Sociological Ambivalence and Other Essays*.
29. Merton and Barber (1963), 'Sociological Ambivalence'.
30. Sharabi (1961), 'Political and Intellectual Attitudes of the Young Arab Generation'; also see van Nieuwenhuijze (1971), *Sociology of the Middle East*, pp. 187, 656-7; and Khalid (1977), 'The Sociocultural Determinants of Arab Diplomacy', pp. 131-4.
31. The other characteristics will be discussed in the final chapter when we examine the implications of this study for expatriates or foreign businessmen.
32. See Chapter 6, section entitled: 'A preference for "informality"', for further comments on the 'business is business' approach.

8 Conclusion and Implications

> This is not the end. It is not even the beginning of the end. But it is, perhaps, the end of the beginning.
>
> W. S. Churchill, 1874–1965
> Speech at the Mansion House,
> 10 November, 1942

In the preceding chapters we have explored many topics at different levels of analysis: societal, organizational and individual. The aim was to sketch a portrait of the Arab executive against the background of a changing social landscape.[1] It is time now to stand back, as it were, and survey the main themes of that landscape. Themes that kept insisting upon being dragged into many of the topics we have been discussing.

THE IMPORTANCE OF ENVIRONMENTAL FACTORS

Throughout this book, we have seen the pervasive influence of the environment on business conditions, on social behaviour and on the attitudes of the Arab executive. Our approach has been to view the executive as part of a business-oriented social system (that is his organization) which, in turn, is embedded in his wider environment. Again, this environment is made up of socio-cultural values and norms, and social structural elements (institutions, groups and sets of social relations and roles). In each of the preceding chapters we have witnessed how the environment (despite its diversity and variety) is influencing the thinking and behaviour of the Arab executive.

For example, earlier in this book we saw how the economic and political instability as well as the recent economic boom are affecting business conditions. Furthermore, we examined how the formal institutions and groups are superimposed on the more powerful family and friendship groups. As a result there is a strong incentive for the Arab executive to rely upon family and friendship ties (connections) in managing his business.

The executive's time and performance are also influenced by socio-cultural values and norms. One of the most serious problems for the executive was the low value placed on time by people around him. We also found that the executive's role in the community and organization is congruent with society's paternalistic and familial nature. The environmental influence was apparent in the executive's styles of decision making and conflict management. We discovered the strong influence of traditional consultation on decision-making styles, and how the authority structure outside the organization is reflected by the executive's attitudes towards conflict management.

The environmental influence was perhaps most prominent when the Arab executive's interpersonal style was examined. Here we found that social values and norms, as well as social structural elements, encourage the executive to use 'personalized' and 'informal' approaches when dealing with his employees and with people outside his organization. Finally, the economic development and the modernization processes which are now taking place in Arab countries are creating ambivalent feelings for the Arab executive.

In short, the environment has a great influence on the executive's thinking and behaviour. This is not to advocate societal or social structural determinism. On the contrary, throughout the book we have attempted to highlight the strain and tension experienced by the executive, and we have repeatedly emphasized the executive's role, not only as a target of social influence but also as an agent of social change. In fact, had we considered only one side of what is obviously at least a two-sided phenomenon, we would have been committing a serious error. Hence, our second theme: the role of the executive in social change.

THE EXECUTIVE AS A CHANGE AGENT

Although the Arab executive is constrained to a large extent by societal and social structure forces, it is clear that these forces are not immune from change. Values, norms, institutions, groups, roles and so on do indeed change. Even the Islamic *Sharī'a* (Sacred Law) is seen 'metaphorically as an organic creature, growing, developing and evolving; attached with a strong link of interdependence to its society, adapting to its needs, and changing with different circumstances'.[2]

Arab executives can, and often do, play an important role in this social change. They may do that consciously or unconsciously, and they may also do it for self-interests or community interests. Whatever their motives, we have seen that the executives are indeed agents of social change in several of the topics we have discussed. For example, some executives are minimizing the fusion of their business, social, and personal lives – trying to separate or compartmentalize these main aspects of their lives. Other executives are actively discouraging the traditional open-door policy by insisting that their employees go through the organizational hierarchy. Still others are attempting to overcome the barriers to better utilization of time. Finally, nearly all executives are encouraging the use of highly sophisticated equipment and machinery within their organizations.[3]

There is, however, one area worthy of special mention to which some Arab executives felt they could increase their present contribution, namely, education.[4] Here education is used in the broadest sense of the word to include acquisition of knowledge and skills, especially managerial and vocational skills. Development of human resources is a never ending process and the executives, as employers and members of society, take over this heavy responsibility where the schools and universities leave off.

Finally, as change agents, Arab executives are bound to influence the process of modernization which is now taking place in Arab countries. The nature of this emerging modernization is the concern of our third theme.

MODERNIZATION WITHOUT SACRIFICING TRADITIONS

With modernization and the concomitant use of science and technology, it is very likely that Arab society will lose some of its traditional ways. Most Arabs, including our executives, would welcome the loss of certain characteristics which they perceive as obstacles to progress. For instance, the low value of time, poor organizational and work habits and the dislike of manual work. The predicament for the Arabs, however, is how to preserve their society's specifically Arab identity or character; also how to avoid the potential ills which often accompany extensive industrialization such as alienation and anomie;[5] emotional and spiritual decadence;[6] and other related problems which for many social scientists have marked the decline or end of ideology in post-industrial societies.[7]

In the preceding chapter, we have discussed various aspects of the intricate modernization process. The plausibility of a 'mixture' of the traditional and modern was suggested; and the ambivalent feelings of executives towards the old and new were discussed. We have also pointed out that there are no easy answers to the perplexing questions posed by modernization. There is, however, one thought worth emphasizing, namely, that social change can have both positive and negative aspects for the members of a given society, as so many social scientists have observed.[8] More specifically, that social change when pushed too rapidly may result in a negative backlash, especially if traditional values and norms are threatened.[9]

Clearly it is difficult to ascertain what the future holds for the Arab world. Social changes are not uniform in all parts of the Arab world, and are not likely to be so in the near future. Various ideologies exist (see Chapter 2) which range from secular to non-secular, from rightist to leftist, and so on – all searching for an *Arab* ideology. Most Arab political leaders, businessmen, academics and the like, would probably agree with the following conclusions reached by a writer on Arab history and contemporary affairs:

> No one can tell what political and social institutions the Arab people will have developed by the end of this momentous century. All that can be said with certainty is that, however much they derive from foreign movements and ideas, they will have a specifically Arab and Islamic character.[10]

IMPLICATIONS

Throughout this study the author has attempted, whenever feasible, to point out the implications of the findings for the several parties to whom this study may be of interst. The parties include: the Arab executive himself; his Arab employees; expatriates and foreign businessmen; management consultants and teachers; and finally social scientists and researchers. Many of the implications were clear and self-explanatory; spelling them out here would simply lead to lengthy recapitulation. There are, however, three important subjects for which the implications of this study must be explicitly emphasized and discussed:

I. management training and development;
II. expatriate employees and foreign businessmen;
III. future research.

I. Management Training and Development

Before we discuss the implications of this study for training and development of Arab managers, we must examine briefly the current debate on what constitutes 'management principles' and whether these are transferable across nations.

For the past twenty years, management teachers and researchers have been engaged in a debate over the extent to which Western (usually American) management principles, practices and knowhow are exportable to other cultures.[11] Although there seems to be some agreement about what functions are performed by managers and organizations, there is disagreement about the skills, styles and techniques needed for performing these functions. The managerial functions are usually defined as the basic 'classical' ones of planning, organizing, controlling and directing (some management writers include other activities such as staffing, coordinating, and so on).[12] It is also agreed that business organizations appear to differentiate their activities by their specialized functions such as production, marketing, finance, personnel, and so on.

The debate, however, is mainly due to questions such as these: what constitutes 'good' management principles and practices? What about the recent contingency (situational) theories? Do we really know enough about the management process within a given culture to justify exporting it to other cultures? And if so, do we know enough about these other cultures to enable us to judge which management practices are applicable and which are not? These, then, are the issues which are likely to keep the above debate topical and lively.

The findings of this study strongly suggest that certain managerial styles and skills required in the Arab world may differ from those advocated or practised in Western cultures. Let us look at some of the practices which may not be applicable in most Arab organizations.

1. Joint decision making (or participative leadership style) is unlikely to be widely adopted by Arab managements, even for decisions which are best suited for this style. The major reasons for this are: (a) subordinates might view it as a sign of weakness on part of the executive: they expect to be consulted, but not to make the final decision; (b) Arab executives prefer and feel more at ease with the consultative decision-making style; and (c) Arab executives and subordinates tend to dislike team-work.
2. Conflict resolution and problem-solving techniques which rely on open confrontation such as T-Groups or Managerial Grid are unlikely to succeed in Arab organizations. Most Arabs are very sensitive to criticism, open confrontation, directness, and frankness especially when in front of a group. Deference to authority, face-saving, manliness, pride and loyalty – all of these act as serious obstacles to open confrontation.
3. Personnel selection or promotion based only on efficiency or achievement may frequently be violated in view of the importance in the Arab world of nepotism, loyalty, and personal connections.
4. Impersonal and formal systems or styles would be at a great disadvantage in an organizational and societal environment which is more person-oriented than task or role-oriented. The paternalistic nature of management would also discourage formality and impersonality.
5. Certain quantitative management systems or decision-making techniques (for example, Operational Research) which rely on stable or advanced infrastructures are often not usable. The business, economic, and governmental infrastructures in the Arab world are not well developed yet. Accurate information and data are scarce; manpower and materials are not easily available; governmental laws and regulations are unstable (changing on short notice); and governmental red tape is widespread. Executives often rely on intuition, 'gut feelings', or connections to get things done.

Indeed some of the Western managerial practices may not only be inapplicable but may also be harmful if applied without adaptation to Arab environments. This would apply particularly to those managerial practices which deal with the personal aspects of management (points 1 to 4, above).

What, then, is needed for the training and development of Arab executives? There are at least five managerial skills which the present author feels can be beneficial to the development of present and especially future Arab executives.

1. *Conceptual skills.* The conceptual skills encourage the executive to see the 'whole' picture in terms of its detail. We have suggested earlier the analogy of the executive as a radar scanning his environment, and the increased use of the 'helicopter view' both of which increase the sensitivity to the complex processes in a fast-changing environment. The conceptual skills would lead to improved corporate policies and strategies which are in keeping with Arab environments.
2. *Delegation.* By more frequent use of delegation the executive can (a) save his time; (b) train his employees; (c) utilize his employees' existing skills and resources; and (d) motivate his employees. We have discussed this issue in Chapter 4 where the findings indicated a low level of delegation.
3. *Conflict management.* In Chapter 5 we suggested that executives should encourage opposition (devil's advocate and so on) from subordinates. Training can help the executive change his own attitudes, as well as his employees' expectations, towards 'reasonable and constructive' opposition.
4. *Management of time.* The management of time in the Arab business world is as much a management of social relations problem as it is proper utilization of one's working hours. Time is precious but it has many competing factors (Chapter 7) which constrain and complicate management of time. Skills must be learnt to deal with both facets of this problem.
5. *Change agent skills.* Earlier in this chapter we discussed the role of the executive as an agent of change. Skills appropriate to this role would include skills of introducing change, managing resistance to change, and understanding the process of change and its consequences.

These five skills have been selected for special emphasis because of their relevance to the findings of this study. Clearly, there are many other managerial skills and functions of equal significance ranging from leadership or human relations skills to the functional skills in marketing or finance.

II. Expatriate Employees and Foreign Businessmen

A deeper understanding of the Arab executive and his environment can be extremely beneficial to expatriates and foreign businessmen. The cost of failure to adjust to a new culture or the cost of business mistakes can be very high for non-Arabs wishing to work in or with Arab organizations. The need for cooperation between Arabs and non-Arabs is mutual. There is a great shortage of skilled manpower in the oil-producing countries; and the huge oil wealth has created trade and business opportunities in the whole region for both Arab and foreign enterprises.

Although the scope of the present study did not include the examination of problems facing expatriates/foreign businessmen who are engaged in business in the Arab world, it did, however, examine the attitudes of a few expatriates towards the Arab executive, and also the attitudes of the Arab executive towards expatriates/foreign businessmen. This was done mainly to increase our understanding of the Arab executive, but it has also provided information which may have important implications for expatriates/foreign businessmen.

This information helps the non-Arab in two ways. First, by understanding the Arab executive (and the environmental elements which influence him), the non-Arab should be able to reduce the culture shock which is so often experienced by people interacting with members of a society different from their own. This should speed the adaptation and adjustment process, and is likely to yield benefits to both the Arab and non-Arab. A second way of reducing the cultural barrier would be for the non-Arab to receive feedback about his own image as perceived by Arab executives. This study provides some feedback. It was accomplished by asking Arab executives which characteristics they admired most and which they strongly disliked about expatriates/foreign businessmen. Most of the responses were presented in the various sections of the previous two chapters. Let us now summarize these responses in Table 8.1. The strongly disliked characteristic of arrogance and sense

TABLE 8.1 The image of expatriates/foreign businessmen as perceived by Arab executives

*Most admired characteristics**	*Frequency of mention†*	*Strongly disliked characteristics*	*Frequency of mention†*
1. High value and respect for time	18	1. Arrogance and sense of superiority	21
2. Productivity and hard work	15	2. Inability or unwillingness to understand or respect local traditions/mentality	15
3. Technical know-how and competence	10	3. 'Inhumane' treatment of employees	11
4. Organized and systematic approach to work	10	4. Extremism in 'business is business' approach	9
5. Dedication and conscientiousness to work	9	5. Money-orientation only	6
6. Discipline	5		
7. Accuracy and precision	5		

* As presented and discussed in Chapter 7.
† Characteristics mentioned by five or more executives.

of superiority warrants a brief remark. There are at least three possible explanations for this image: (1) the behaviour of non-Arabs toward Arabs is actually arrogant; (2) the behaviour seems to be arrogant to some Arabs because they feel they are lacking in certain skills; or (3) the non-Arab's behaviour is so impersonal and formal that it unintentionally conveys arrogance. Of course, it is likely that a combination of these explanations is at work here.[13] The investigation of this characteristic, and all the others shown in Table 8.1, is clearly an important future research project, which of course must take into account not only the Arab executive's perceptions but also those held by the expatriates and foreign businessmen.

Finally, the findings presented in this study are merely a start to the necessary and valuable cross-cultural training for expatriates (and their spouses) as well as foreign businessmen wishing to work in the Arab world.

III. Future Research

The approach used in this study has influenced the suggestions for future research. Let us, therefore, briefly restate the reasoning behind this approach. The present study of the Arab executive has been exploratory. It has also avoided direct comparison of Arab executives with those from other societies. References to Western societies were occasionally made only to illuminate the topics under discussion. Thus the reader was encouraged to compare the Arabs with whichever society he is most familiar. There were two reasons for this type of approach. First, the dearth of systematic research on business and management in the Arab world encourages exploratory work and discourages premature comparison. Second, having examined most of the recent literature on cross-cultural research, the present author is persuaded that Karlene Roberts' conclusion, based on her critical review ten years ago of cross-cultural research, is still applicable today. Roberts concluded at that time that:

> Organizations are rarely viewed as parts of their environments, yet understanding organizational-environmental interactions seems a major practical reason for engaging in cross-cultural research.[14]

Roberts went on to recommend that:

> . . . more effort be invested in understanding behaviour in a *single culture*, developing middle-level theories to guide explorations, and seeking the *relevant questions* to ask across cultures (p. 347, emphasis added).

This study is only the beginning of the quest towards a better understanding of the Arab executive. Future research is direly needed into several areas of which the following seem to be the most urgent:

1. Following up, elaborating and testing the large number of hypotheses suggested by this study. Added emphasis must be placed on explaining the similarities and differences between executives from the various Arab countries.[15]
2. In order to complement the present findings, future research must focus on the expectations and attitudes of Arab employees at the middle and lower organizational levels.
3. Future studies of the adjustment and adaptation problems of expatriates working in the Arab world will add a new and different perspective to this subject. The results should be valuable both to expatriates and Arab executives.
4. As more empirical data on the behaviour and thinking of Arab executives and their employees become available, cross-cultural research will then become more feasible and meaningful.

The researcher, like the management consultant and teacher, must bear in mind the main findings of this book. These findings emphasized the strong links that exist between the Arab executive and his environment. Further, the researcher must become aware and sensitive to the fact that both the environment and members of Arab society are going through a critical period in their history. Indeed, the Arabs have now left the 1970s, their *decade of awareness*, and have entered the 1980s, their *decade of action* and rapid change.

NOTES

1. To use R. Nisbet's metaphors of the sociological portraits and landscapes; see Nisbet (1976), *Sociology as an Art Form.*

2. Yamani (1972), 'Islamic Law and Contemporary Issues', p. 53.
3. See especially Chapters 3, 6, and 7 for more examples.
4. Several large organizations have their own vocational training centres; in addition, as mentioned in Chapter 7, several companies pay for the university education of prospective managers.
5. Black (1966), *Dynamics of Modernization: A Study in Comparative History*, pp. 27–34.
6. Nisbet (1976), pp. 132–5.
7. Lipset (1976), 'Social Structure and Social Change', pp. 190–203.
8. Robock *et al.* (1977), *International Business and Multinational Enterprise*, p. 338.
9. Events in Pakistan, and more recently in Iran, support this observation.
10. Peter Mansfield (1976), *The Arabs*, p. 552.
11. Richman (1965), 'Significance of Cultural Variables', p. 292. See also Newman (1970), 'Is Management Exportable?'; and Evan (1976), *Organization Theory*, Chapter 15.
12. The 'classical' functions of management were introduced by Henri Fayol in 1916.
13. One expatriate felt that this arrogance has been reversed in some Arab countries in the past few years.
14. Roberts (1970), 'On Looking at an Elephant', p. 347.
15. At least one more North African country should be included in future studies, such as Algeria, Libya, Morocco, or Tunisia.

Appendix 1: Methodology and Data Analysis

METHODOLOGY

The fifty-two Arab executives interviewed for this study were purposefully selected to meet a number of requirements. First, they came from three non-oil exporting countries: Egypt, Jordan, and Lebanon; and from three oil-exporting countries: Kuwait, Saudi Arabia, and the United Arab Emirates. Second, an attempt was made to select executives from three organizational size categories: small (180–499 employees), medium (500–999 employees), and large (over 1000 employees). Third, from each country we attempted to select top executives from organizations whose nature of business was classified as follows: manufacturing; trade and services (many of these firms were in construction and contracting);[1] and conglomerate (firms with diversified activities, usually including manufacturing). For the other variables, see Table A.1.

Some of the executives were selected from *Major Companies of the Arab World*;[2] others were suggested by various chambers of commerce, friends, relatives, or business associates. In each country, the author typically began the field work with a list of fifteen to twenty executives of whom six to ten, depending on the country, were interviewed. The typical semi-structured interview lasted 1 hour and 20 minutes. The executives were given the choice of conducting the interview in either Arabic or English. About 40 per cent chose Arabic, 40 per cent English, and about 20 per cent used both languages. Most of the interviews took place in ten Arab cities (in six countries), but a few were conducted in London.

DATA ANALYSIS

Due to the exploratory nature of this study, most of the data collected were based on nominal- and ordinal-level scales. The simple χ^2 test was used on such data.

TABLE A.1 A statistical profile of Arab executives and their organizations

Country	N	Executives' age: mean (range)	University education				Social background			Status		Organizational size*				Organizational ownership			Nature of business		
			None	Arab	Western	Mixed	Tribal	Rural	Urban	Owner	Non-owner	Small	Medium	Large	Mean Size	Family	Partnership	Government	Mfg.	Trade and service	Conglomerate
Egypt	9	52 (40–62)	—	7	1	1	—	1	9	3	6	2	2	5	3561	3	—	6	7	2	—
Jordan	10	52 (39–69)	1	5	1	3	—	7	3	7	3	7	2	1	527	4	5	1	7	2	1
Kuwait	9	42 (33–52)	2	—	1	6	—	8	2	6	3	1	4	4	2457	7	1	1	1	5	3
Lebanon	8	44 (33–53)	1	5	1	1	—	4	4	4	4	4	2	2	2287	1	7	—	3	5	—
Saudi Arabia	10	42 (29–50)	2	—	2	6	1	4	5	6	4	2	2	6	1402	3	3	4	5	3	2
UAE	6	45 (38–53)	2	1	—	3	2	1	3	3	3	2	2	2	1872	2	4	—	1	4	1
Totals	52	46 (29–69)	8	18	6	20	3	25	24	29	23	18	14	20	2482	20	20	12	24	21	7

* Organizational size: Small=180–499 employees; Medium=500–999 employees; Large=over 1000 employees.

In Chapter 4, however, the power-sharing continuum (Figure 4.1) was defined and measured by a four-point equal interval scale. The equal interval assumption allowed us to use multiple regression and correlational techniques.

Interval Scale

The assumption of interval scale is consistent with assumptions made by other researchers. Thus, Heller,[3] using a similar continuum, assumed a five-point equal interval scale. While Vroom and Yetton[4] developed an ordered metric scale which resulted in equal intervals between their three major decision styles, excluding their two minor styles A11 and C11 (see Table 4.1). The values for the three major styles were: autocratic (A1)=0, consultative (C1)=5, and group decision (G11)=10; styles which closely correspond to our styles 1, 2, and 3. Vroom and Jago[5] have extended the Vroom and Yetton model to include individual problems and have, therefore, included delegation (D1) on their scale assigning a value of 10 to it. The present research assumes that delegation, Style 4, is also separated from Style 3 by an equal distance (see Figure 4.1).

Decisional categories

The seven decisions given to the executives were broken down into three categories: personnel, departmental, and organizational. This was based on the nature of the decisions as well as on the high intercorrelation between the decisions within each category. For example, the first three decisions were highly interrelated, and were not consistently related to any other category of decisions (see Figure A.1).

Multiple regression analysis

Some of the independent variables were interrelated.[6] To control for any spurious relationships and to isolate only those variables which contribute substantially to the variation in decision-making styles, multiple regression statistical technique was used.

First, dummy variables were created in order to dichotomize the nominal-scale variables and to incorporate them in the parametric analyses. Second, Pearson product–moment corre-

	Personnel decisions			*Departmental decisions*			*Organizational decisions*
Decision*	1	2	3	4	5	7	6
1	–						
2	0.59	–					
3	0.52	0.62	–				
4	0.38	0.09	0.24	–			
5	0.06	0.07	-0.07	0.28	–		
7	0.08	0.29	0.08	0.15	0.30	–	
6	0.07	0.13	-0.04	0.10	0.25	0.19	–

Coefficient alpha = 0.884 (Decisions 1, 2 and 3)

Coefficient alpha = 0.746 (Decisions 4, 5 and 7)

FIGURE A.1 Pearson correlation matrix (7 decisions)

* For details of decisions 1 to 7, see Interview Schedule, Appendix 2, or Chapter 4.

lation coefficients were calculated between all independent variables and the three categories of decisions (the dependent variables). This gave us zero-order correlations. Next, partial correlation methods provided us with first-order and second-order correlations. Finally, variables were retained in the regression equation if their marginal contribution to the proportion of the variance accounted for was significantly greater than zero, all other variables being controlled.

Table A.2 illustrates the calculations of the amount of variance explained by the independent variables for the organizational decision category (Decision 6). The significant contributions came from the first and second variables only; accounting for 20.31 per cent of the variance in decisional style (for Decision 6). The same procedure as above was used for the other two decisional categories; see Table 4.6.

TABLE A.2 Analysis of variance (organizational decision 6)

Independent variable	*Explained sums of squares*	*Unexplained sums of squares*	AR^2	*F ratio*	*df*	*Significance*
1. Lebanon	146.94	—	9.55	6.38	1,50	0.025
2. No university education	304.25	993.82	10.76	7.76	1,49	0.01
3. Kuwait	358.05	940.03	2.75	2.75	1,48	N.S.

AR^2 is the adjusted square of multiple correlation coefficient. It is adjusted for the number of independent variables in the equation and the number of cases.

N.S. = not significant.

NOTES

1. Organizations whose business was restricted to management of banks, hospitals, and hotels were not included.
2. *Major Companies of the Arab World*, Graham and Trotman Ltd., London, 1977.
3. Heller (1971), *Managerial Decison-Making*, p. 53.
4. Vroom and Yetton (1973), *Leadership and Decision-Making*, pp. 65–71.
5. Vroom and Jago (1974), 'Decision Making as a Social Process', pp. 743–69.
6. The intercorrelations were not high enough to cause problems of multicollinearity. The highest correlation among independent variables was 0.46.

Appendix 2: The Interview Schedule

THE ARAB EXECUTIVE

This research work is intended for the doctorate degree in business management, University of London. Personal interviews are needed with senior Arab executives in several Arab countries. Each interview will cover the following topics:

I. General information
II. The executive and his environment
III. Decision making
IV. Interpersonal relations
V. Attitude towards time and change

Your personal help would be deeply appreciated. It would also contribute to the advancement of knowledge on this subject.

Farid A. Muna

I. General information

Code number: ....

Nature of business: ....
Location of head office: ....
Principal countries of operation: ....
Total number of employees: ....
Number of other Arabs:................. Non-Arabs:.....................
Age of company: .... Type of ownership: ....
How long have you been with the company?: ....
Present position: .... How long in this position?: ....
To whom do you report (if applicable)?: ....
Number of managers reporting directly to you: ....
Previous positions with this organization: *Duration*
....
....
....

Where *Positions* *Duration*
Other work experience: ....
....
....

Where *Public or Private*
Education: High School...

Where *Degree* *Subject*
College or University...
....

Who ran courses *Subject* *Duration*
Training courses: ....
....

Languages:...
Age:.................... Place of birth:.............. Nationality: ....
In which place did you spend most of your *first* 18 years of life?:...
Marital status:.................... Wife's nationality: ....
Is she a close relative?: ....
No. of children:........... Age range:...

No. of children:............ Age range:..
How would you describe your relations with your extended family?:..
....
Outside activities (hobbies, clubs, groups, etc.): ....
....

II. The Executive and His Environment

1. What are the main business activities, duties or responsibilities on which you find yourself spending most of your time (in and out of the organization)?:

	Approx. % of time
....	....
....	....
....	....
....	....

2. When making the following decisions what are the main factors you would take into consideration:
   (a) Hiring a national manager:
   (a manager at the lowest level you would normally be concerned with)
   (b) Hiring a non-national manager: Other Arabs..............
   Non-Arabs................

3. In your community (social and business circles) who are the one or two persons whose thoughts and opinions you respect most highly? Why? (No names needed, only role or social status):

4. Do you ever consult persons/groups from outside your firm when making business decisions? If so, whom, under what circumstances and why?

5. Because of your high position in this company, what are some of the things that are expected of you by:
   (a) people in your community?:
   (b) top people in government?:
   (c) your extended family?:
   (d) your employees?:

6. Could you please mention some of the ideas, programmes, or changes that you as an executive would like to implement, but find yourself restricted from doing so because of Arab traditions, customs, and values (in and out of the organization):

7. Do you find that your work and your position as a senior executive influence your family life or your community life? How and in what ways? Please, give some examples:

8. When making serious *personal* decisions individuals often ask themselves: 'What would *people* think or say if I do this or that?' If and when this happens to you, could you please rank in the order of importance the type of people you would have in mind:

9. How do you perceive your role as a senior executive both inside and outside your company?:

10. What do you consider to be the main problems or obstacles which you, as a senior executive in the Arab world, are facing at the present time (with examples)?

III. Decision making

Decision making can be considered as a prime factor in management. In fact, some writers go to the extent of defining management and decision making as synonymous terms. There are, however, many ways and methods in which business decisions are made. Rarely is there one perfect method that can be applied to all decisions in all situations. Below are four alternative methods that apply to relations with subordinates:

I. The decision is made by you, no consultation or discussion with subordinate(s).
II. Prior consultation with subordinate(s); he/they may or may not influence your final decision.
III. You and your subordinate(s) *together* analyse the problem and come to a decision – subordinates have as much influence as you have on the final (majority) decision.
IV. Ask subordinate(s) to make decision on his/their own.

The above possible alternatives can be applied not only to subordinates, but also to colleagues, superiors, and others (both in and out of the organization). Please indicate which of these alternatives you would normally use to arrive at the following decisions:

1. The decision to promote one of the employees directly supervised by one of your subordinates.
2. The decision to discipline one of the employees directly supervised by one of your subordinates.
3. The decision to terminate the services of one of the employees directly supervised by one of your subordinates.
4. The decision to reduce the total workforce by 20 per cent.
5. The decision to increase the workforce in a subordinate's department/division.
6. The decision to introduce a new product/enter a new market/take on a new project/expand existing work facilities.
7. The decision to alter/modify the formal organization chart (changes in job and/or responsibilities, re-organization) in your subordinate's department/division.

In your role as a senior Arab executive, you may occasionally be called upon to deal with disagreements between yourself and a person reporting directly to you. Could you please tell me how you have handled such disagreements in the past. For example, let us suppose that you and one of your staff completely disagree about the promotion of a key employee working for him. Please indicate how you would in the end deal with this conflict:

(a) When you favour it and he opposes it:
(b) You oppose it and he favours it:

As a second example, let us suppose that you and one of the employees who reports directly to you completely disagree about an expansion plan (or a new product or a new project) which involves and affects his department/division. Please indicate how you would in the end deal with this conflict:

(a) When you favour it and he opposes it:
(b) You oppose it and he favours it:

Finally, can you think of proverbs or sayings (in Arabic or English) which guide you or influence your thinking when handling these types of disagreement?

IV. Interpersonal Relations

1. In your own community, to what extent do people rely on family ties, friendships or other means of influence to get things done, or done faster? Examples, please.

   Do you feel that this is a help or a hindrance to you in the performance of your duties as a senior Arab executive? Examples, please:

2. When would you use *formal* methods of getting business done within the Company, and why?:

   When would you use *informal* methods of getting business done within the Company, and why?:

3. Let us suppose that a foreign friend of yours wants to do business in this country; what would you tell him about our customs and practices regarding the giving and taking of gifts and other acts of reciprocity, especially how these practices are used in business?:

4. The ideal employee would be, among other things, *both* loyal and efficient. But, unfortunately, this does not always occur. In such cases, then, which would you prefer to have, *employees* in your company who are:
   (a) more loyal to the company?:....................................
   (b) more efficient on the job?:..

   What about your preference concerning your own immediate subordinate... Would you prefer your *immediate subordinate* to be:
   (a) more loyal to you?:..
   (b) more efficient in his work?: ....

5. During the past few weeks or so, please think of the employees who have asked, and were able to contact you or have a meeting (interview) with you. Do they belong to:
   ____ Any level of the company (without going through hierarchy)?

____ Any level, provided they go through proper hierarchy (channels)?
____ Managerial level only?
____ Immediate subordinates only?

6. How often do you personally give instructions to employees at the middle or lower levels without going through their immediate supervisors?:
____ Very often
____ Occasionally
____ Seldom

7. (a) When starting a business discussion, would you normally spend a period of time offering greetings, refreshments, and social talk of a general nature?:

(b) In which situations and with whom would you do this?:

(c) Do you feel that this custom is beneficial or is it mostly a waste of time? Why?

8. What are some of the characteristics of the expatriates employed here (if no expatriates, then foreign businessmen) which you admire most? Why?

What about characteristics which you strongly dislike? Why?

9. What are some of the managerial practices of foreign businessmen working in the major industrial nations which you believe can be learned and then applied to your business here? Why?

10. If you were to describe the personal traits and characteristics that contributed to your success, which would be the most important ones?:

V. Attitude Towards Time and Change

1. What are the most common reasons which occasionally cause you to be late to:
   A business meeting or appointment?:
   A social occasion (lunch, dinner)?:

2. What proverb or saying would best represent your views and attitudes towards time (in Arabic or English)?:

3. Please indicate on the scale below which period of time best describes your expectations when undertaking the following:

   (a) Payback on capital investment

______	______	______	______	______
Under 1 yr.	1–2 yr.	3–5 yr.	6–10 yr.	Over 10 yr.

   (b) Company-wide planning

______	______	______	______	______
Under 1 yr.	1–2 yr.	3–5 yr.	6–10 yr.	Over 10 yr.

   (c) Looking ahead in managerial training and development

______	______	______	______	______
Under 1 yr.	1–2 yr.	3–5 yr.	6–10 yr.	Over 10 yr.

4. Could you please name some of the happenings that have had a direct effect on your business, but over which you have had little control:

5. Do you ever take steps or measures to prevent undesirable events from occurring? Examples, please?

6. Do you carry life insurance? ____ Yes ____ No
   If not, why not?

7. Change and innovation in the Arab world are phenomena which are fairly easy for a person to see and feel. In your position as a senior executive, where do you get your ideas about changes and innovations which you feel can be introduced in your company? Please name these sources of ideas:

8. How do you feel about the following changes?:

(a) Women holding high managerial positions in business firms.

	______	______	______	______
Do you:	Strongly favour	Favour	Oppose	Strongly oppose

Likelihood of it happening in the next 5–10 years:

______	______	______	______
Very likely	Likely	Not likely	Highly unlikely

(b) An increase in the introduction of sophisticated scientific systems and equipment to business (computers, latest machinery, etc.) when and where applicable.

	______	______	______	______
Do You:	Strongly favour	Favour	Oppose	Strongly oppose

Likelihood of it happening in the next 5–10 years:

______	______	______	______
Very likely	Likely	Not likely	Highly unlikely

(c) The newer generation to gain more freedom and independence from family, customs, religion, and traditions. (For example, a move from the extended family to the nuclear one and so on.)

	______	______	______	______
Do you:	Strongly favour	Favour	Oppose	Strongly oppose

Likelihood of it happening in the next 5–10 years:

______	______	______	______
Very likely	Likely	Not likely	Highly unlikely

9. Before we end this interview (we have indeed covered many topics and subjects) is there anything else you would like to discuss, or voice an opinion on, which is related to this subject?

Bibliography

Ali, Abdullah Yusuf (1975), *The Holy Qur'ān: Text, Translation and Commentary* (The Muslim Students' Association of the USA and Canada).

Antoun, R. T. (1965), 'Conservatism and Change in the Village Community: A Jordanian Case Study', *Human Organization*, 24, pp. 1–10.

Al-Awaji, Ibrahim M. (1971), 'Bureaucracy and Society in Saudi Arabia', Ph.D. dissertation, University of Virginia.

Ayoub, Victor F. (1965), 'Conflict Resolution and Social Reorganization in a Lebanese Village', *Human Organization*, 24, pp. 11–17.

Badre, A. Y. and Siksek S. G. (1960), *Manpower and Oil in Arab Countries* (Beirut: American University of Beirut).

Barnard, Chester I. (1938), *The Functions of the Executive* (Cambridge, Mass.: Harvard University Press).

Berger, Morroe (1957), *Bureaucracy and Society in Modern Egypt: A Study of the Higher Civil Service* (Princeton, NJ: Princeton University Press).

—— (1962), *The Arab World Today* (London: Weidenfeld & Nicolson).

Bill, James and Leiden, Carl (1974), *The Middle East, Politics and Power* (Boston: Allyn & Bacon).

Black, C. E. (1966), *Dynamics of Modernization: A Study in Comparative History* (New York: Harper & Row).

Blau, Peter M. (1964), *Exchange and Power in Social Life* (New York: Wiley).

—— (1976), 'Parameters of Social Structure', in P. M. Blau (ed.) *Approaches to the Study of Social Structure* (London: Open Books).

Cartwright, D. (1965), 'Influence, Leadership and Control', in J. G. March (ed.) *Handbook of Organizations* (Chicago: Rand McNally).

Casadio, Gian Pablo (1976), *The Economic Challenge of the Arabs* (London: Saxon House/D. C. Heath).

Central Statistical Office (1979), *Financial Statistics* (London: HMSO). (March).

Coon, Carleton S. (1958), *Caravan: The Story of the Middle East* (rev. ed.) (New York: Holt).

Coser, L. A. (1956), *The Functions of Social Conflict* (New York: Free Press).

—— (1976), 'Structure and Conflict' in P. M. Blau (ed.) *Approaches to the Study of Social Structure* (London: Open Books).

Dahl, R. A. (1957), 'The Concept of Power', *Behavioural Science*, 2, pp. 201–8.

Desai, A. R. (ed.) (1971), *Modernization of Underdeveloped Societies*, 2 vols. (Bombay: Thacker).

Eisenstadt, S. N. (1964), 'Social Change, Differentiation and Evolution' in L. Coser and B. Rosenberg (eds.), *Sociological Theory: A Book of Readings*, 4th ed. (New York: Macmillan, 1976).

—— (1973), *Tradition, Change and Modernity* (New York: Wiley).

—— (1977), 'Convergence and Divergence of Modern and Modernizing Societies: Indications from the Analysis of the Structure of Social Hierarchies in Middle Eastern Societies', *International Journal of Middle Eastern Affairs*, 8, pp. 1–27.

Eliot, T. S., 'Burnt Norton', *Four Quartets* (London: Faber & Faber, 1944) ll. 1–3.

Europa Publications (1978), *The World of Learning, 1978–79*, vols. 1 and 2 (London).

Evan, William M. (1976), *Organization Theory* (New York: Wiley).

Farmer, R. and Richman, B. (1965), *Comparative Management and Economic Progress* (Homewood, Ill.: Irwin).

Farsoun, Samih K. (1970), 'Family Structure and Society in Modern Lebanon' in Louise E. Sweet (ed.), *Peoples and Cultures of the Middle East*, vol. 2 (Garden City, New York: The Natural History Press).

Fayerweather, John (1960), *Management of International Operations* (New York: McGraw-Hill).

Fiedler, F. E. (1967), *A Theory of Leadership Effectiveness* (New York: McGraw-Hill).

French, J. R. P., Jr., and Raven, B. H. (1959), 'The Bases of Social Power' in D. Cartwright (ed.), *Studies in Social Power* (Ann Arbor, Mich.: Institute of Social Research).

Geertz, Clifford (1963), *Peddlers and Princes: Social Development and Economic Change in Two Indonesian Towns* (Chicago: University of Chicago Press).

Goldthorpe, J. E. (1975), *The Sociology of the Third World* (Cambridge: Cambridge University Press).

Graham & Trotman Ltd. (1977), *Major Companies of the Arab World* (London).

Gulick, John (1976), *The Middle East: An Anthropological Perspective* (Pacific Palisades, California: Goodyear).

Gusfield, J. R. (1978), 'Review Essay', *American Journal of Sociology*, 82, No. 2, pp. 443–8.

Hall, Edward T. (1959), *The Silent Language* (New York: Doubleday).

——and Whyte, W. F. (1960), 'Intercultural Communication: A Guide to Men of Action', *Human Organization*, 19, No. 1, pp. 5–12.

Hall, J. (1971), 'Decisions, Decisions, Decisions', *Psychology Today*, 5 (November).

Hazen, William E. and Mughisuddin, Mohammed (1975), *Middle Eastern Subcultures* (Lexington, Mass.: D. C. Heath).

Heidenheimer, A. J. (1971), *Political Corruption: Readings in Comparative Analysis* (New York: Holt, Rinehart & Winston).

Heller, Frank A. (1971), *Managerial Decision-Making* (London: Tavistock).

Hitti, Philip K. (1970), *History of the Arabs*, 10th edn. (London: Macmillan).

—— (1971a) *Islam: A Way of Life* (London: Oxford University Press).

—— (1971b) *The Arabs: A Short History* (London: Macmillan).

Hobday, Peter (1978), *Saudi Arabia Today* (London: Macmillan).

Homans, George C. (1961), *Social Behaviour* (New York: Harcourt).

Hourani, Albert (1962), *Arabic Thought in the Liberal Age, 1798–1939* (London: Oxford University Press).

Inkeles, Alex and Smith, David H. (1974), *Becoming Modern: Individual Changes in Six Developing Countries* (Cambridge, Mass.: Harvard University Press).

Jabra, Jabra I. (1971), 'Arab Language and Culture' in Michael Adams (ed.) *The Middle East: A Handbook* (New York: Praeger).

Jacoby, N. H., Nehemkis, P., and Eells, R. (1977), *Bribery and Extortion in World Business* (New York: Macmillan).

Katz, Daniel and Kahn, Robert L. (1978), *The Social Psychology of Organizations*, 2nd ed. (New York: Wiley).

Kelman, H. C. (1958), 'Compliance, Identification and Internalization: Three Processes of Attitude Change', *Journal of Conflict Resolution*, 2, pp. 51–60.

Kent, Raymond (1969), *Corporate Financial Management*, 3rd edn. (Homewood, Ill.: Irwin).

Kerr, C., Dunlop, J., Harbison, F. and Meyers, C. (1960), *Industrialism and Industrial Man* (Cambridge, Mass.: Harvard University Press).

Khalaf, S. and Shwayri, Emile (1966), 'Family Firms and Industrial Development: The Lebanese Case', *Economic Development and Cultural Change*, 15 (October), pp. 59–69.

Khalid, Mansour (1977), 'The Sociocultural Determinants of Arab Diplomacy' in G. N. Atiyeh (ed.) *Arab and American Cultures* (Washington D.C.: American Enterprise Institute for Public Policy Research).

Kluckhohn, F. and Strodbeck, F. (1961), *Variations in Value Orientation* (New York: Row, Peterson).

Lauer, Robert H. (1971), 'The Scientific Legitimation of Fallacy: Neutralizing Social Change Theory', *American Sociological Review*, 36, pp. 881–9.

Lerner, Daniel (1958), *The Passing of Traditional Society: Modernizing the Middle East* (Glencoe, Ill.: Free Press).

Levy, M. J. (1965), *Modernization and the Structure of Societies: A Setting for International Affairs* (Princeton, N.J.: Princeton University Press).

Lewin, Kurt; Lippitt, Ronald; and White, Robert K. (1939), 'Patterns of Aggressive Behaviour in Experimentally Created Social Climates', *Journal of Social Psychology*, 10, pp. 271–99.

Lewis, Bernard (1970), *The Arabs in History*, 5th edn. (London: Hutchinson).

Likert, R. (1967), *The Human Organization* (New York: McGraw-Hill).

Lipset, Seymour Martin (1976), 'Social Structure and Social Change' in P. M. Blau (ed.), *Approaches to the Study of Social Structure* (London: Open Books).

Mabro, Robert and Radwan, Samir (1976), *The Industrialization of Egypt, 1939–1973* (Oxford: Oxford University Press).

MacDonald, Robert W. (1965), *The League of Arab States: A Study in the Dynamics of Regional Organization* (Princeton, N.J.: Princeton University Press).

Maier, N. R. F. (1955), *Psychology in Industry*, 2nd edn. (Boston: Houghton-Mifflin).

Mann, F. C. (1964), 'Toward an Understanding of the Leadership Role in Formal Organizations', in R. Dubin, G. Homans and D. Millar (eds.) *Leadership and Productivity* (San Francisco: Chandler).

Mansfield, Peter (1976), *The Arabs* (London: Allen Lane).

McClelland, D. (1961), *The Achieving Society* (Princeton, N.J.: Van Nostrand).

MEIRC, S.A. (1975), 'Attitude Survey of Saudi and Kuwaiti Employees', unpublished report, Beirut, Lebanon.

MEIRC, S.A. (1976a), 'Job Attitude Survey of Omani National Staff', July 1976, unpublished report, Beirut, Lebanon.
—— (1976b), 'Das Island Attitude and Motivation Survey', September 1976, unpublished report, Beirut, Lebanon.
—— (1976c), 'Labour and Social Insurance Regulations: Saudi Arabia', Law Division, November 25, 1976, unpublished report, Beirut, Lebanon.
—— (1977), 'A Summary Analysis of the Labor Movement in the Middle East and North Africa', January 1977, unpublished report, Athens, Greece.
—— (1978), 'A Summary Analysis of the Labor Movement in the Middle East and North Africa', January 1978, unpublished report, Athens, Greece.
Melikian, Levon H. (1977), 'The Modal Personality of Saudi College Students: A Study in National Character', in L. C. Brown and N. Itzkowitz (eds.), *Psychological Dimensions of Near Eastern Studies* (Princeton, N.J.: Darwin Press).
—— and Diab, Lutfy N. (1959), 'Group Affiliations of University Students in the Arab Middle East', *Journal of Social Psychology*, 49, pp. 145–59.
—— ——, (1974), 'Stability and Change in Group Affiliations of University Students in the Arab Middle East', *Journal of Social Psychology*, 93, pp. 13–21.
Merton, Robert K. (1976), *Sociological Ambivalence and Other Essays* (New York: Free Press).
—— and Barber, E. (1963), 'Sociological Ambivalence', in E. A. Tiryakian (ed.), *Sociological Theory, Values, and Sociocultural Change* (New York: Free Press).
Middle East Economic Survey 'Atiqi on Investment in Arab World' (7 November, 1977), Vol. XXI, No. 3, pp. i–vi.
Mills, C. Wright (1959), *The Sociological Imagination* (New York: Oxford University Press).
Mintzberg, Henry (1973), *The Nature of Managerial Work* (New York: Harper & Row).
—— (1973), 'The Manager's Job: Folklore and Fact', *Harvard Business Review*, July–August, pp. 49–61.
Moore, W. E. (1969), 'Social Structure and Behaviour', in G. Lindzey and E. Aronson (eds.), *The Handbook of Social Psychology* (2nd edn.), vol. 4 (Reading, Mass.: Addison Wesley).
Morris, Desmond (1967), *The Naked Ape* (New York: McGraw-Hill).
Muna, Farid A. (1979), 'The Arab Executive Mind', Ph.D. thesis, University of London.
Naim, Samir (1978), 'Towards a Demystification of Arab Social Reality', *Review of Middle East Studies*, No. 3 (London: Ithaca Press).
Newman, W. H. (1970), 'Is Management Exportable?', *Columbia Journal of World Business*, Jan.–Feb. 1970.
Nieuwenhuijze, C. A. O. van (1971), *Sociology of the Middle East* (Leiden: Brill).
Nightingale, Donald (1976), 'Conflict and Conflict Resolution', in George Strauss *et al.* (eds.), *Organizational Behaviour* (Belmont, California: Wadsworth).
Nisbet, Robert (ed.) (1972), *Social Change* (Oxford: Basil Blackwell).
—— (1976), *Sociology as an Art Form* (London: Heinemann).

Nuseibeh, Hazam Z. (1956), *The Ideas of Arab Nationalism* (Ithaca, N.Y.: Cornell University Press).

Nutting, Anthony (1964), *The Arabs* (New York: Mentor, The New American Library).

Ogionwo, W. W. (1969), 'The Adoption of Technological Innovations in Nigeria: A Study of Factors Associated with Adoption of Farm Practices', Ph.D. thesis, University of Leeds.

Onyemelukwe, C. C. (1973), *Men and Management in Contemporary Africa* (London: Longman).

Owen, Roger (1976), 'Islam and Capitalism: A Critique of Rodinson', *Review of Middle East Studies,* No. 2 (London: Ithaca Press).

Parsons, Talcott (1966), *Societies: Evolutionary and Comparative Perspectives* (Englewood Cliffs, N.J.: Prentice-Hall).

Patai, Raphael (1973), *The Arab Mind* (New York: Scribners).

Prothro, E. Terry and Diab, Lutfy N. (1974), *Changing Family Patterns in the Arab East* (Beirut: American University of Beirut).

Radcliffe-Brown, A. R. (1940), 'On Social Structure', *Journal of the Royal Anthropological Institute,* 70, pp. 1–12.

—— (1957), *A Natural Science of Society* (New York: Free Press).

Richman, B. M. (1965), 'Significance of Cultural Variables', *Academy of Management Journal,* 8, No. 4.

Riggs, Fred W. (1964), *Administration in Developing Countries: The Theory of Prismatic Society* (Boston: Houghton Mifflin).

—— (1966), *Thailand: The Modernization of Traditional Polity* (Honolulu: University Press of Hawaii).

Roberts, Karlene H. (1970), 'On Looking At an Elephant: An Evaluation of Cross-Cultural Research Related to Organizations', *Psychological Bulletin,* 74, No. 4 (November 1970).

Robock, S., Simmonds, K. and Zwick, J. (1977), *International Business and Multinational Enterprises* (rev. edn.), (Homewood, Ill.: Irwin).

Rodinson, Maxime (1974), *Islam and Capitalism,* English edn. (Harmondsworth, Middlesex: Penguin).

Sampson, Anthony (1975), *The Seven Sisters* (London: Hodder & Stoughton).

—— (1977), *The Arms Bazaar* (London: Hodder & Stoughton).

Sayigh, Yusif (1962), *Entrepreneurs of Lebanon* (Cambridge, Mass.: Harvard University Press).

Shaker, Fatina Amin (1972), 'Modernization of the Developing Nations: The Case of Saudi Arabia', Ph.D. dissertation, Purdue University.

Sharabi, Hisham B. (1961), 'Political and Intellectual Attitudes of the Young Arab Generation', in Tibor Kerekes (ed.), *The Arab Middle East and Muslim Africa* (New York: Praeger).

—— (1966), *Nationalism and Revolution in the Arab World* (New York: Van Nostrand Reinhold).

Simon, Herbert A. (1957), *Administrative Behavior* (New York: Macmillan).

Stinchcombe, Arthur L. (1965), 'Social Structure and Organizations', in J. G. March (ed.), *Handbook of Organizations* (Chicago: Rand McNally).

Tannenbaum, R. and Schmidt, W. H. (1958), 'How to Choose a Leadership Pattern', *Harvard Business Review,* 36, pp. 95–101.

Thomas, J. M. and Bennis, W. G. (eds.) (1972), *Management of Change and Conflict* (London: Penguin Books).

Thomas, K. (1976), 'Conflict and Conflict Management', in M. D. Dunnette, (ed.), *Handbook of Industrial and Organizational Psychology* (Chicago: Rand McNally).

—— and Walton, R. E. (1971), 'Conflict-Handling Behaviour in Interdepartmental Relations', Research Paper No. 38, Graduate School of Business Administration, University of California, Los Angeles.

Tomeh, Aida K. (1970), 'Reference-Group Supports Among Middle Eastern College Students', *Journal of Marriage and the Family*, 32, pp. 156–65.

United Nations (1977), *Yearbook of Labour Statistics* (New York).

—— (1978), *Demographic Yearbook* (New York).

Vroom, Victor (1976), 'Leadership', in M. D. Dunnette (ed.), *Handbook of Industrial and Organizational Psychology* (Chicago: Rand McNally).

—— and Jago, A. G. (1974), 'Decision Making as a Social Process: Normative and Descriptive Models of Leader Behavior', *Decision Sciences*, 5, pp. 743–69.

—— and Yetton, Philip (1973), *Leadership and Decision-Making* (Pittsburgh: University of Pittsburgh Press).

Weber, Max (1947), *The Theory of Social and Economic Organization* (Oxford: Oxford University Press).

Yamani, Ahmed Zaki (1972), 'Islamic Law and Contemporary Issues' in Charles Malik (ed.), *God and Man in Contemporary Islamic Thought* (Beirut: American University of Beirut).

MAGAZINES AND NEWSPAPERS:

Al-Ahrām (Cairo), 15 January 1978.

Alam Attijarat, vol. 13, No. 2 (London), February 1978.

Al-Bilād (Riyadh), 15 October 1976.

The Financial Times (London), 18 December 1978; 26 February 1979.

Time Magazine, Europe edition, 9 October 1978.

The Times, (London), 12 June 1978; 16 and 27 November 1978.

Al-Ummāl (Cairo), 17 July 1978.

Index

Abassid empire, 7–8
Agent of change, Arab executive as, 1, 33, 42, 82, 91, 98, 114–15, 119
Al-Ahrãm, 62n, 147
Alam Attijarat, 43n, 147
Algeria, 10, 14, 25n, 124n
Ali, Abdullah Yusuf, 70n, 111n, 142
Ambivalence, 1, 4, 67–8, 104, 106–10, 114
American University of Beirut, 10, 36, 61n, 107
Amman Stock Exchange, 9
Antoun, R. T., 43n, 142
Arab
- identity, 1, 5–7, 109, 116, *see also* History; Arabic language; Religion
- nationalism, 13–15
- socialism, 10, 14
- unity, 14–15

Arab Labour Organization (ALO), 22–3
Arab League, 6, 8
Arab Maritime Petroleum Transport Company, 19
Arab Petroleum Investments Corporation, 19
Arab Petroleum Services Company, 19
Arab Shipbuilding & Repair Yard Company, 19
Arab-Israeli conflict, 14, 16–18
Arabic language, as a basis of identity, 5–7
Al-Atiqi, Abd al-Rahman, 16
Authority, deference to, 70n, 118
Al-Awaji, Ibrahim M., 87n, 142
Ayoub, Victor F., 70n, 142
Al-Azhar University, 24n

Badre, A. Y., 25n, 142
Bahrain, 25n
Barber, E., 112n, 145
Barnard, Chester I., 61n, 142
Beirut Stock Exchange, 9
Bennis, W. G., 70n, 146
Berger, Morroe, 23–4n, 86n, 142
Al-Bilãd, 25n, 147
Bill, James, 13, 24n, 142
Black, C. E., 124n, 142
Blau, Peter M., 24n, 86n, 142
Bribery, 76–8
Buqra (tomorrow) attitude, 29
Business agents, *see* Middlemen
'Business is Business' attitude, 85–6, 110, 112n

Capital investment, *see* Time horizons
Cartwright, D., 61n, 142
Casadio, Gian Pablo, 25n, 142
Change
- agent, *see* Agent of change
- attitudes towards, 88, 98–110
- social, 86, 98, 102–6, 116
- technological, 98, 102–6
- types of, 99–100, 111n

Classical managerial functions, 117, 124n
Commercial and industrial tradition, 5, 8–9
Communication, 82
Community, types of social communities, 11, 13, *see also* Social structure
Comparative management, 3, 122
Conceptual skills, 38, 119
Conflict
- dyadic, 63–4, 68
- management of, 1, 4, 63–9, 114, 118–19
- proverbs on, 64, 68–9
- role of third party (mediator), 63, 65
- *see also* Power tactics

Confrontation, as taboo, 63, 65, 69, 118
Connections, 22, 37–8, 71, 74–8, 83, 114, 118
  bribery, 76–8
  corruption, 76–7
  reciprocity, 75–8
Consultation, 36, 49, 58–60, 63, 85, 114
  as a tactic for conflict reduction, 59, 65, 68–9
  in decision making, *see* Decision-making styles
  reasons for, 59–60
Contacts, *see* Connections
Contingency approach, 45, 53, 58, 61–2n, 117
Coon, Carleton, S., 24n, 142
Corruption, 76–7
Coser, L. A., 70n, 142
Cross-cultural research, 3, 98, 117, 122–3
Cultural bias, 4n
Culture, 27, *see also* Socio-cultural values and norms
Culture shock, 21, 83, 120

Dahl, R. A., 61n, 142
Decision-making
  departmental decisions, 51–2, 54–8, 127
  organizational decisions, 52, 55, 57–8, 127–9
  personnel decisions, 51, 53–5, 58, 127
  socio-psychological variables affecting, 52–8
  variables affecting, 45, 53–8
Decision-making profile, 47–53
Decision-making styles, 1, 4, 44–50, 53–61 *passim*, 85, 114, 127
  consultative, 46–50, 58, 118, 127
  delegation, 45–50, 58, 127
  joint decision (democratic), 46–50, 58, 60, 118. 127
  own decision (autocratic) 45–50, 58, 127
Delegation
  advantages of, 45, 47, 61, 119
  and decision making, *see* decision-making styles
  low levels of, 60–1, 91
Desai, A. R., 111n, 142
Diab, Lutfy N., 24n, 35, 43n, 112n, 145–6
Differentiation
  partial, 12–13, 84, 100
  social and economic, 11–13, 99

Economic
  boom, 14, 18–23, 45, 113, 120
  developments, 4, 5, 13, 18–23
  infrastructure, 19, 21, 23, 91, 118
  instability, 21, 23, 92, 97, 108, 113, 118
Economically active population, 105, 112n
Eells, R., 144
Egypt, 3, 7, 10, 14, 25n, 50–3, 55–7, 62n, 86n, 101, 103–4, 112n, 125–6
Eisenstadt, S. N., 24n, 111n, 142
Eliot, T. S., 88, 143
Environment
  importance of environmental factors, 113–14, 120
  sensitivity to, 38–9, 119 123
Evan, William M., 124n, 143
Executive role in the organization
  chief executive role, 39–40
  family role, 40–1
Expatriates, 3, 20–1, 71, 83–6, 86–7n, 89, 107–10, 112n, 124n
  image of, 120–2
  implications for, 4, 117, 120–2
  see also Culture shock, and 'Business is Business' attitude
Expectations, of Arab executives and employees,
  see Role of executive
  see also Self-fulfilling prophecy
Extended Family, *see* Family

Face-saving, 60, 118
Faisal, King of Saudi Arabia, 16, 87n, 101
Familial, *see* Paternalistic
Family
  expectations of, 1, 36–7

extended family, 11, 33, 35–6, 42, 91
freedom from family and traditions, 102–6
importance of, 11–13, 22, 35–7, 71, 74–5
Farmer, R., 110n, 143
Farsoun, Samih K., 24n, 43n, 70n, 86n, 111n, 143
Fatalism
myth of, 4, 93–8
and preventive measures, 96–8
and uncontrollable events, 97–8
Fayerweather, John, 78, 87n, 143
Fayol, H., 124n
Fiedler, F. E., 61n, 143
Foreign businessmen, *see* Expatriates
Formal system, *see* Informality
French, J. R. P., Jr., 61n, 70n, 143
Friendship ties, 12–13, 22, 74–5, 90, 114
Future, attitudes towards the, *see* Change; *see also* Time

Geertz, Clifford, 111n, 143
Gifts and bribery, 77–8
Goldthorpe, J. E., 24n, 143
Governmental bureaucracy, 22, 108, 118
development plans, 19, 92–3
laws and regulations, 21, 118
Group
affiliation and interaction, 12, 36
patterns, 12, 113
reference groups, 31
role of small groups, 12–13, 113
Gulick, John, 24n, 43n, 143
Gusfield, J. R., 112n, 143

Ḥadīth, 59, 95
Hall, Edward T., 73, 86n, 110n, 143
Hall, J., 70n, 143
Harbison, F., 144
Hayward, H. C., 25n
Hazen, William E., 25n, 143
Heidenheimer, A. J., 87n, 143
Helicopter view, 38, 119, *see also* Conceptual skills
Heller, Frank A., 45–7, 52, 61n, 127, 130n, 143
Hierarchy
downward bypassing, 82–3
upward bypassing, 81–2, 115
see also Open-door tradition
History of the Arabs, as a basis of identity, 5–7
Hitti, Philip K., 2, 9, 23–4n, 70n, 143
Hobday, Peter, 87n, 143
Homans, George C., 86n, 143
Hospitality, 11, 33, 77, 90
Hourani, Albert, 7, 143

Ijmā', 23n
Impersonal, *see* Person-oriented
Individual variables
age of executive, 41, 52–8, 79, 126
education, 10, 41, 52–8, 79–80, 126
social background, 11, 52–8, 79, 126
status in organization, 9, 52–8, 79–80, 126
Indonesia, 25n, 100
Industrialization, potential ills of, 116
Informality, 4, 13, 60, 71, 83–6, 109, 114, 118
Inkeles, Alex, 111n, 143
Inshā' Allāh, 96
Insurance, life, 98, 111n
Inter-Arab conflict, 8, 14–15, 17, 108
Intermediary role, 36–8, 43n, 75, 86n
International Confederation of Arab Trade unions (ICATU), 22
International Labour organization (ILO), 22–3
Interpersonal styles, 1, 4, 71–86 *passim*, 91, 114
Interview Schedule, 4, 68, 70n, 131–41
Iran, 25n, 101, 124n
Iraq, 10, 14, 18, 25n
Islam, 6–8, 15–16, 59, 94–6, 101
Islamic fundamentalism, 15–16, 112n
Israel, *see* Arab–Israeli conflict

Jabra, Jabra I., 23n, 144

Jacoby, N. H., 86n, 143, 144
Jago, A. G., 61n, 127, 130n, 147
Japan, 36, 101, 109
Jordan, 3, 14, 17, 25n, 29, 33, 50–3, 103–4, 125–6

Kahn, Robert L., 38, 43n, 69–70n, 144
Katz, Daniel, 38, 43n, 69–70n, 144
Kelman, H. C., 70n, 144
Kent, Raymond, 110n, 144
Kerr, C., 111n, 144
Khalaf, S., 111n, 144
Khalid, Mansour, 112n, 144
Kinship, *see* Family
Kluckhohn, F., 110n, 144
Kuwait, 3, 14, 16, 25n, 33–4, 50–2, 98, 100, 103–4, 125–6, 129
Kuwait Stock Exchange, 9

Labour unions, 14, 22–3, 25n
Lauer, Robert H., 111n, 144
Leadership styles, 44, 61n, 118, *see also* Decision-making styles
Lebanon, 3, 17, 33, 50–2, 55, 57, 86n, 100, 103–4, 125–6, 129
Leiden, Carl, 13, 24n, 142
Lerner, Daniel, 111n, 144
Level of analysis, 3–4, 26, 113
Levy, M. J., 111n, 144
Lewin, Kurt, 47, 144
Lewis, Bernard, 24n, 144
Libya, 23n, 25n, 124n
Likert, R., 47, 144
Lippitt, Ronald, 47, 144
Lipset, Seymour Martin, 124n, 144
Loyalty
  and efficiency, 79–80, 83
  importance of, 11, 71, 78–80, 118

Mabro, Robert, 62n, 144
McClelland, D., 110n, 144
MacDonald, Robert W., 23n, 144
Maier, N. R. F., 47, 144
Majlis, 81, 87n
Managerial Grid, 118
Managerial training and development, *see* Time horizons
Mann, F. C., 43n, 144
Manpower
  shortage, 19–20, 45, 105, 120
  supply, 18, 25n
Mansfield, Peter, 111n, 124n, 144
MEIRC, S.A., 25n, 43n, 144–5
  research studies by, 41–2
Melikian, Levon H., 24n, 43n, 70n, 145
Merton, Robert K., 112n, 145
Meyers, C., 144
Middle East Economic Survey, 25n, 145
Middlemen (business agents), 8, 76–7
Mills, C. Wright, 5, 145
Mintzberg, Henry, 38, 42–3n, 61n, 145
Modernity – *see* Modernization
Modernization, 1, 4, 16, 35, 37, 88, 98, 100–2, 106–10, 114, 115–16
Moore, W. E., 24n, 145
Morocco, 23n, 124n
Morris, Desmond, 73, 86n, 145
Motivation, *see* Delegation
Mu'āwiyah, the Caliph, 63, 68–9
Mughisuddin, Mohammed, 25n, 143
Muhammad, the Prophet, 7–8, 23n, 59
Multiple regression analysis, 53, 127–9
Muna, Farid A., 4n, 47, 131, 145
Muslim, *see* Islam

Nai'f, Prince of Saudi Arabia, 16, 25n
Naim, Samir, 111n, 145
National employee
  side-business opportunities for, 22
  training of, 37, 42, 108–9, 115, 119
Nationalism, *see* Arab nationalism
Nehemkis, P., 144
Newman, W. H., 124n, 145
Nieuwenhuijze, C. A. O. van, 23–4n, 112n, 145
Nigeria, 25n, 100
Nightingale, Donald, 69n, 145
Nisbet, Robert, 111n, 123–4n, 145
Non-decision making, as a power tactic, 65–6, 69
Norms, *see* Socio-cultural values and norms

Nuseibeh, Hazem Z., 23n, 146
Nutting, Anthony, 23n, 146

Ogionwo, W. W., 111n, 146
Oil, *see* Petroleum
Oman, 25n
Onyemelukwe, C. C., 111n, 146
Open-door tradition, 71, 80–3, 91, 115
Organization of Arab Petroleum Exporting Countries (OAPEC), 19, 24–5n
Organization of Petroleum Exporting Countries (OPEC), 18, 25n
Organizational structure, 68, 81, 83–5
Organizational variables
  country, 3, 52–8, 79, 125–6
  nature of business, 52–8, 79
  ownership, 3, 40, 52–8, 79, 125–6
  size, 3, 40, 52–8, 61, 62n, 79, 125–6
  see also Individual variables
Organized chaos, 84
Ottoman Turks, 7, 14
Owen, Roger, 111n, 146

Pakistan, 101, 124n
Palestine, *see* Arab–Israeli conflict
Parsons, Talcott, 87n, 111n, 146
Participation, 46–7, 118
Patai, Raphael, 110–11n, 146
Paternalistic, 1, 40–2, 45, 78, 80, 85, 110, 114, 118
Personal ties, 71, 74–8, 83, 90
Personalism, *see* Person-oriented
Personalized, *see* Person-oriented
Personnel selection, 80, 118
Person-oriented, 4, 13, 60, 71, 73–4, 80, 83, 86, 91, 109, 114, 118
Petroleum, discovery of, 9, 14, 18
Planning, *see* Time horizons
Political
  developments, 4, 5, 13–18
  instability, 14, 23, 92, 97, 108, 113
Power
  in conflict management, 63–9
  position, 65–6
  tactics, 4, 65–6, 69
Power-sharing, 4, 44–5, 51, 64
  continuum, 45, 47, 50, 127
  see also Decision-making styles
Pride, 11, 118
Prothro, E. Terry, 24n, 35, 43n, 112n, 146

Qatar, 25n
Qiyās, 23n
Quran, Holy, 8, 23n, 44, 59, 68–9, 95, 111n

Radcliffe-Brown, A. R., 24n, 111n, 146
Radwan, Samir, 62n, 144
Raven, B. H., 61n, 70n, 143
Religion, as a basis of identity, 5–7
Research
  future, 4, 28, 67, 106, 117, 122–3
  methodology, 4, 125
Richman, B. M., 110n, 124n, 143, 146
Riggs, Fred W., 12, 24n, 84, 87n, 100, 111n, 146
Rituals, in conducting business, 71–4, 86n, 91
Roberts, Karlene H., 122–3, 124n, 146
Robock, S., 110n, 124n, 146
Rodinson, Maxime, 24n, 94–5, 110–11n, 146
Role of executive
  in community, 1, 4, 26, 35–9, 42, 74, 91, 114
  in organization, 1, 4, 26, 39–42, 81, 91, 114
  see also Executive role in the organization
Role-oriented, 73, 80, 83, 118
Rural, 11–13, 78

Sampson, Anthony, 25n, 87n, 146
Saudi Arabia, 3, 7, 14–16, 18, 20, 25n, 29–30, 33, 50–2, 55–7, 84, 98, 100–1, 102–4, 111n, 125–6
Sayigh, Yusif, 111n, 146
Schmidt, W. H., 47, 146
Self-fulfilling prophecy, 41–2
Shaker, Fatina Amin, 111–12n, 146
Sharabi, Hisham B., 24n, 112n, 146
Sharī'a, 7, 15–16, 23n, 112n, 114

Sharjah Group Company, 9, 24n
Shūra, 59
Shwayri, Emile, 111n, 144
Siksek, S. G., 25n, 142
Simmonds, K., 110n, 146
Simon, Herbert A., 61n, 146
Smith, David H., 111n, 143
Social exchange, *see* Connections
Social influence, Arab executive as *agent* and *target* of, 26, 34, 42, 44, 98, 114
  see also Agent of change
Social pressures, 26–34, 42, 44, 75, 91
  dislike of manual work, 28, 30, 34, 115
  fusion of business, social and personal, 28, 30–1, 34, 91, 115
  high expectations for success, 28, 33–4
  individualistic approach to work, 28–30
  industrial mentality, 28–9, 34, 108–9, 115
  low value of time, 28–9, 34, *see also* Time
  marketing constraints, 28, 30
  nepotism, 28, 33–4, 78, 80, 118
  reputation in community, 28, 31–2
  restrictions on women, 28–9, 34, 42n, 102–3, 105
  social visits at the office, 28, 32–4, 91
  top-man syndrome, 28, 32, 91
  weekend problem, 28, 30
Social responsibility, 37
Social structure, 1–3, 5, 10–13, 24n, 71, 74, 78, 86, 99–100, 113–14
Socio-cultural pressures, *see* Social pressures
Socio-cultural values and norms, 1, 4, 11, 27, 34, 42, 69, 78, 80, 86, 99, 108, 113–14
Stinchcombe, Arthur L., 24n, 146
Strodbeck, F., 110n, 144
Subordinates
  bypassing, 81–3
  compliance by, 67
  opposition from, 63–9, 119
Sunna, 23n
Sūra, 59
Syria, 10, 14, 25n
System, business-oriented social, 2, 26, 60, 113

Tannenbaum, R., 47, 146
T-Groups, 118
The Financial Times, 24–5n, 147
The Times, 43n, 111–12n, 147
Thomas, J. M., 70n, 146
Thomas, K., 69–70n, 147
Time
  attitudes towards, 4, 88–98
  constraints on, 26, 31, 42, 44, 72–4, 76, 90–1, 119
  management of, 47, 91, 115, 119
  proverbs on value of, 89–90
  value of, 1, 89–91, 108, 114–15
Time horizons
  capital investment, 91–3, 96
  corporate planning, 91–3, 96
  managerial training and development, 91–3, 96, 108–9, 115
Time Magazine, 111n, 147
Tomeh, Aida K., 24n, 43n, 147
Traditions
  neo-traditionalist, 102, 112n
  sacrificing, 16, 101, 104, 109–10, 115–16
Training and development of Arab executives, 4, 39, 93, 117–20
  harmful Western managerial practices, 118–19
  managerial skills, 119–20
Tribal, 11–13, 78
Tunisia, 14, 124n

Umayyad empire, 7, 68
Al-Ummāl, 112n, 147
United Arab Emirates, 3, 25n, 30, 50–2, 85, 89, 100, 103–4, 125–6
United Nations, 23n, 112n, 147
Urban, 11–13, 78

Values, *see* Socio-cultural values and norms
Vroom, Victor, 45, 47, 53, 61n, 127, 130n, 147

Walton, R. E., 70n, 147
Wastah, 43n, *see also* Connections
Weber, Max, 61n, 147
White, Robert K., 47, 144
Whyte, W. F., 73, 86n, 143
Women
  in management, 102–6
  restrictions on 28–9, 34, 42n, 102–3, 105

Yamani, Sheikh Ahmed Zaki, 15–16, 25n, 124n, 147
Yetton, Philip, 45, 47, 53, 127, 130n, 147

Zwick, J., 110n, 146